EXSULTEMUS

REJOICING WITH GOD

IN THE

HYMNS OF THE ROMAN BREVIARY

EXSULTEMUS

REJOICING WITH GOD

IN THE

HYMNS OF THE ROMAN BREVIARY

Translated by

Martin D. O'Keefe, S.J.

SAINT LOUIS

THE INSTITUTE OF JESUIT SOURCES

Number 4 in Series V:
Prayer

©2002, The Institute of Jesuit Sources
3601 Lindell Boulevard
Saint Louis, MO, 63108
TEL: 314-977-7257
FAX: 314-977-7263
e-mail: ijs@slu.edu
Website: www.jesuitsources.com

Library of Congress Catalog Card Number: 2002113309
ISBN 1-880810-47-6

For Clare and David,
and in fond memory of Tom.

Given peers and friends like these,
one can only be grateful,
and rejoice with God.

CONTENTS

PROPER OF THE SAINTS   183

PREFACE

Some years ago, I undertook to compose a translation of certain liturgical texts. I had in mind the collects, prayers over the gifts, and the prayers after communion (all 1534 or so of them!) that were then (and are now) in use in the Mass. (Later on, other things were added: the 80 prefaces, the 4 canons, and the 5 sequences.) I did not intend for my translation to be an official one, for public liturgical use; rather, it was intended for private study and prayer. But I did intend to make the translation as accurate, dignified, and reverent as I could. And I admit that all this arose out of a degree of dissatisfaction on my part with the official translation given in the English *Sacramentary,* which impressed me as being an approximation or paraphrase rather than a translation, and moreover as being needlessly pedestrian in tone. The result of my efforts was a book, entitled *Oremus: Praying to God in the Words of the Roman Rite,* published by the Institute of Jesuit Sources in 1993.

The present book is like that earlier book in some ways, and unlike it in others. It too is a translation of certain liturgical texts. It is not intended for official use, but rather for private study and prayer. And it is intended to be as reverent, accurate, and dignified as I can make it. But there are two differences between this book and the earlier one. First, this book does not deal with prayers of the Mass; rather, it is concerned with the almost 300 hymns that occur in the Breviary (or *Liturgy of the Hours,* as it is called in English). Secondly, it does not stem from any dissatisfaction with an existing translation. A comment on each of these differences might be helpful.

Anyone familiar with the Breviary knows that each day's office is made up of five "hours" (Office of Readings, Morning Prayer, Midday Prayer, Evening Prayer, Night Prayer). Each of these "hours" is structurally similar, in that each begins with a hymn, followed by psalmody, followed by a reading or readings, followed by a response to the readings, followed by a concluding prayer. The first element of each hour, the hymn, is the principal interest of this book. In general, the hymn for each hour is a poem, expressing to God sentiments that are appropriate to that particular hour.

I have no quarrel with existing translations. My problem arises from the lack of existing translations. For when the 1970 English version of the *Roman Breviary* was published, the decision was made not to translate into English the existing Latin hymns; rather, good English poetry and good English hymns would be substituted instead.

The decision was a laudable one, particularly given the less-than-felicitous translations of some of the hymns that had been published in English-language experimental breviaries in the years immediately preceding 1970. But the decision did entail one undesirable consequence: inevitably, the Latin hymns would gradually fall into disuse and would cease to be known throughout the English-speaking world. For the number of people who could read the Latin hymns and understand them was to decrease gradually and continues to decrease even now.

That has the potential of being a tragedy. These hymns form a precious part of every Catholic's patrimony; some of them are very ancient indeed, and all of them express the Church's faith as it has been stated down through the ages. They need to continue to be available to English-speaking Catholics, even if only by means of a translation.

And so this book tries to provide such a translation. It does so, however, on terms that are peculiar to itself, and perhaps the reader would appreciate knowing the conditions (presuppositions, if one will) that I have adopted in undertaking the task.

First, the Latin poetry of the Breviary does not, in large measure, make use of a rhyme scheme. There are some poems that are exceptions to that norm (one thinks of some of Saint Thomas Aquinas's poems, for example), but they are not numerous. Thus an English translation of a Latin Breviary poem is perhaps best not held to the sort of rhyme scheme that characterizes much of poetry written originally in English.

Latin poetry does, however, have a metric scheme: lines and stanzas are very much subject to a definite rhythm (or, more exactly, sets of rhythms). And here a translator must make a choice. For attempting to duplicate these Latin rhythms in English guise can result in just about anything from superb poetry (once in a rare while) to utter doggerel (most of the time). One need only read the disastrous translation of the *Te lucis ante terminum* (the hymn at Night Prayer) that appeared in some of the English experimental editions prior to 1970 to have that fact demonstrated.

So what is a translator to do? Something like this seems reasonable. First, these poems are not simply Latin poetry (though they are superb examples of that); they are, most importantly, Latin prayers. They are expressions of a soul's rejoicing in the Lord as he or she undertakes the task of reciting one or the other of the Hours of the Office.

Very well, then: they should be translated as prayers. That is to say, they should be translated, first of all: as accurately as possible, so that their meaning comes through clearly. But they should be translated in the sort of dignified diction that properly characterizes a public prayer. Let the translation be done in a sort of free verse; if out of this a sort of rhythm develops on its own accord, then so be it. But the translation, and the dignified translation, are primary and the rhythm is not. (Actually, such a rhythm does tend to develop—iambic in character, for the most part—in most though not all of the translations: one ends up with an interesting mixture of free verse and blank verse.)

Some of the hymns have variant versions in the Latin. I have chosen not to take account of these, but rather simply to follow the version that was given in the 1974 version of the *Liturgia Horarum (Editio Typica, Typis Polyglottis Vaticanis)*. The reason is that my interest is in the hymns *as prayers*; and variant versions, in general, do not greatly affect that character of the hymns.

Two final thoughts. First, traditionally the breviary is to be recited "with at least incipient speech, i.e., with some movement of the lips," as opposed to being read merely with the eyes. I could not prove this, but I suspect that at least part of the reason for that regulation was the hymns, which come across quite differently if vocalized (even if only minimally), rather than being simply read ocularly. For that reason I encourage any who use the translations in this book to vocalize them, too, even if only incipiently; it will make quite a difference in how the hymns are intended to be understood.

Secondly, I need to acknowledge here the kindness and expertise of Fr. John L. McCarthy, S.J., of the Institute of Jesuit Sources. He has read through the entire manuscript carefully (and most sections of it more than once), and his extraordinarily sharp eye and exquisite knowledge of Latin have contributed immeasurably to making the translations as accurate and error-free as they are. Such failings in accuracy, or any other errors, as may manage to make their way into print, however, are the exclusive property of the translator.

Martin D. O'Keefe, S.J.
The Institute of Jesuit Sources
Fall, 2002.

PROPER OF THE SEASONS

ADVENT (A): UNTIL DECEMBER 17
ADVENT (B): DECEMBER 17-23

CHRISTMAS (A): CHRISTMAS TO EPIPHANY
CHRISTMAS (B): EPIPHANY TO THE BAPTISM OF THE LORD
THE FESTIVALS OF CHRISTMAS:
Christmas Day
Holy Family
Solemnity of the Blessed Virgin Mary, Mother of God
Epiphany
Baptism of the Lord

LENT (A): ASH WEDNESDAY TO HOLY WEEK
LENT (B): HOLY WEEK
THE FESTIVALS OF LENT:
Palm Sunday
Holy Thursday
Good Friday
Holy Saturday

EASTER (A): EASTER THROUGH ASCENSION
EASTER (B): FROM ASCENSION THROUGH PENTECOST
THE FESTIVALS OF EASTER
Easter Sunday
Ascension
Pentecost

SEASON OF ADVENT (A)
EVENING PRAYER
Conditor Alme Siderum / Gracious Maker of the Stars Above

Conditor alme siderum,
aeterna lux credentium,
Christe, redemptor omnium,
exaudi preces supplicum.

Gracious maker of the stars above,
Light everlasting for believers true,
Christ God, Redeemer of us all,
hear the prayers of those
who plead with you.

Qui condolens interitu
mortis perire saeculum,
salvasti mundum languidum,
donans reis remedium,

Aggrieved were you that the world
was near lost
to death's dark destruction,
and so you rescued a tottering universe
and granted healing to the guilt-filled.

Vergente mundi vespere,
uti sponsus de thalamo,
egressus honestissima
Virginis matris clausula.

As the world's very eve was tumbling
into dark, you came: a spouse
springing forth from bridal chamber,
coming from that most honored womb
of the Virgin Mother kind.

Cuius forti potentiae
genu curvantur omnia;
caelestia, terrestria
nutu fatentur subdita.

Before your fearsome power
all things bend at the knee;
in heaven, on earth,
let all in subjection profess you
by their humble stance.

Te, Sancte, fide quaesumus,
venture iudex saeculi,
conserva nos in tempore
hostis a telo perfidi.

In faith, most Holy One,
we bring our prayer to you:
you are the judge
of the world who is to come.
Preserve us in time's deep space
from the stinging dart
of the foe most foul.

Sit, Christe, rex piissime,
tibi Patrique gloria
cum Spiritu Paraclito
in sempiterna saecula.
Amen.

O Christ, King most faithful,
may glory be given you,
and to the Father as well,
with the Holy Spirit blest for endless
ages to come.
Amen.

SEASON OF ADVENT (A): NIGHT PRAYER
Te Lucis ante Terminum / Before Day's Finish

Te lucis ante terminum
rerum Creator, poscimus,
ut solita clementia
sis praesul ad custodiam.

Before day's finish, Creator most high,
we implore:
with your wonted mercy,
be you our guardian guide.

Te corda nostra somnient,
te per soporem sentiant,
tuamque semper gloriam
vicina luce concinant.

May our hearts dream of you;
may they know you
even in their slumber.
May they ever sing of your glory
when next light draws nigh.

Vitam salubrem tribue,
nostrum calorem refice,
taetram noctis caliginem
tua collustret claritas.

Grant us a health-filled life;
restore to us the warmth of day.
Let your own bright light illumine
the fell darkness of our night.

Praesta, Pater omnipotens,
per Iesum Christum Dominum,
qui tecum in perpetuum
regnat cum Sancto Spiritu.
Amen.

Grant this, Father most powerful,
through Jesus Christ our Lord,
who with the Holy Spirit
rules with you
for endless days.
Amen.

SEASON OF ADVENT (A): OFFICE OF READINGS
Verbum Supernum Prodiens / Word Most High, Arising

Verbum supernum prodiens,
a Patre lumen exiens,
qui natus orbi subvenis
cursu declivi temporis:

Word most high, arising
from the Father, coming forth
as Light itself,
by your birth you come to the aid
of the world in its last stages
of desperation time.

Illumina nunc pectora
tuoque amore concrema;
audita per praeconia
sint pulsa tandem lubrica.

Enlighten now our darkened hearts;
consume them now with love for you.
Now at long last
let worldly lore's treacherous teaching
be driven far from them
by what we hear
in your word proclaimed.

Iudexque cum post aderis
rimari facta pectoris,
reddens vicem pro abditis
iustisque regnum pro bonis,

And when later
you come to us as judge,
to uncover each heart's secret deeds,
to render what is due for hidden sins,
to grant the just regal reward for their
good deeds,

Non demum artemur malis
pro qualitate criminis,
sed cum beatis compotes
simus perennes caelites.

Then by the evil we have done
may we not,
at thy final call, be enstraitened to sin's
thin measure of worth
but rather, along with the blessed,
be enabled to live in heaven's
e'erlasting bliss.

Sit, Christe, rex piissime,
tibi Patrique gloria
cum Spiritu Paraclito,
in sempiterna saecula.
Amen.

O Christ, king most faithful,
may glory be to you,
and to the Father too,
to the Holy Spirit as well
for all ages e'er to tell.
Amen.

SEASON OF ADVENT (A): MORNING PRAYER
Vox Clara Ecce Intonat / Lo, a Clarion Call Rings Forth

Vox clara ecce intonat,
obscura quaeque increpat:
procul fugentur somnia;
ab aethre Christus promicat.

Lo, a clarion call rings forth,
reproving whate'er may darkling be:
let dim dreams be driven far away;
from heaven above
shines forth Christ the Lord.

Mens iam resurgat torpida
quae sorde exstat saucia;
sidus refulget iam novum,
ut tollat omne noxium.

Let slumber-filled mind
now wake once more,
mind once wounded
by sin's foul stain.
Now gleams forth a new star bright
to take from us whate'er would do ill.

E sursum Agnus mittitur
laxare gratis debitum;
omnes pro indulgentia
vocem demus cum lacrimis.

From on high the Lamb is sent,
freely to shatter
the bond that was due.
For such gracious kindness let us
one and all
join voice in tearful gratitude.

Secundo ut cum fulserit
mundumque horror cinxerit,
non pro reatu puniat,
sed nos pius tunc protegat.

So that, when for the second time
that Lamb shall appear on high,
when terror fell shall embrace
this sinful world,
he may not punish
what our guilt deserves,
but may, in his faithful love,
guard and protect us instead.

Summo Parenti gloria
Natoque sit victoria,
et Flamini laus debita
per saeculorum saecula.
Amen.

To the Father most high be glory given
and to the Son be triumph accorded;
To the Spirit too be praise well due
for ages e'en not yet recorded.
Amen.

SEASON OF ADVENT (A): MIDMORNING PRAYER
Nunc, Sancte, Nobis, Spiritus / And Now, Spirit Most Holy

Nunc, Sancte, nobis, Spiritus,
unum Patri cum Filio,
dignare promptus ingeri
nostro refusus pectori.

And now, Spirit most Holy,
united ever
with the Father and with the Son,
be pleased to be sent forth willingly
and poured out into our hearts.

Os, lingua, mens, sensus, vigor
confessionem personent,
flammescat igne caritas,
accendat ardor proximos.

May mouth, may tongue,
may understanding, may senses five,
may strength of frame
make to resound our confession
of your name;
may charity flash forth
with brightest blaze,
its brilliance inflaming
our neighbors' souls.

Per te sciamus da Patrem,
noscamus atque Filium,
te utriusque Spiritum
credamus omni tempore.
Amen.

Grant that, by your inspiration,
we may know the Father,
know also His only Son;
and, Spirit of Father and of Son,
grant us to place our faith firmly in you
now and for all ages to come.
Amen.

SEASON OF ADVENT (A): MIDDAY PRAYER
Rector Potens, Verax Deus / Ruler Most Powerful, God of All Truth

Rector potens, verax Deus,
qui temperas rerum vices,
splendore mane instruis
et ignibus meridiem.

Ruler most powerful, God of all truth,
you govern the successive cycles
your creatures pursue.
The morning
you establish in majesty;
and the noontime you set
in blaze of fire.

Exstingue flammas litium,
aufer calorem noxium
confer salutem corporum
veramque pacem cordium.

Quench the fires of querulous strife;
take far from us
hatred's unholy high heat.
Grant us, rather, health of body,
and true peace within our hearts.

Praesta, Pater piissime,
Patrique compar Unice,
cum Spiritu Paraclito
regnans per omne
saeculum.
Amen.

Grant this, Father most faithful;
grant this, equal to the Father
and only-begotten Son,
as you reign together
with the Spirit Advocate
for endless ages to come.
Amen.

SEASON OF ADVENT (A): MIDAFTERNOON PRAYER
Rerum, Deus, Tenax Vigor / God Most Holy, Unyielding Strength

Rerum, Deus, tenax vigor
immotus in te permanens,
lucis diurnae tempora
successibus determinans,

God most holy, unyielding strength
of all your creatures,
unmoved, steadfast unto yourself,
you establish the times for light of day
in all its changes;

Largire clarum vespere,
quo vita numquam decidat,
sed praemium mortis sacrae
perennis instet gloria.

Grant that our evening
may be bright and clear;
from it may life never fall away;
but may the abiding glory
of a holy death
shine forth from it as our reward.

Praesta, Paster piissime,
Patrique compar Unice,
cum Spiritu Paraclito
regnans per omne saeculum.
Amen.

Grant this, most faithful Father; grant it,
O co-equal and sole-begotten Son,
with the Spirit Paraclete
ruling for endless ages to come.
Amen.

SEASON OF ADVENT (B): EVENING PRAYER
Verbum Salutis Omnium / The Word: It Brings Salvation

Verbum salutis omnium,
Patris ab ore prodiens,
Virgo beata, suscipe
casto, Maria, viscere.

That Word: it brings salvation
to the whole of humankind;
it comes forth from the mouth
of the Father most high.
Receive it, O Virgin blest, Mary,
within thy most pure womb.

Te nunc illustrat caelitus
umbra fecundi Spiritus,
gestes ut Christum Dominum,
aequalem Patri Filium.

The o'ershadowing
of the Spirit, fruitful-making,
now comes upon you alone
from on high,
that you might bear Christ the Lord,
that Son to the exalted Father
full equal.

Haec est sacrati ianua
templi serata iugiter,
soli supremo Principi
pandens beata lumina.

Lo, this is the doorway
of the sacred temple,
a doorway e'er firm barred:
for the Supreme Lord alone
does it open; then streams forth
blessed light.

Olim promissus vatibus,
natus ante luciferum,
quem Gabriel annuntiat,
terris descendit Dominus.

Of old promised
to prophets full faithful,
before the daystar born,
the one whom Gabriel foretold,
the Lord:
He comes down upon the earth.

Laetentur simul angeli,
omnes exsultent populi:
excelsus venit humilis
salvare quod perierat.

Let the angel choirs
be at one in praise;
let all the nations rejoice.
For the Most High has come
in humble estate
to rescue what had been lost.

Sit, Christe, rex piissime,
tibi Patrique gloria
cum Spiritu Paraclito,
in sempiterna saecula.
Amen.

To you, Christ, O King most faithful
and to the Father be glory given,
in company with the Spirit blest,
for ages e'er to come.
Amen.

SEASON OF ADVENT (B): NIGHTTIME PRAYER
Christe, Qui, Splendor et Dies / Christ our Lord, Brightness

Christe, qui, splendor et dies,
noctis tenebras detegis,
lucisque lumen crederis,
lumen beatis praedicans,

Christ our God,
brightness, daylight itself,
you lay bare the darkness of night.
We believe that you are
the very light of light,
proclaiming brilliance supreme
to your blessed ones.

Precamur, sancte Domine,
hac nocte nos custodias;
sit nobis in te requies,
quietas horas tribue.

We ask you, most holy Lord,
to guard us this night.
May we find rest in you;
grant us peaceful hours
of quiet repose.

Somno si dantur oculi,
cor semper ad te vigilet;
tuaque dextra protegas
fideles, qui te diligunt.

If our eyes are given over to slumber,
yet let our hearts
ever be watchful for you.
With your strong right hand
protect your faithful ones,
who love you so.

Defensor noster, aspice,
insidiantes reprime,
guberna tuos famulos,
quos sanguine mercatus es.

You are our defender.
Be on guard; restrain those
who would lie in wait for us.
Govern us who are your people,
whom you have purchased
with your own blood.

Sit, Christe, rex piissime,
tibi Patrique gloria,
cum Spiritu Paraclito,
in sempiterna saecula.
Amen.

May glory be to you, Christ,
King most faithful;
may it likewise be given
to your Father most high,
with the Spirit Advocate,
for endless ages to come.
Amen.

SEASON OF ADVENT (B): OFFICE OF READINGS
Veni, Redemptor Gentium / Come, Savior of All Nations

Veni, Redemptor gentium,
ostende partum Virginis;
miretur omne saeculum;
talis decet partus Deum.

Non ex virili semine,
sed mystico spiramine
Verbum Dei fac*tum* est caro
fructusque ventris floruit.

Alvus tumescit Virginis,
claustrum pudoris permanet,
vexilla virtutum micant,
versatur in templo Deus.

Procedat e *thala*mo suo,
pudoris aula regia,
*gemi*nae gigas substantiae
alacris ut currat viam.

Aequalis aeterno Patri,
carnis tropaeo cingere,
infirma nostri corporis
virtute firmans perpeti.

Praesepe iam fulget tuum
lumenque nox spirat novum,
quod nulla nox interpolet
fideque iugi luceat.

Sit, Christe, rex piissime,
tibi Patrique gloria
cum Spiritu Paraclito,
in sempiterna saecula.
Amen.

Come, Savior of all the nations,
show forth to us
the Virgin giving birth.
Let the ages all in turn
be wonder-struck, for such a child
befits the God that is ours.

Not through seed
derived from human man, nay,
but by heaven's breath from on high
was the Word of God made flesh,
did the fruit of the mother-virgin's
womb flourish true.

That womb of the Virgin grows large,
but the guardian gate of chastity
remains untouched:
virtue's ensign unfurls full, and
God dwells in his temple most fair.

Let him now come forth
from the chamber he has chosen,
from those regal halls
of purity most firm;
so that, a giant he
of dual substance,
both God and man,
might eagerly course the life
that is his to live.

Equal to the Father
who knows no term,
Be thou girded
with victorious sign of flesh,
giving power to the weakness
of our mortal frame
with strength that knows no fail.

[continued]

Veni, Redemptor Gentium / Come, Savior of All Nations
[concluded]

Now glows forth your stable crib;
now the night sends forth
a light hereto unknown;
may no darkness
render that light untrue,
nay, may it shine
with a faith that never ends.

To you, O Christ, King most faithful,
may glory be
and to the Father too,
with the Spirit Advocate
for ages ere yet to run .
Amen.

SEASON OF ADVENT (B): MORNING PRAYER
Magnis Prophetae Vocibus / With Voices Stern and Clear

Magnis prophetae vocibus
venire Christum nuntiant,
laetae salutis praevia,
qua nos redemit, gratia.

With voices stern and clear,
the prophets proclaim
that Christ is coming.
and that the grace
of blessed salvation
whereby he redeemed us,
leads his way.

Hinc mane nostrum promicat
et corda laeta exaestuant,
cum vox fidelis personat
praenuntiatrix gloriae.

And so our morning-time
brightens fair,
our hearts glow hot
with joy unbounded,
when that faithful voice sounds forth,
foreteller of the glory soon to come.

Adventus hic primus fuit,
punire quo non saeculum
venit, sed ulcus tergere,
salvando quod perierat.

In his first coming, he aimed not
to punish the world,
but to heal its wounds,
to make sound once more
whate'er had been destroyed.

At nos secundus praemonet
adesse Christum ianuis,
sanctis coronas reddere
caelique regna pandere.

But He will come a second time:
we are warned that Christ
is e'en now present at the gates,
to award crowns to his holy ones,
to fling open wide
the kingdom of heaven.

Aeterna lux promittitur
sidusque salvans promitur;
iam nos iubar praefulgidum
ad ius vocat caelestium.

Eternal light is sent down to us;
a shining, salvific star comes forth.
Now a splendor most brilliant
summons us
to righteousness celestial.

Te, Christe, solum quaerimus
videre, sicut es Deus,
ut perpes haec sit visio
perenne laudis canticum.
Amen.

You alone, O Christ, do we ask
to make us see that,
just as you are God most high,
so this heavenly sight
might have no end, but
might rather stir
a perpetual song of praise.
Amen.

SEASON OF ADVENT (B): MIDMORNING PRAYER
Certum Tenentes Ordinem / Maintain We Now a Steady Path

Certum tenentes ordinem, pio poscamus pectore hora diei tertia trinae virtutis gloriam,	Maintain we now a steady path and, with faithful heart, beg we at this third hour of day to know the glory of the Triune power,
Ut simus habitaculum illi Sancto Spiritui, qui quondam in apostolis hac hora distributus est.	So that we might be a fit dwelling place for that Holy Spirit who, at this hour, was of old poured forth upon the Apostles.
Hoc gradiente ordine, ornavit cuncta splendide regni caelestis conditor ad nostra aeterna praemia.	As this day's pathway wends along, the Author of the heavenly realm lends beauty prodigal to all his creation, leading us thus to our eternal reward.
Deo Patri sit gloria eiusque soli Filio cum Spiritu Paraclito in sempiterna saecula. Amen.	To God the Father be glory, and to His only Son, with the Spirit Paraclete for endless ages to come. Amen.

SEASON OF ADVENT (B): MIDDAY PRAYER
Dicamus Laudes Domino / By Heartening Spirit Inspired

Dicamus laudes Domino
fervente prompti spiritu;
hora voluta sexies
nos ad orandum provocat.

By heartening Spirit inspired,
let us sing our praises to the Lord.
The hours' course
has now come to six,
and it calls us forth to prayer.

In hac enim fidelibus
verae salutis gloria,
beati Agni hostia,
crucis virtute redditur.

For at this hour the glory
of salvation true,
the Sacred Lamb who is immolated,
is granted to the faithful
through the power of the Cross.

Cuius luce clarissima
tenebricat meridies,
sumamus toto pectore
tanti splendoris gratiam.

In the brilliant light thus shed,
noontime itself pales into darkness.
Let us, with all our hearts,
receive the grace
of such shining glory.

Deo Patri sit gloria
eiusque soli Filio
cum Spiritu Paraclito
in sempiterna saecula.
Amen.

To God the Father be glory,
and to his only Son,
with the Spirit Paraclete ruling
for endless ages to come.
Amen.

SEASON OF ADVENT (B): MIDAFTERNOON PRAYER
Ternis Horarum Terminis / Now That, As Gift of the Lord

Ternis horarum terminis
volutis dante Domino,
trinum perfecte et unicum
ipsum devoti psallimus.

Now that, as gift of the Lord,
the third of the three
measures of the hours
with stately pace has come,
we sing our faithful hymn to Him
who is perfect Threesome
and yet perfect One.

Sacrum Dei mysterium
puro tenentes pectore,
Petri magistri regula
signo salutis prodita,

As we hold in cleansed hearts
the holy mystery of
God most high,
and as the example of Peter our teacher
is handed down to us
as a sign of our salvation,

Et nos psallamus spiritu,
haerentes sic apostolis,
ut plantas adhuc debiles
Christi virtute dirigant.

We too sing forth in spirit
and place our confidence
in the Apostles,
that they may guide
our still-faltering footsteps
with the power of Christ.

Deo Patri sit gloria
eiusque soli Filio
cum Spiritu Paraclito
in sempiterna saecula.
Amen.

To God the Father be glory,
and to his sole-begotten Son,
with the Spirit Paraclete
for endless ages to come.
Amen.

SEASON OF CHRISTMAS (A): EVENING PRAYER
Christe, Redemptor Omnium / Christ God, Redeemer of Us All

Christe, redemptor omnium,
ex Patre, Patris Unice
solus ante principium
natus ineffabiliter,

Christ God, Redeemer of us all,
the Father's only-begotten Son,
sole-born of the Father
in manner inexpressible
ere all else came to be,

Tu lumen, tu splendor Patris,
tu spes perennis omnium,
intende quas fundunt preces
tui per orbem servuli.

Light itself are you,
very brilliance of the Father
most high,
Unending hope are you
for all that live:
listen to the prayers which,
through the length and breadth
of the world, your faithful ones
e'er pour out to you.

Salutis auctor, recole
quod nostri quondam corporis,
ex illibata Virgine
nascendo, formam sumpseris.

Hic praesens testatur dies,
currens per anni circulum,
quod solus a sede Patris
mundi salus adveneris;

Sole Source of Salvation,
deign to recall
that once upon a time
you took unto yourself the very form
of our human frame,
for born were you
of the stainless Virgin blest.

Hunc caelum, terra, hunc mare,
hunc omne quod in eis est,
auctorem adventus tui
laudat exsultans cantico.

Nos quoque, qui sancto tuo
redempti sumus sanguine,
ob diem natalis tui
hymnum novum concinimus.

Today, this very day,
racing in brilliant power throughout the course of the entire year,
gladsome witness bears:
you, who alone are
the world's salvation,
have truly come
from the exalted throne
of the Father most high.

Iesu, tibi sit gloria,
qui natus es de Virgine,
cum Patre et almo Spiritu
in sempiterna saecula. Amen.

[continued]

Christe, Redemptor Omnium / Christ God, Redeemer of Us All
[concluded]

Heaven, earth, and sea,
and everything that lives
within their bounds as well,
laud with exultant song
this Father-God:
for His command is why you came.

And we as well,
redeemed by your blood most sacred,
sing together a new hymn of praise
because of this, the day of your birth.

Jesus Lord, to you be glory,
born now of the Virgin most pure,
with the Father and the kindly Spirit,
for ages e'er to come.
Amen.

SEASON OF CHRISTMAS (A): OFFICE OF READINGS
Candor Aeternae Deitatis Alme / Kindly Radiance of the Godhead Eternal

Candor aeternae Deitatis alme,
Christe, tu lumen venis atque vita,
advenis morbis hominum medela,
porta salutis.

Kindly radiance
of the Godhead eternal,
Christ Lord, as light and as life
are you here.
As cure for humankind's ills
do you come,
as their gateway to salvation.

The angel choir sings
to the earth below
a song brand new:
of a new age they tell,
of the Father's glory, and of the joys
that peace will bring to our race.

Intonat terrae chorus angelorum
caelicum carmen, nova saecla
dicens,
gloriam Patri, generique nostro
gaudia pacis.

You lie in your crib
as a babe most small,
yet you rule over the entire earth:
fruit of the womb of the Virgin
without stain,
Christ, master now
of the whole wide world,
much to be loved
for all time to come.

Qui iaces parvus dominans et orbi,
Virginis fructus sine labe sanctae,
Christe, iam mundo potiaris omni,
semper amandus.

Now born, you will give us
the heavens themselves
as our homeland,
for you are one of us, of our own flesh
truly formed.
Renew our spirits;
draw our hearts to you
by the gentle bonds of love.

Nasceris caelos patriam daturus,
unus e nobis, caro nostra factus;
innova mentes, trahe caritatis
pectora vinclis.

Lo, in joy we gather together
to sing our song,
joined together with the angels
in exultant lay;
to the Father, to you, and to the Spirit,
coequal in love,
we render bright paean of praise.
Amen.

Coetus exsultans canit ecce noster,
angelis laeto sociatus ore,
et Patri tecum parilique Amori
cantica laudis.
Amen.

SEASON OF CHRISTMAS (A): MORNING PRAYER
A Solis Ortus Cardine / From the World's East Side

A solis ortus cardine
adusque terrae limitem,
Christum canamus principem,
natum Maria Virgine.

Beatus auctor saeculi
servile corpus induit,
ut carne carnem liberans
non perderet quod condidit.

Clausae parentis viscera
caelestis intrat gratia;
venter puellae baiulat
secreta quae non noverat.

Domus pudici pectoris
templum repente fit Dei;
intacta nesciens virum
verbo concepit Filium.

Enixa est puerpera
quem Gabriel praedixerat,
quem matris alvo gestiens
clausus Ioannes senserat.

Feno iacere pertulit,
praesepe non abhorruit,
parvoque lacte passus est
per quem nec ales esurit.

Gaudet chorus caelestium
et angeli canunt Deum,
palamque fit pastoribus
pastor, creator omnium.

Iesu, tibi sit gloria,
qui natus es de Virgine,
cum Patre et almo Spiritu,
in sempiterna saecula.
Amen.

From the world's east side, the point
where rises bright the sun,
thence to the place where the earth
comes finally to its end,
Christ our Prince do we praise in song,
Christ Prince, born now of Mary
the Virgin blest.

The holy maker of the universe so broad
now takes upon himself
the body of a slave:
so that by means of flesh itself
might he flesh set free,
and thus not lose
what he himself had made.

Heavenly grace invades
the inmost parts
of the well-guarded parent mother;
the young girl's womb
now carries a hidden burden;
would she explain it,
she could not call upon
knowledge of man.

The home-site of a chaste breast
suddenly becomes the temple of God:
untouched, no carnal intercourse here,
she none the less
by only a simple word of assent,
conceives God's Son in human form.

In labor brings she forth the one
whom Gabriel had foretold,
the one whom, while still living
peaceably in his mother's womb,
John, himself yet unborn,
had recognized and proclaimed.

[continued]

A Solis Ortus Cardine / From the World's East Side
[concluded]

He endured lying in the straw;
from the stable shrank he not.
With a bit of milk
did he let himself be nourished,
he, through whom e'en
the birds of the air
find freedom from savage hunger.

The heavenly choir rejoices;
the angels sing their praise to God.
To the shepherds
there appears openly
the Shepherd Supreme,
the creator of us all.

Jesus, to you be all glory,
for you are of the blest Virgin born,
with the Father
and the Spirit most faithful,
for ages fore'er to come.
Amen.

Note: During Christmas (A) season:
     For NIGHT PRAYER: see *Te Lucis ante Terminum*, p. 4
     For MIDMORNING PRAYER: see *Nunc, Sancte, Nobis, Spiritus*, p. 7
     For MIDDAY PRAYER: see *Rector Potens, Verax Deus*, p. 8
     For MIDAFTERNOON PRAYER: see *Rerum, Deus, Tenax Vigor*, p. 9

SEASON OF CHRISTMAS (B): EVENING PRAYER
Hostis Herodes Impie / Herod, Wicked Foe

Hostis Herodes impie,
Christum venire quid times?
Non eripit mortalia
qui regna dat caelestia.

Herod, wicked foe,
why fear you the coming of the Christ?
He who grants heavenly kingdoms
does not take away earthly ones.

Ibant magi, qua venerant
stellam sequentes praeviam,
lumen requirunt lumine,
Deum fatentur munere.

The Magi traveled on, following the star
that had led them
along the way they had come.
By a heavenly light, they seek
the Light of Heaven;
their God they proclaim
by the gifts they bring.

Lavacra puri gurgitis
caelestis Agnus attigit;
peccata quae non detulit
nos abluendo sustulit.

At the rebirth bath
of Jordan stream most pure
did the Lamb of Heaven arrive:
in washing us clean,
he took upon himself
sins whose guilt belonged not to him.

Novum genus potentiae:
aquae rubescunt hydriae,
vinumque iussa fundere
mutavit unda originem.

A new type of powerful sign:
vessels of water glow bright red,
and the water within,
bidden to pour itself out as wine,
changes its lineage, its stock, its kind.

Iesu, tibi sit gloria,
qui te revelas gentibus,
cum Patre et almo Spiritu,
in sempiterna saecula.
Amen.

Jesus, to you be all glory
as you make yourself known
to the nations far and wide;
to the Father too,
and the Spirit most kind
for ages fore'er to run.
Amen.

SEASON OF CHRISTMAS (B): OFFICE OF READINGS
Magi Videntes Parvulum / The Magi Espy the Child

Magi videntes parvulum
eoa promunt munera,
stratique votis offerunt
tus, myrr*am* et aurum regium.

Agnosce cl*a*ra insignia
virtutis et regni tui,
Puer, cui trinam Pater
praedestinavit indolem:

Regem Deumque annuntiant
thesaurus et fragrans odor
turis Sab*ae*i, et myrrhus
pulvis sepulchrum praedocet.

O sola magnar*um* urbium
maior Bethlem, cui contigit
ducem salutis caelitus
incorporatum gignere!

Hunc et prophetis testibus
isdemque signatoribus
testator et sator iubet
adire regn*um* et cernere:

Regnum quod ambit omnia
di*a* et marin*a* et terrea
a solis ort*u* ad exitum
et tartar*a* et caelum supra.

Iesu, tibi sit gloria,
qui te revelas gentibus,
cum Patre et almo Spiritu
in sempiterna saecula.
Amen.

The Magi espy the Child:
lo, they proffer gifts they have brought
from the distant East.
Prostrate in devotion
they offer as homage
incense, myrrh, and regal gold.

O Child, recognize the shining symbols
of your kingly power—
for the Father has preordained for you
a threefold role:

Rich and fragrant the aroma
of the incense of Araby:
it, and the proffered treasure of gold,
proclaim you as both King and God,
while the dusty myrrh warns darkly
of the tomb that lies in wait for you.

O Bethlehem! of all great cities
alone yet greater,
to you did it befall to bring forth
the Chieftain of Salvation
in human form
from spirit state in heaven above.

The prophets serve as witnesses,
and likewise guarantors of the deed:
Mandator Father, Creator Father,
bids him
approach his kingdom, behold it all.

[continued]

Magi Videntes Parvulum / The Magi Espy the Child
[concluded]

That kingdom which embraces all,
sky, ocean, land,
from the sun's bright rising
to dusky eve,
yes, e'en hell-land and heaven above.

Jesus, to you be glory
as you reveal yourself to nations far,
in company with Father and kindly Spirit
for all ages to come.
Amen.

SEASON OF CHRISTMAS (B): MORNING PRAYER
Quicumque Christum Quaeritis / You Who Seek the Anointed One

Quicumque Christum quaeritis
oculos in altum tollite:
illic licebit visere
signum perennis gloriae.

You who seek the Anointed One,
whoe'er ye be,
Lift up your gaze
to the heavens above:
there can you behold, in splendor fair,
the sign of a glory that has no end.

Haec stella, quae solis rotam
vincit decore ac lumine;
venisse terris nuntiat
cum carne terrestri Deum.

This sign, this star: in brilliant beauty
it o'erpowers e'en
the gleaming path of the Sun itself;
and it proclaims that to this earth
has come our God,
in mortal flesh enclosed.

En, Persici ex orbis sinu
Sol unde sumit ianuam,
cernunt periti interpretes
regale vexillum Magi.

Lo, from the heart
of far-distant land,
whence finds the sun its gateway
to the world,
the eyes of expert diviners,
e'en the Persian-born
Magi themselves,
behold that symbol so regal,
that symbol so sublime.

"Quis iste tantus"—inquiunt—
"regnator astris imperans,
quem sic tremunt caelestia,
cui lux et aethra inserviunt?

"Illustre quiddam cernimus
quod nesciat finem pati,
sublime, celsum, interminum
antiquius caelo et chao,

"Hic ille rex est gentium
populique rex Iudaici
promissus Abrahae patri
eiusque in aevum semini."

"Who is this awesome sovereign" —
say they—
"who gives commands
e'en to the stars above?
Before whom the heavens themselves
tremble in fear,
Whom light itself and the farthest
reaches of the sky as well
obey in thrall most fair?

Iesu, tibi sit gloria
qui te revelas gentibus,
cum Patre et almo Spiritu
in sempiterna saecula.
Amen.

[continued]

Quicumque Christum Quaeritis / You Who Seek the Anointed One
[concluded]

"Brilliant it is, whatever it is,
that comes into our view:
it knows not how to suffer an end
to its light so clear:
exalted, coming from on high,
with neither start nor finish,
more ancient than
famed heaven above, yes,
older e'en than the unformed mass
that went before.

"The one it proclaims is He:
the king of nations,
and king as well of Jewish people all—
the king promised to Abraham,
his ancestral sire,
and to descendants of his
for all time to come."

Jesus, to you be all glory,
as you reveal yourself to nations far,
in company with Father and kindly Spirit
for all ages to come.
Amen.

Note: During the Season of Christmas (B):
    For NIGHT PRAYER, see *Christe, Qui Splendor,* p. 11
    For MIDMORNING PRAYER, see *Certum Tenentes Ordinem,* p. 15
    For MIDDAY PRAYER, see *Dicamus Laudes Domino,* p. 16
    For MIDAFTERNOON PRAYER, see *Ternis Horarum Terminis,* p. 17.

THE FESTIVALS OF CHRISTMAS (A and B)

DECEMBER 25: CHRISTMAS DAY
All hymns are taken from the Proper of the Season (A), pp. 7-9 and 18-22.

SUNDAY WITHIN THE OCTAVE OF CHRISTMAS: HOLY FAMILY
MIDMORNING, MIDDAY, MIDAFTERNOON PRAYERS: pp. 7-9
NIGHT PRAYER, p. 4.

HOLY FAMILY: EVENING PRAYER
O Lux Beata Caelitum / O Light, Great Delight

O lux beata caelitum
et summa spes mortalium,
Iesu, cui domestica
arrisit orto caritas:

Maria, dives gratia,
o sola quae casto potes
fovere Iesum pectore,
cum lacte donans oscula;

Tuque ex vetustis patribus
delecte custos Virginis,
dulci patris quem nomine
divina Proles invocat:

De stirpe Iesse nobili
nat*i in* salutem gentium,
audite nos, qui supplices
ex corde vota fundimus.

Qua vestra sedes floruit
virtutis omnis gratia,
hanc detur in domesticis
referre posse moribus.

Iesu, tuis oboediens
qui factus es parentibus,
cum Patre summo ac Spiritu
semper tibi sit gloria.
Amen.

O light, great delight of those
who live in high heaven above,
and brightest hope for us
who dwell here on earth below,
Jesus Lord, at your birth
the love of a happy home
smiled fully upon you.

Mary, rich in grace!
Only to you is it given
to dandle the infant Jesus
at your most chaste breast,
mingling loving kisses
with maiden-mother's milk
as tenderly you feed him
with utmost care.

And you,
chosen guardian of the Virgin,
born of a royal race from of old:
you are the one
whom the divine Infant
calls upon with blessed title of father.

[continued]

O Lux Beata Caelitum / O Light, Great Delight
[concluded]

You, the holy family, all three
sprung from Jesse's noble line
for the salvation of the peoples:
hear us, as in humble petition
we pour forth our prayers to you
from hearts' fullest depths.

Your household flowered forth
with bedeckment
of every grace and virtue high.
Through these let it be granted us
to have such richness
in our homes and habits too.

Jesus, you became obedient
to your parents.
To you, in company
with the Father most high,
and the most high Spirit as well,
let glory and praise be forever given.
Amen.

HOLY FAMILY: OFFICE OF READINGS
Dulce Fit Nobis Memorare Parvum / Most Pleasant It Is for Us

Dulce fit nobis
memorare parvum
Nazarae tectum
tenuemque cultum;
expedit Iesu tacitam referre
carmine vitam.

Most pleasant it is for us
to call to mind
the little house at Nazareth,
and to ponder its modest way of life;
it is fitting to relate in song
the hidden life that Jesus led.

Arte qua Ioseph
humili excolendus,
abdito Iesus iuvenescit aevo,
seque fabrilis socium laboris
adicit ultro.

In the humble trade that was Joseph's
was Jesus to be trained,
as he grew up
in that life so far from the public eye;
willingly did he make himself
one with his father
in doing the things that carpenters do.

Assidet nato pia mater almo,
assidet sponso bona nupta, felix
si potest curas relevare lassis
munere amico.

O neque expertes operae et
laboris,
nec mali ignari, miseros iuvate;
quotquot implorant columen,
benigno cernite vultu.

At the side of her dutiful son
stands a mother, fond and caring;
stands she too next to her husband,
loving wife that she is,
delighted if by her companion role
she can ease the cares
of her weary son,
of her weary spouse.

Sit tibi, Iesus, decus
atque virtus,
sancta qui vitae
documenta praebes,
quique cum summo Genitore
et almo Flamine regnas.
Amen.

[continued]

Dulce Fit Nobis Memorare Parvum / Most Pleasant It Is for Us
[concluded]

O threesome blest,
not inexperienced in work and toil,
nor unaware of hardship dire,
come to the aid of the poor wretches
who call upon you;
with benign gaze look upon
whoever makes plea to you
in your high station above.

Praise be to you, Jesus,
and power as well,
for you give us a model,
shining sacred-bright,
for what our lives should be,
and you reign eternally
with the almighty Father
and the kindly Spirit.
Amen.

HOLY FAMILY: MORNING PRAYER
Christe, Splendor Patris / Christ, Brilliant Splendor

Christe, splendor Patris,
Dei mater Virgo,
Ioseph, tam sacrorum
pignorum servator,

Nitet vestra domus
floribus virtutum,
unde gratiarum
fons promanat ipse.

Angeli stupentes
Natum Dei cernunt
servi forma indutum
servis famulantem.

Imus praees, Ioseph,
humilisque iubes;
iubes et Maria
et utrique servis.

Cunctis praestant aulis
haec egena saepta,
salus unde coepit
generis humani.

Iesu, Mater, Ioseph,
mansionis vestrae
nostras date sedes
donis frui sanctis.

Tibi laudes, Christe,
spem qui nobis praebes,
tuos per parentes
caeli adire domum.
Amen.

Christ, brilliant splendor
of the Father most high,
Mary, Virgin, truly termed
Mother of God,
Joseph, faithful guardian
of God's salvation-pledge so sacred,

Your home spills over, full-laden,
with all the flowers
of the virtues so many, so diverse;
and from it flows richly forth
the true teeming fountain
of graces Himself.

Awe-struck are the angels:
they gaze upon
God's own and only Son,
now in the form of a servant;
now indeed a servant
serving servants.

Joseph, least of the three,
it has pleased God
to place you in charge;
and in great humility
you voice your commands.
Mary, you too tell what must be done,
and you watch carefully
over your husband and your Son.

E'en all palaces on earth
does this humble home surpass,
for from it came forth
the beginnings of salvation
for the whole human race.
[continued]

Christe, Splendor Patris / Christ, Brilliant Splendor
[concluded]

Jesus Lord, Mary Mother,
and Joseph Just:
grant that our homes too may enjoy
those holy gifts
that adorn your blessed abode.

To you, O Christ, be full praise given!
You give us great hope that,
through your holy parents,
we too may come to find a home
in the halls of heaven on high.
Amen.

JANUARY 1: SOLEMNITY OF THE BLESSED VIRGIN MARY
MIDMORNING, MIDDAY, AND MIDAFTERNOON PRAYER: pp. 7-9
NIGHT PRAYER: p. 4

EVENING PRAYER
Corde Natus ex Parentis / Born Was He from the Heart of the Father

Corde natus ex Parentis
ante mund*i* exordium,
Alph*a* et Omega vocatus,
ipse fons et clausula
omnium quae sunt, fuerunt
quaeque post futura sunt.

Corporis formam caduci,
membra morb*i* obnoxia
induit, ne gens periret
primoplasm*i* ex germine,
merserat quam lex profundo
noxialis tartaro.

O beatus ortus ille,
Virgo cum puerpera
edidit nostram salutem
feta Sancto Spiritu,
et puer redemptor orbis
os sacratum protulit.

Ecce, quem vates vetustis
concinebant saeculis,
quem prophetarum fideles
paginae spoponderant,
emicat promissus olim:
cuncta collaudent eum!

Gloriam Patri melodis
personemus vocibus;
gloriam Christo canamus,
matre nato virgine,
inclitoque sempiternam
gloriam Paraclito.
Amen.

Born was he
from the heart of the Father
before the world began;
"Alpha" and "Omega"
were the names given him.
In him everything has beginning,
everything has end:
things now, things then,
things that were yet to be.

With form of perishable body,
with limbs
that death could overcome,
did he clothe himself:
so that the race
sprung from Adam-seed
might not perish—
for the law of death held it in thrall
in deepest Sheol.

How blessed
that wondrous beginning,
when the Virgin,
made fertile by the Holy Spirit,
brought forth to birth our salvation—
when the child,
the Redeemer of the world,
showed forth his visage sublime.
[continued]

Corde Natus ex Parentis / Born Was He from the Heart of the Father
[concluded]

Lo! The one of whom
the seers in ancient ages
used to sing—whom the faithful writings
of the prophets had pledged!
Foretold of old, now he shines forth;
let all that has being render him praise!

Let us give full song
to the Father's glory
in music and in voice;
let us sing as well of the glory
to be given to Christ,
born of his Virgin Mother.
To the glorious Advocate as well
be e'erlasting praise e'erlastingly given.
Amen.

SOLEMNITY OF THE B.V.M.: OFFICE OF READINGS
Radix Jesse Floruit / The Root of Jesse Has Blossomed

Radix Jesse floruit
et virga fructum edidit;
fecunda partum protulit
et virgo mater permanet.

The root of Jesse has blossomed;
the branch has brought forth its fruit.
A woman, heavy with child,
has brought it to birth—
but, though a mother indeed,
she remains yet a virgin most pure.

Praesepe poni pertulit
qui lucis auctor exstitit;
cum Patre caelos condidit,
sub matre pannos induit.

In a manger
did he allow himself to be placed,
the very One
who was the brilliant creator of light—
yea,
the very One
who with his Father all-powerful,
established the heavens:
that very One
at the tender hands of his mother,
in swaddling clothes
is now humbly garbed.

Legem dedit qui saeculo,
cuius decem praecepta sunt,
dignando factus est homo
sub legis esse vinculo.

Iam lux salusque nascitur,
nox diffugit, mors vincitur;
venite, gentes, credite:
Deum Maria protulit.

The very One
who gave to the world its ruling law,
the very One
whose commandments ten we have:
that very One
has chosen to be one of humankind,
and so be ruled
by the law that he himself gave.

Iesu, tibi sit gloria,
qui natus es de Virgine,
cum Patre et almo Spiritu
in sempiterna saecula.
Amen.

[continued]

Radix Jesse Floruit / The Root of Jesse Has Blossomed
[concluded]

Now indeed is light born;
so is salvation.
Night flees; death is overcome.
Come, all ye nations:
see and believe
that Mary has given birth to God.

Jesus, to you be glory e'er given.
for you are born of the Virgin.
Glory be too, along with you,
to the Father most high
and the Spirit most benign,
for ages all e'er yet to come.
Amen.

SOLEMNITY OF THE B.V.M.: MORNING PRAYER
Fit Porta Christi Pervia / The Gateway Christ the Lord Would Use

Fit porta Christi pervia
omni referta gratia,
transitque rex, et permanet
clausa, ut fuit, per saecula.

The gateway
Christ the Lord would use
now grants him passage free,
a gateway filled with every grace.
The king passes through;
the gate remains firm closed,
forever so to be, as e'er it has been.

Summi Parentis Filius
processit aula Virginis,
sponsus, redemptor, conditor,
suae gigas Ecclesiae:

The Son of the Father most high
comes forth now
from the royal chamber
of the Virgin's womb:
spouse is he, redeemer, creator,
colossus of his Church:

Honor matris et gaudium,
immensa spes credentium,
lapis de monte veniens
mundumque replens gratia.

The great joy and honor, too,
of his maiden mother fair,
the boundless hope of those
who put their trust in him,
the stone tumbling down
from the mountaintop,
filling the whole world with its favor.

Exsultet omnis anima,
quod nunc salvator gentium
advenit mundi Dominus
redimere quos condidit.

Let every soul rejoice,
for now has the Savior of the nations,
the very Lord of the world,
come to redeem those
that He himself did in truth create.

Christo sit omnis gloria,
quem Pater Deum genuit,
quem Virgo mater edidit
fecunda Sancto Spiritu.
Amen.

To Christ be all glory,
Christ whom the Father begat
as divine,
Christ whom the Virgin Mother,
made fruitful by the Holy Spirit,
brought forth into this
human world of ours.
Amen.

EPIPHANY

EVENING PRAYER I: *Quicumque,* pp. 26-27

NIGHTTIME PRAYER: *Christe, Qui Splendor,* p. 11

OFFICE OF READINGS: *Magi Videntes,* pp. 24-25

MORNING PRAYER: *Quicumque,* pp. 26-27

MIDMORNING PRAYER: *Certum Tenentes,* p. 15
MIDDAY PRAYER: *Dicamus Laudes Domino,* p. 16
MIDAFTERNOON PRAYER: *Ternis Horarum Terminis,* p. 17

EVENING PRAYER II: *Hostes Herodes Impie,* p. 23

BAPTISM OF THE LORD

EVENING PRAYER I:
A Patre Unigenite / Christ God, Sole-begotten

A Patre Unigenite,
ad nos venis per Virginem,
baptismi rore consecrans
cunctos, fide regenerans.

Christ God, sole-begotten
from the Father most high,
you come to us:
The Virgin provides the path.
You sanctify all
by blessed baptizing bath,
you give new life to all
by a faith that stands most firm.

De caelo celsus prodiens
excipis formam hominis,
facturam morte redimens,
gaudia vitae largiens.

When you came forth
from heaven on high,
you took to yourself a human form:
by your own cruel death
you redeemed the people
you had made,
and bestowed on them
the gift of joyous life.

Hoc te, Redemptor, quaesumus:
illabere propitius,
clarumque nostris cordibus
lumen praebe deificum.

Redeemer blest, grant this boon to us:
in your great mercy,
enter deep into our hearts;
pour out into them your clear
and sanctifying light.

Mane nobiscum, Domine,
noctem obscuram remove,
omne delictum ablue,
pie medelam tribue.

Remain with us, Lord God!
Take away the darkness of the night.
Wash away every sin;
in your faithful mercy,
grant us cure for all our ills.

O Christe, vita, veritas,
tibi sit omnis gloria,
quem Patris atque Spiritus
splendor revelat caelitus. Amen.

Christ! Our life, our light!
May all glory be given unto you,
for upon you has the brilliant radiance
of the Father and the Spirit
shone full fair from far on high. Amen.

BAPTISM OF THE LORD: OFFICE OF READINGS
and EVENING PRAYER II
Implente Munus Debitum / As John, the Baptizer Blest

Implente munus debitum
Ioanne, rerum conditor
Iordane mersus hac die
aquas lavando diluit,

As John, the baptizer blessed,
goes about the tasks
he has been given,
lo, into Jordan's murky waters
goes down this day
the Creator of heaven and earth and,
by his own baptismal bath,
cleanses the very cleansing waters
themselves.

Non ipse mundari volens
de ventre natus Virginis,
peccata sed mortalium
suo lavacro tollere.

Not his wish was it
to be made clean himself,
for of a Virgin's chaste womb
had he been born;
instead, by the waters
of his baptism by John
would he take away the sins
of frail humankind.

Dicente Patre quod "Meus
dilectus hic est Filius,"
sumente Sancto Spiritu
formam columbae caelitus,

As the Father spoke the words,
"This is my beloved Son";
As the Holy Spirit took unto himself
the form of a dove
in high heaven above,

'Neath this event so mysterious,
'neath this power that cannot be told,
there shines forth
the salvation that is the Church;
threefold are the Persons,
but only one God remains
at event's beginning,
at event's unfolding,
at event's final end.

Hoc mystico sub nomine
micat salus Ecclesiae;
Persona trina commanet
unus Deus per omnia.

O Christe, vita, veritas,
tibi sit omnis gloria,
quem Patris atque Spiritus
splendor revelat caelitus.
Amen.

Christ! Our life, our light!
May all glory be given unto you,
for upon you has the brilliant radiance
of the Father and the Spirit
shone full fair from far on high. Amen.

BAPTISM OF THE LORD: MORNING PRAYER
Iesus Refulsit Omnium / In Brilliance He Stands Forth

Iesus refulsit omnium
pius redemptor gentium;
totum genus fidelium
laudis celebret canticum.

In brilliance He stands forth:
Jesus, faithful redeemer
of the mass that is humankind;
and so let the whole tribe
of ever faithful people
shout forth to him
a hymn of loving praise.

Denis ter aevi circulis
iam parte vivens corporis
lympham petit baptismatis
cunctis carens contagiis.

For three cycles of years times ten
has he lived in bodily form;
now he seeks the bath of baptism,
howe'er so much he lacks
all stain of sin.

Felix Ioannes mergere
illum tremescit flumine,
potest suo qui sanguine
peccata mundi tergere.

Blessed Saint John fears
to immerse Him
in the waters of Jordan-flow,
for he is the one who, by his blood,
can wipe away the sins of the world.

Vox ergo Prolem de polis
testatur excelsi Patris,
fluitque virtus Spiritus
sancti datrix charismatis.

And so a voice,
from the Father on high,
rings out from heaven above;
it proclaims Him as beloved Son.
And the power of the Spirit—
the giver of the holy gift—
rushes forth from heaven as well.

Nos, Christe, voce supplici
precamur, omnes protege,
ac mente fac nitescere
tibique mundos vivere.

Now, O Christ,
with humble voice we pray to you:
protect us all,
make our spirits thrive
and live unto you purified full well.

O Christe, vita, veritas,
tibi sit omnis gloria,
quem Patris atque Spiritus
splendor revelat caelitus.
Amen.

Christ! Our life, our light!
May all glory be given unto you,
for upon you has the radiant brilliance
of the Father and the Spirit
shone full fair from far on high.
Amen.

THE SEASON OF LENT (A)
EVENING PRAYER: SUNDAYS
Audi, Benigne Conditor / Creator Most Gracious, Grant Merciful Ear

Audi, benigne Conditor,
nostras preces cum fletibus,
sacrata in abstinentia
fusas quadragenaria.

Creator most gracious,
grant merciful ear
to the prayers we pour forth
with the tears that we shed,
which we bring unto you
during this time of sacred Lenten fast.

Scrutator alme cordium,
infirma tu scis virium;
ad te reversis exhibe
remissionis gratiam.

Kindly reader of hearts, you know well
how little in our weakness we can do:
grant precious forgiveness' grace
to those who struggle back to you.

Surely, in many things have we sinned.
But do you have mercy on those
who call upon you;
for the praise of your holy name
grant healing to us,
who languish in soul-sickness drear.

Multum quidem peccavimus,
sed parce confitentibus,
tuique laude nominis
confer medelam languidis.

And thus, by abstinence stern, grant
that our body may to humbled state
be brought down:
so that our sobered spirit
may fast its way far distant
from slightest stain of sin.

Sic corpus extra conteri
dona per abstinentiam,
ieiunet ut mens sobria
a labe prorsus criminum.

Grant this, blessed Trinity;
Grant this, Unity in Three.
And so may this gift of self-denial
truly aid
the people you have made your own.
Amen.

Praesta, beata Trinitas,
concede, simplex Unitas,
ut fructuosa sint tuis
haec parcitatis munera.
Amen.

LENT (A): EVENING PRAYER, WEEKDAYS
Iesu, Quadragenariae / Jesus Lord, Loving Mandator

Iesu, quadragenariae
dicator abstinentiae,
qui ob salutem mentium
praeceperas ieiunium,

Jesus Lord, loving mandator
of forty-day strictures stern,
it was for the well-being of our souls
that you had decreed
that this fast be held.

Adesto nunc Ecclesiae,
adesto paenitentiae,
qua supplicamur cernui
peccata nostra dilui.

Be present now
to your penitent Church;
witness now our acts
of repentance sincere.
By them we humbly pray,
with heads bowed low,
that our sins
may fully be washed away.

Tu retroacta crimina
tua remitte gratia
et a futuris adhibe
custodiam mitissime.

By your saving grace grant forgiveness
for the guilt of our sins in the past;
and in your merciful kindness grant us
protection from any wrongdoing
yet to come.

Ut, expiati annuis
compunctionis actibus,
tendamus ad paschalia
digne colenda gaudia.

And so, washed clean
by repentance deeds
we undertake each year
at this holy but fearful time,
may we go forward in holy haste
to celebrate worthily
joys paschal and sublime.

Te rerum universitas,
clemens, adoret, Trinitas,
et nos novi per veniam
novum canamus canticum.
Amen.

You, most merciful Trinity,
does the entire universe of creatures
adore most profoundly;
and may we especially, through
your own forgiveness renewed,
sing unto you a new song of praise.
Amen.

LENT (A): OFFICE OF READINGS, SUNDAYS
Ex More Docti Mystico / By Mystic Lore Well Taught

Ex more docti mystico
servemus abstinentiam,
deno dierum circulo
ducto quater notissimo.

By mystic lore well taught,
let us observe the fast,
in the tenfold cycle of days
four times led
by command well known.

Lex et prophetae primitus
hanc protulerunt, postmodum
Christus sacravit, omnium
rex atque factor temporum.

At the very first,
the law and the prophets
proclaimed the fast full far;
afterward, Christ the Lord,
the king and creator of all the ages,
rendered it sacred.

Utamur ergo parcius
verbis, cibis et potibus,
somno, iocis et arctius
perstemus in custodia.

Let us therefore use more sparingly
our speech, our food, our drink,
our time of rest, our laughter:
with all these,
let us be diligent, be vigilant
be guardians well watchful,
be guardians well wakeful.

Vitemus autem pessima
quae subruunt mentes vagas,
nullumque demus callido
hosti locum tyrannidis.

Now, let us shun those vilest evils
that subvert our wandering minds;
nor let us yield any place whatever
to the canny enemy
from tyranny's realm.

Praesta, beata Trinitas,
concede, simplex Unitas,
ut fructuosa sint tuis
haec parcitatis munera.
Amen.

Grant this, blessed Trinity;
bestow this upon us,
O Unity most sublime,
so that for your people
this gift of scarcity self-imposed
may bear fruit most plentiful.
Amen.

LENT (A): OFFICE OF READINGS, WEEKDAYS
Nunc Tempus Acceptabile / Now Shines Forth, from Heaven Above

Nunc tempus acceptabile
fulget datum divinitus,
ut sanet orbem languidum
medela parsimoniae.

Now shines forth, from heaven above,
that time approved, wherein
the saving remedy of frugal self-denial
may come to the aid
of a world sluggish and spirit-slow.

Christi decoro lumine
dies salutis emicat,
dum corda culpis saucia
reformat abstinentia.

By the seemly light of Christ most high
does the day of salvation
now flash forth,
as self-denial sets about its work
of healing hearts gashed
by sin most foul.

Hanc mente nos et corpore,
Deus, tenere perfice,
ut appetamus prospero
perenne pascha transitu.

Make us, O God most exalted,
hold firmly in mind and body
to the penance we undertake:
thus through the successful journey
through stark Lent
may we approach the Paschal feast
that has no end.

Te rerum universitas,
clemens, adoret, Trinitas,
et nos novi per veniam
novum canamus canticum.
Amen.

Trinity most merciful,
let the entire universe
fall down and adore You;
and may we,
renewed through
your gracious pardon,
sing unto you a renewed song of joy.
Amen.

LENT (A): MORNING PRAYER, SUNDAYS
Precemur Omnes Cernui / Let Us All Bow Down Low

Precemur omnes cernui,
clamemus atque singuli,
ploremus ante iudicem,
flectamus iram vindicem:

Let us all bow down low
as we offer our prayer,
let each and every one
bring heartfelt cry unto you:
let us plead
at the feet of our judge most just;
thus may we turn aside
his avenging wrath most dire.

Nostris malis offendimus
tuam, Deus, clementiam;
effunde nobis desuper,
remissor, indulgentiam.

By our wicked deeds
we have offended, O God,
that mercy of yours so great, so kind.
Pour out upon us from above,
kindly forgiver,
that mercy of yours,
so gracious, so mild.

Memento quod sumus tui,
licet caduci, plasmatis;
ne des honorem nominis
tui, precamur, alteri.

Bear in mind, we beg:
born of your own molding are we,
albeit frail and fallen;
let it not happen, we beg,
that you allow
the honor of your sacred name
to be given to some other.

Laxa malum quod fecimus,
auge bonum quod poscimus,
placere quo tandem tibi
possimus hic et perpetim.

Free us from the bonds
of the evil we have done,
augment the good
that we ask from you now,
that so we may be able,
both now and in eternity,
at long last to be pleasing unto you.

Praesta, beata Trinitas,
concede, simplex Unitas,
ut fructuosa sint tuis
haec parcitatis munera.
Amen.

Grant this, Trinity most blessed;
Bestow it, Unity most pure,
so that for your people
these gifts of Lenten self-denial
may bear abundant fruit
unto life eternal.
Amen.

LENT (A): MORNING PRAYER, WEEKDAYS
Iam, Christe, Sol Iustitiae / And Now, O Christ, Blazing Sun

Iam, Christe, sol iustitiae,
mentis dehiscant tenebrae,
virtutum ut lux redeat,
terris diem dum reparas.

And now, O Christ,
blazing Sun of justice stern,
let the inky blackness of our minds
be rent asunder,
so that virtues' bright light
might return once more,
as you begin to restore
for darkling earth
its grim-spirited day.

Dans tempus acceptabile
et paenitens cor tribue,
convertat ut benignitas
quos longa suffert pietas;

You grant us a suitable time: so too
bestow upon us a repentant heart;
and so may your generous favor
change the hearts
of those sons and daughters of yours
to whom your lasting fidelity
e'en now still grants tolerance kind.

Quiddamque paenitentiae
da ferre, quo fit demptio,
maiore tuo munere,
culparum quamvis grandium.

Grant that we may bear
whate'er sort of penance
may bring us blessed forgiveness,
by your unmeasured gracious gift,
however great be the burden
of our faults and sins.

Dies venit, dies tua,
per quam reflorent omnia;
laetemur in hac ut tuae
per hanc reducti gratiae.

The day has now come: that day
that belongs to you, that day
through which all things
bloom forth once more;
let us rejoice in it, as those who have,
by means of it, been brought back
to your graced life.

Te rerum universitas,
clemens, adoret, Trinitas,
et nos novi per veniam
novum canamus canticum.
Amen.

Most merciful and holy Trinity,
let all of your creatures bend low
in adoration of you;
so may we too,
by your forgiveness made new,
sing a new song of praise to you.
Amen.

LENT (A): MIDMORNING PRAYER, SUNDAYS AND WEEKDAYS
Dei Fide, Qua Vivimus / With the Faith in God

Dei fide, qua vivimus,
qua spe perenni credimus,
per caritatis gratiam
Christi canamus gloriam.

With the faith in God
whereby we live,
with the ne'er failing hope
whereby we trust,
through the graced gift
of charity most high
let us proclaim in song
the glory of Christ the Lord.

Qui ductus hora tertia
ad passionis hostiam,
crucis ferens suspendia
ovem reduxit perditam.

He it was, that very Christ, who,
at the third hour.
was forced to victim state,
as his passion required,
and endured even the dread
of hanging from a cross:
and so led safely back to the fold
the sheep that had been lost.

Precemur ergo subditi,
redemptione liberi,
ut eruat a saeculo
quos solvit a chirographo.

Let us therefore, in subjection humble,
but freed by Christ's redemptive deed,
pray that he may save us
from worldly snares:
us, whom He has freed
from all our acts' consequences fell
that had been
direfully sealed and signed.

Christum rogamus et Patrem,
Christi Patrisque Spiritum,
unum potens per omnia,
fove precantes, Trinitas,
Amen.

Christ do we beseech,
and the Father as well,
the Spirit too of Christ and Father:
O Trinity, alone most powerful
in all things,
grant gracious care to those
who call upon your name.
Amen.

LENT (A): MIDDAY PRAYER, SUNDAYS AND WEEKDAYS
Qua Christus Hora Sitiit / At the Hour When Thirst Beset

Qua Christus hora sitiit
crucem vel in qua subiit,
quos praestat in hac psallere
ditet siti iustitiae.

At the hour
when thirst beset Christ the Lord,
at the hour
when He took upon himself the cross:
may He enrich with a thirst for justice
those whose happy task it is
at this hour
to offer songs of praise.

Simul sit his esuries,
quam ipse de se satiet,
crimen sit ut fastidium
virtusque desiderium.

Let them likewise feel hunger,
that hunger which
he himself assuages
with his very self;
thus may deeds of sin
become deeds despised,
deeds of virtue
become deeds desired.

Charisma Sancti Spiritus
sic influat psallentibus,
ut carnis aestus frigeat
et mentis algor ferveat.

Let the gift of the Spirit most holy
so flow into those
who now chant praise,
that for them
carnal passion's white-hot breath
may chill,
for them
mind's tepid state become inflamed.

Christum rogamus et Patrem,
Christi Patrisque Spiritum;
unum potens per omnia,
fove precantes, Trinitas.
Amen.

Christ do we implore,
and the Father as well,
as also the Spirit
of both Christ and Father:
one in essence, all-powerful one,
graciously grant loving care to those
who call upon you,
Trinity most high.
Amen.

LENT (A): MIDAFTERNOON PRAYER, SUNDAYS AND WEEKDAYS
Ternis Ter Horis Numerus / Now Is That Sacred Number

Ternis ter horis numerus
nobis sacratus panditur,
sanctoque Iesu nomine
munus precemur veniae.

Now is that sacred number,
that thrice-three
in the count of the hours,
made open to us:
and in the holy name of Jesus
let us beg the boon of full forgiveness.

Latronis, en, confessio
Christi meretur gratiam;
laus nostra vel devotio
mercetur indulgentiam.

For lo, at this hour,
a thief's faith-offering
earns him Christ's freely given favor;
may our praise,
yea, our prayerful praise
likewise now gain for us too
his gracious forgiveness.

Mors per crucem nunc interit
et post tenebras lux redit;
horror dehiscat criminum,
splendor nitescat mentium.

Through the Cross
is death itself now put to death;
after the darkness,
light returns once more.
May our mouths now gape open wide
in revulsion at sin,
and the beauty of our spirits
shine forth in splendor.

Christum rogamus et Patrem,
Christi Patrisque Spiritum;
unum potens per omnia,
fove precantes, Trinitas.
Amen.

Christ do we beg, the Father too,
and the Spirit of Christ and Father
as well:
Trinity in unity, most powerful over all,
grant your loving favor
to those who call upon you.
Amen.

Note: During the Season of Lent (A):
    For NIGHT PRAYER:
        During weeks 1, 3, and 5: see *Te Lucis ante Terminum,* p. 4
        During other weeks: see *Christe, Qui Splendor,* p. 11.

THE SEASON OF LENT (B)
EVENING PRAYER, SUNDAYS AND WEEKDAYS
Vexilla Regis Prodeunt / The Royal Standard of the King

Vexilla regis prodeunt,
fulget crucis mysterium,
quo carne carnis conditor
suspensus est patibulo;

Quo, vulneratus insuper
mucrone diro lanceae,
ut nos lavaret crimine,
manavit unda et sanguine.

Arbor decora et sanguine
ornata regis purpura,
electa digno stipite
tam sancta membra tangere!

Beata, cuius bracchiis
saecli pependit pretium;
statera facta est corporis
praedam tulitque tartari.

Salve, ara, salve, victima,
de passionis gloria,
qua vita mortem pertulit
et morte vitam reddidit!

O crux, ave, spes unica!
hoc passionis tempore
piis adauge gratiam
reisque dele crimina.

Te, fons salutis, Trinitas,
collaudet omnis spiritus;
quos per crucis mysterium
salvas, fove per saecula.
Amen.

The royal standard of the King
does now appear:
the mystery of the Cross
flashes forth full fair,
that mystery when
the very creator of our human frame
was, in human flesh himself,
hanged on yoke cruciformed:

On that gibbet-cross, where,
wounded further by harsh point
of soldier's piercing lance,
He bled forth water,
bled forth life-blood too,
so as to cleanse us all
of sin's foul guilt-bane.

Tree penal, but tree most beautiful,
made lovely with regal purple blood,
chosen from a worthy stock
to embrace limbs so holy,
limbs so divine.

Blessed tree, from whose branches
the ransom-cost of this world
hung suspended;
now are you the balance-beam
on which hangs the ransom body;
now have you stolen away the booty
that hell had claimed in vain
as its own.

Hail to you, O altar;
hail to you, yourself made part
of the sacrifice by the splendor
of the Savior's suffering,
for on you Life itself endured death,
and by that death,
restored the victory of life!
[continued]

Vexilla Regis Prodeunt / The Royal Standard of the King
[concluded]

O sacred cross, hail to thee!
For you stand as our only hope.
At this time
of the Savior's doleful suffering,
increase God's kindly grace
for his faithful children,
and for the guilty
wipe their sins full away.

Trinity most sacred,
source of salvation most blessed,
let every soul offer praise to you.
May your loving care guard,
for all ages to come,
those whom you rescue
by the mystery
of this sacred, blessed rood.
Amen.

LENT (B): OFFICE OF READINGS, SUNDAYS AND WEEKDAYS
Pange, Lingua, Gloriosi Proelium / Sing, My Tongue, of That Clash

Pange, lingua, gloriosi
proelium certaminis,
et super crucis tropeo
dic triumphum nobilem,
qualiter redemptor orbis
immolatus vicerit.

De parentis protoplasti
fraude factor condolens,
quando pomi noxialis
morte morsu corruit,
ipse lignum tunc notavit
damna ligni ut solveret.

Hoc opus nostrae salutis
ordo depoposcerat,
multiformis perditoris
arte ut artem falleret,
et medelam ferret inde,
hostis unde laeserat.

Quando venit ergo sacri
plenitudo temporis,
missus est ab arce Patris
Natus, orbis conditor,
atque ventre virginali
carne factus prodiit.

Lustra sex qui iam peracta
tempus implens corporis,
se volente, natus ad hoc,
passioni deditus,
agnus in crucis levatur
immolandus stipite.

Aequa Patri Filioque,
inclito Paraclito,
sempiterna sit beatae
Trinitati gloria,
cuius alma nos redemit
atque servat gratia.
Amen.

Sing, O my tongue, of that clash,
of that glorious strife;
tell of the noble triumph
shown in the victory-trophy
of the holy Cross:
Say how the Redeemer of the world,
though offered as sacrifice,
yet triumphed full well.

Long ago was the Creator
sore aggrieved
at the deceit our earliest parent;
Adam the first-born, suffered,
Adam who fell in death
by his taste of the baneful fruit
of the tree.
And so the Creator himself
then chose the wood he would use
to cure that first tree's
grim and hurtful ills.

The proper manner
of how we should be saved
demanded this work of tree for tree,
so that craft anew, craft divine,
might overturn craft of old,
craft of deceiver many-wiled
and a cure might be wrenched
from the very same wooden source
that the archfiend had of old
used to inflict his fatal wound.
[continued]

Pange, Lingua, Gloriosi Proelium / Sing, My Tongue, of That Clash
[concluded]

And thus, when dawned the fullness
of the sacred time,
by heaven itself decreed,
from the Father's high citadel
was sent the Son,
the Creator of the world:
Taking human flesh
from a virgin's womb,
he came forth unto us.

When he had fulfilled
the appointed years, and
after thirty twelvemonths
had run their course,
he then, with freedom sovereign
and born to such a fate,
surrendered to his passion:
the Lamb is raised
to be sacrificed on the cross.

To the Father and to the Son,
and to the Advocate most glorious,
be equal praise given:
eternal laud to the Blessed Trinity,
whose faithful love brings us salvation,
brings us constant care.
Amen.

LENT (B): MORNING PRAYER, SUNDAYS AND WEEKDAYS
En Acetum, Fel, Arundo / Behold: the Sour Vinegar, the Bitter Gall
(Pange, Lingua, Gloriosi Proelium [pp. 54-55] [continuation])

En acetum, fel, arundo,
sputa, clavi, lancea;
mite corpus perforatur,
sanguis, unda profluit;
terra, pondus, astra, mundus
quo lavantur flumine!

Crux fidelis, inter omnes
arbor una nobilis!
Nulla talem silva profert
flore, fronde, germine.
Dulce lignum, dulci clavo
dulce pondus sustinens!

Flecte ramos, arbor alta,
tensa laxa viscera,
et rigor lentescat ille
quem dedit nativitas,
ut superni membra regis
miti tendas stipite.

Sola digna tu fuisti
ferre saecli pretium,
atque portum praeparare
nauta mundo naufrago,
quem sacer cruor perunxit
fusus Agni corpore.

Aequa Patri Filioque
inclito Paraclito,
sempiterna sit beatae
Trinitati gloria,
cuius alma nos redemit
atque servat gratia.
Amen.

Behold: the sour vinegar, the bitter gall,
the prickly reed,
See the spittle so foul,
the nails so sharp,
the spear with burnished point:
This gentle body, so humble, so meek,
is harshly pierced;
blood and water in rivulets
gush flashing forth:
look ye, at what flood
are earth, sea, stars, cosmos entire
washed full and sparkling clean!

Cross most faithful,
tree of all trees alone most noble!
None that e'er in grove has dwelt
did bear on itself
such a burden
from flower, from branch, from root.
Precious indeed the wood
precious the burden it sustains
on so precious a nail!

Bend low your branches,
O tree most exalted;
comfort the body
that lies so rigid against thee.
Let those unyielding boughs,
nature's gift to thee,
soften now: reach out in gentle gift
to the limbs
of heaven's own suffering king.

[continued]

En, Acetum, Fel, Arundo / Behold the Sour Vinegar, the Bitter Gall
[concluded]

You alone were worthy
to bear upon yourself
the full cosmic ransom-price;
you alone the mariner
who could prepare
safe-harbor for shipwrecked world:
you whom the holy blood,
poured out from the body of the Lamb,
did in truth crimson-stain,
did holily anoint.

Equal be the glory given Father, Son,
and Advocate most renowned:
eternal be the glory
given to the Blessed Trinity,
whose faithful and gracious care
redeems us, and protects us all as well.
Amen.

NOTE: During the Season of Lent (B):
    For NIGHT PRAYER, see *Christe, Qui Splendor,* p. 11
    For MIDMORNING PRAYER, see *Dei Fide Qua Vivimus,* p. 49
    For MIDDAY PRAYER, see *Qua Christus Hora Sitiit,* p. 50
    For MIDAFTERNOON PRAYER, see *Ternis Ter Horis Terminus,* p. 51.

THE FESTIVALS OF LENT (B):

PASSION (PALM) SUNDAY
All as in the Season of Lent (B) (pp. 52-57), except for the following:

MIDMORNING, MIDDAY, OR MIDAFTERNOON PRAYER:
Celsae Salutis Gaudia / Confident in Exultation

Celsae salutis gaudia
mundus fidelis iubilet:
Iesus, redemptor omnium,
mortis peremit principem.

Confident in exultation,
let the world cry out
at the joys of heavenly salvation:
Jesus, Savior of the world,
has placed in firmest bondage
the prince of death most dire.

Palmae et olivae surculos
coetus viando deferens,
"Hosanna David Filio"
claris frequentat vocibus.

Carrying with them tender shoots
of palm, of olive sleek and fair,
the crowd, as it moves along, oft says,
"Hosanna to the Son of David!"
in voices loud and clear.

Nos ergo summo principi
curramus omnes obviam;
melos canentes gloriae,
palmas geramus gaudii.

Now let us too all hasten
to meet this prince most high;
let us chant the strains of glory,
and proudly hold
the palms of gladsome joy.

Cursusque nostros lubricos
donis beatis sublevet,
grates ut omni tempore
ipsi feramus debitas.

With gifts most blessed may he
sustain our hazardous way,
so that wherever, whenever
we may be,
we might render fitting thanks to him.

Deo Patri sit gloria
eiusque soli Filio
cum Spiritu Paraclito,
in sempiterna saecula.
Amen.

To God the Father be glory,
and to his sole-begotten Son,
with Advocate most blessed,
for ages e'er to run.
Amen.

THE FESTIVALS OF LENT (B): HOLY THURSDAY
All as in the Season of Lent (B) (pp. 52-57), except the following:

EVENING PRAYER
O Memoriale Mortis Domini / Remembrance Most Holy
(stanzas 5, 6, 7 of St. Thomas Aquinas's *Adoro Te Devote)*

O memoriale mortis Domini,
panis vivus
vitam praestans homini,
praesta meae menti de te vivere
et te illi semper dulce sapere.

Remembrance most holy
of the death of the Lord,
living bread, life-granting
to receiving humankind,
bring to my spirit too
the power to live as you would wish,
the power to savor you
as food in which it full delights.

Pie pellicane, Iesu Domine,
me immundum
munda tuo sanguine,
cuius una stilla salvum facere
totum mundum quit
ab omni scelere.

Loving pellican,
giver of your own life-blood,
Jesus, Lord,
cleanse me of my sin
by that blood of yours;
a single drop of it would suffice
to rid the entire world
of all and every sin.

Te cum revelata cernam facie
visu tandem laetus tuae gloriae,
Patri, tibi laudes et Spiritui
dicam beatorum iunctus coetui.
Amen.

May I look upon you
when that time shall come wherein
your countenance stands full revealed,
when I am blessed
to rejoice at last
in the vision of your glory.
Then may I sing praise to the Father,
to you, and to the Spirit most high,
in company with the throng
that lives in heaven above.
Amen.

THE FESTIVALS OF LENT (B): GOOD FRIDAY
All as in the Season of Lent (B) (pp. 52-57), except the following:

MIDMORNING PRAYER
Salva, Redemptor, Plasma Tuum / O Redeemer Blest

Salva, Redemptor,
plasma tuum nobile,
signatum sancto vultus
tui lumine,
ne lacerari sinas
fraude daemonum,
propter quod mortis
exsolvisti pretium.

O Redeemer blest, preserve
your creature so renowned
that has been marked
with the sacred image
of your own likeness;
do not allow it to be destroyed
by demons' deceit,
for on its behalf have you
paid the price of death.

Dole captivos
esse tuos servulos,
absolve reos, compeditos erige,
et quos cruore redemisti proprio,
rex bone, tecum fac
gaudere perpetim.
Amen.

Be aggrieved, we pray,
that your servants are become
captive to sin;
wash away the fault of the guilty,
and raise up the enshackled.
Those whom you have redeemed
by your own blood,
O good and gentle King—
make them rejoice with you
for ages without end.
Amen.

THE FESTIVALS OF LENT (B): GOOD FRIDAY

MIDDAY PRAYER
Crux, Mundi Benedictio / Cross of Christ, Blessing for the World

Crux, mundi benedictio,
spes certaque redemptio,
olim gehennae baiula,
nunc clara caeli ianua,

Cross of Christ,
blessing for the world,
its fair hope, its ransom price secure,
once you were a tree
that bore souls off to hell so dire,
now you are the shining gateway
of heaven full fair.

In te levatur hostia
ad se qui traxit omnia,
quam mundi princeps impetit
suumque nihil invenit.

Upon you is raised up the victim
who has drawn all things unto himself,
whom the prince of this world attacks
and finds nothing to claim as his own.

Patri, tibi, Paraclito
sit aequa, Iesu, gloria,
qui nos crucis victoria
concedis usque perfrui.
Amen.

To the Father, to you, O Jesus,
and to the Advocate Spirit
be equal praise,
for you grant us ever to rejoice
in the victory of the cross.
Amen.

THE FESTIVALS OF LENT (B): GOOD FRIDAY

MIDAFTERNOON PRAYER
Per Crucem, Christe, Quaesumus / O Christ, We Pray

Per crucem, Christe, quaesumus
ad vitae transfer praemium
quos ligni fixus stipite
dignatus es redimere.

O Christ, we pray:
by means of your cross,
bring to the reward of everlasting life
those you have seen fit to redeem
by being nailed
to the wood of the tree.

Tuae legis articulus
vetus cassat chirographum;
antiqua perit servitus,
vera libertas redditur.

The time of your law is come;
now is made void
the banishment of old.
Gone is the ancient slavery;
true freedom is truly restored.

Patri, tibi, Paraclito
sit aequa, Iesu, gloria,
qui nos crucis victoria
concedis usque perfrui.
Amen.

To the Father, to you, O Jesus,
and to the Spirit Advocate
be equal praise,
for you grant us ever to rejoice
in the victory of the Cross.
Amen.

THE FESTIVALS OF LENT (B): HOLY SATURDAY

OFFICE OF READINGS
Christe, Caelorum Domine / Christ, Great Lord of Heaven on High

Christe, caelorum Domine,
mundi salvator maxime,
qui crucis omnes munere
mortis solvisti legibus,

Christ, great Lord of heaven on high,
Savior unmatched
of the entire wide world,
by bearing the burden of the Cross
you have freed us all
from death's stern rule.

Te nunc ovantes poscimus,
tua conserves munera,
quae sacra per mysteria
cunctis donasti gentibus.

With exultant voice do we now plead:
with great care watch over
those gifts you have given,
through your sacred mysteries,
to every race, to every clan.

You are the Lamb: gentle, without stain,
offered up in sacrifice
for the whole world;
the robes of all your saints
you have washed
in the bath of your blood.

Tu agnus mitis, innocens,
oblatus terrae victima,
sanctorum vestes omnium
tuo lavasti sanguine.

Take then with you, as you rise
into heaven's kingdom above,
those whom you have redeemed
at the cost of your own sacred body.
There they sing to you
the praises that are your due
for ages without end.

Quos redemisti pretio
tui sacrati corporis,
caelo resurgens advehis
ubi te laudant perpetim.

And, to their fair number,
we beg of you, Lord,
add us as well;
for, from every race and people,
you have made us into
a kingdom for the Father on high.
Amen.

Quorum nos addas numero,
te deprecamur, Domine,
qui Patri nos ex omnibus
fecisti regnum populis.
Amen.

THE FESTIVALS OF LENT (B): HOLY SATURDAY

MORNING PRAYER
Tibi, Redemptor Omnium / Redeemer of the Whole World

Tibi, Redemptor omnium,
hymnum deflentes canimus;
ignosce nobis, Domine,
ignosce confitentibus.

Redeemer of our whole world,
to you we sing our sorrowed song.
Forgive us, Lord;
forgive us who name you as our God.

Qui vires hostis veteris
per crucem mortis conteris,
qua nos vexillum fidei,
fronte signati, ferimus,

You are the one who,
through your death-bringing cross,
have shattered the power
of the ancient foe—
that cross wherewith our foreheads
are marked and sealed,
that cross which we raise
aloft on high
as the banner of our faith.

Illum a nobis iugiter
repellere dignaveris,
ne possit umquam laedere
redemptos tuo sanguine.

Qui propter nos ad inferos
descendere dignatus es,
ut mortis debitoribus
vitae donares munera.

In your kindness,
drive far from us e'ermore
that ancient enemy,
lest ever he be able
to wreak foul harm
on those whom you have redeemed
by your sacred blood.

Tu es qui certo tempore
daturus finem saeculo,
iustus cunctorum merita
remunerator statues.

Te ergo, Christe, quaesumus,
ut nostra cures vulnera,
qui es cum Patre et Spiritu
laudandus in perpetuum.
Amen.

You are the one who,
on our behalf, saw fit
to go beneath the earth,
to Sheol itself,
to give those who owed debt to death
the gift of e'erlasting life instead.
[continued]

Tibi, Redemptor Omnium / Redeemer of the Whole World
[concluded]

You it is who,
at a time clearly preordained,
will bring an end to this,
our present age;
just arbiter of humankind,
you will give to all what each deserves.

And so, O Christ our Lord, we beg you
to heal the wounds that we now bear;
in company with the Father
and the Spirit blessed
worthy are you of all praise
through age upon age upon age.
Amen.

THE FESTIVALS OF LENT (B): HOLY SATURDAY

EVENING PRAYER
Auctor Salutis Unice / Sole Source of Soul's Salvation

Auctor salutis unice,
mundi redemptor inclite,
rex, Christe, nobis annue
crucis fecundae gloriam.

Sole source of souls' salvation,
glorious redeemer of the weary world,
Christ, our King most high,
grant unto us
the glory of your life-giving holy cross.

Tu morte mortem diruens
vitamque vita largiens,
mortis ministrum subdolum
deviceras diabolum.

You destroyed death by dying,
and you bestow life
by living once more;
death's deceitful servant,
Lucifer the demon,
have you now conquered full fair.

Piis amoris artibus
somno sepulcri traditus,
sedes recludis inferi
patresque dicis liberos.

In artful hands of friends' faithful love
were you delivered over
to the sleep of the tomb;
but you then flung open wide
the doors to the abode of the dead,
and announced to all our ancestors
that they had now been made free.

Nunc in Parentis dextera
sacrata fulgens victima,
audi, precamur, vivido
tuo redemptos sanguine,

Quo te diebus omnibus
puris sequentes moribus,
adversus omnes impetus
crucis feramus labarum.

Now, as victim most brilliant,
victim most holy,
victim standing
at the Father's right hand,
hear us, we pray:
for with the bright red of your blood
have you wrought
our redemption so fair.

Patri, tibi, Paraclito
sit aequa, Iesu, gloria,
qui nos crucis victoria
concedis usque perfrui.
Amen.

[continued]

Auctor Salutis Unice / Sole Source of Souls' Salvation
[concluded]

As, with conduct becoming,
we strive each day
to be your disciples true,
may we,
through that same precious blood,
hold up on high, whoe'er be the foe,
the glorious standard of the holy cross.

To the Father, to you, to the Spirit blest
be equal glory, Lord Jesus,
for you grant that forever
we may rejoice
in the victory of the cross.
Amen.

NOTE: For Holy Saturday:
  For MIDMORNING PRAYER, see *Salva, Redemptor, Plasma Tuum,* p. 60
  For MIDDAY PRAYER, see *Crux, Mundi Benedictio,* p. 61
  For MIDAFTERNOON PRAYER, see *Per Crucem, Christe, Quaesumus,* p. 62.

THE SEASON OF EASTER (A)
EVENING PRAYER (Sundays and Ferial Days)
Ad Cenam Agni Providi / We Look Forward to the Supper of the Lord

Ad cenam Agni providi,
stolis salutis candidi,
post transitum maris Rubri
Christo canamus principi.

Cuius corpus sanctissimum
in ara crucis torridum,
sed et cruorem roseum
gustando, Deo vivimus.

Protecti paschae vespero
a devastante angelo,
de Pharaonis aspero
sumus erepti imperio.

Iam pascha nostrum
Christus est,
agnus occisus innocens;
sinceritatis azyma
qui carnem suam obtulit.

O vera, digna hostia,
per quam franguntur tartara,
captiva plebs redimitur,
redduntur vitae praemia!

Consurgit Christus tumulo,
victor redit de barathro,
tyrannum trundens vinculo
et paradisum reserans.

Esto perenne mentibus
paschale, Iesu, gaudium
et nos renatos gratiae
tuis triumphis aggrega.

Iesu, tibi sit gloria,
qui morte victa praenites,
cum Patre et almo Spiritu
in sempiterna saecula. Amen.

We look forward
to the supper of the Lord,
wrapped as we are white-robed
in the garment of salvation.
The Red Sea is now safely crossed,
and we sing our praises
to Christ our Prince.

Tasting, as we do, his most holy body,
upon the altar of the Cross
parched dry,
but tasting too his purpling blood,
we live our lives for God.

Guarded are we at paschal eve
from havoc-wreaking messenger grim,
rescued also are we from
harsh rule of Pharaoh most cruel.

Now Christ is our passover Victim;
the lamb, though full innocent,
is slain:
unleavened bread
of truthfulness sublime,
he offered up his own body,
his own flesh.

[continued]

Ad Cenam Agni Providi / We Look Forward to the Supper of the Lord
[concluded]

O offering most true,
offering most worthy,
by you were hell's bonds shatter-broken:
a captive people is ransomed free,
and the crown of life is restored!

Christ arises glorious from the tomb:
the conquering hero returns
from the bottomless abyss;
He binds the tyrant in firmest bonds,
and swings open wide
the gates of heaven most high.

Jesus, Lord, for our minds and spirits
may you be paschal joy that never ends;
unite us together, reborn as we are
in your triumphant victories of grace.

Jesus, may glory be given to you,
for you outshine all
in overcoming death,
with the Father and the Spirit true
for ages yet to come. Amen.

EASTER (A): EVENING PRAYER (Ferial Days)
O Rex Aeterne, Domine / O King Eternal

O rex aeterne, Domine,
semper cum Patre Filius,
iuxta tuam imaginem
Adam plasmasti hominem.

Quem diabolus deceperat
hostis humani generis,
eius et formam corporis
sumpsisti tu de Virgine,

Ut nos Deo coniungeres
per carnis contubernium,
daturus in baptismate,
Redemptor, indulgentiam.

Tu crucem propter hominem
suscipere dignatus es;
dedisti tuum sanguinem
nostrae salutis pretium.

Tu surrexisti, gloriam
a Patre sumens debitam;
per te et nos resurgere
devota mente credimus.

Esto perenne mentibus
paschale, Iesu, gaudium,
et nos renatos gratiae
tuis triumphis aggrega.

Iesu, tibi sit gloria,
qui morte victa praenites,
cum Patre et almo Spiritu,
in sempiterna saecula.
Amen.

O King eternal,
Lord God without end,
Son never absent
from the Father most high,
you made the man Adam
in the likeness
of what you yourself
have from all eternity been.

Adam, whom the evil one deceived,
that evil spirit
who despises the human race,
Adam: the selfsame sort of flesh
that he had
you took unto yourself
from the Virgin blest.

And this so that,
by firm fellowship of flesh,
you might join us to a God unfleshed:
Redeemer most blest,
you it was who would grant,
by baptism's cleansing flow,
forgiveness' blessed, yearned-for,
pined-for boon so dear.

For the sake of fallen man
you bent low
to take upon yourself
the weight of the Cross;
you poured out your blood
as ransom-cost of our salvation.
[continued]

O Rex Aeterne, Domine / O King Eternal
[concluded]

You arose! You received from the Father
the glory that was yours.
With full-faithful heart, we believe
that, through you,
we too shall arise one day.

Jesus Lord, be thou our spirits'
constant paschal joy;
unite us, renewed, reborn
to the victories your grace has won.

Jesus, to you
be constant praise and laud,
for your glory flashes forth,
blinds all in brilliance,
since death is overcome;
with the Father and the Spirit most kind,
for ages ne'er to end.
Amen.

EASTER (A): NIGHT PRAYER (Sundays and Ferial Days)
Iesu, Redemptor Saeculi / Jesus, Redeemer God

Iesu, redemptor saeculi,
Verbum Patris altissimi,
lux lucis invisibilis,
custos tuorum pervigil:

Jesus, Redeemer God
of this world of ours,
Word ineffable
of the Father most high,
Light of light,
yet light no one can fully see,
Unsleeping guardian of those
whom you have made your own:

Tu fabricator omnium
discretor atque temporum,
fessa labore corpora
noctis quiete recrea.

You are the maker of all the ages;
you are their judge as well.
these bodies of ours, then,
worn out with toil:
renew them, we beg,
with the peaceful silence of night.

Qui frangis ima tartara,
tu nos ab hoste libera,
ne valeat seducere
tuo redemptos sanguine.

You it is who shatter the grip
of the regions infernal;
free us, we beg,
from the enemy most foul,
so that he cannot lead us astray,
for we are redeemed by your holy,
your precious blood.

Ut, dum gravati corpore
brevi manemus tempore,
sic caro nostra dormiat
ut mens soporem nesciat.

And so, while for yet a short time
we remain weighed down by burdens
brought on by body's banes,
may our flesh yet know
such rest secure,
that our minds know no cloud,
no darkness, no ill.

Iesu, tibi sit gloria,
qui morte victa praenites,
cum Patre et almo Spiritu
in sempiterna saecula.
Amen.

[continued]

Iesu, Redemptor Saeculi / Jesus, Redeemer God
[concluded]

Jesus, to you be glory:
you outshine all by death o'ercome,
with the Father as well,
and the kindly Spirit
for endless ages e'er to come. Amen.

EASTER (A): OFFICE OF READINGS (Sundays and Ferial Days)
His Est Dies Verus Dei / This, Truly Is God's Own Day

Hic est dies verus Dei,
sancto serenus lumine,
quo diluit sanguis sacer
probrosa mundi crimina.

This, truly, is God's own day,
peaceful and resplendent in holy light
that day when the sacred blood-flow
washed away the shameful sinfulness
of the world.

Fidem refundit perditis
caecosque visu illuminat;
quem non gravi solvit metu
latronis absolutio?

To those who were lost,
it restores faithful trust
and the blind
it brightens with blessed sight.
Who is there whom the forgiveness
granted to the thief on the cross
does not rescue from trembling fear?

Opus stupent et angeli,
poenam videntes corporis
Christoque adhaerentem reum
vitam beatam carpere.

Mysterium mirabile,
ut abluat mundi luem,
peccata tollat omnium
carnis vitia mundans caro.

The angels themselves
gape in wonder at the event
as they gaze upon the punishments
his body endured,
looking too at the thief who,
confessing Christ,
snatched as his reward
blessed life eternal.

Quid hoc potest sublimius,
ut culpa quaerat gratiam,
metumque solvit caritas,
reddatque mors vitam novam?

Esto perenne mentibus
paschale, Iesu, gaudium,
ut nos renatos gratiae
tuis triumphis aggrega.

Mystery most marvelous!
To wash away
the world's calamitous guilt,
to take away the sins of all,
flesh cleanses the crimes of flesh.

Iesu, tibi sit gloria
qui morte victa praenites,
cum Patre et almo Spiritu
in sempiterna saecula.
Amen.

What could be more exalted than this,
that fault could seek forgiveness,
that love could dissolve fear,
that death could grant newness of
life?
[continued]

Hic Est Dies Verus Dei / This, Truly, Is God's Own Day
[concluded]

Jesus Lord, be thou
our souls' constant Easter joy,
and so join us, too,
in our rebirth unto grace
to the glorious victories
you have already won.

Jesus, to you be all glory,
for you surpass all
by the death you have overcome,
with the Father and the kindly Spirit
for ages e'er yet to run.
Amen.

EASTER (A): OFFICE OF READINGS (Ferial Days)
Laetare, Caelum, Desuper / Rejoice, O Heaven

Laetare, caelum, desuper,
applaude, tellus ac mare:
Christus resurgens post crucem
vitam dedit mortalibus.

Iam tempus acceptum redit,
dies salutis cernitur,
quo mundus Agni sanguine
refulsit a caligine.

Mors illa, mortis passio,
est criminis remissio:
illaesa virtus permanet
victus dedit victoriam.

Nostrae fuit gustus spei
hic, ut fideles crederent
se posse post resurgere,
vitam beatam sumere.

Nunc ergo pascha candidum
causa bonorum talium
colamus omnes strenue
tanto repleti munere.

Esto perenne mentibus
paschale, Iesu, gaudium,
et nos renatos gratiae
tuis triumphis aggrega.

Iesu, tibi sit gloria,
qui morte victa praenites,
cum Patre et almo Spiritu
in sempiterna saecula.
Amen.

Rejoice, O Heaven,
from your place on high;
clap your hands,
solid earth and oceans profound:
for Christ has endured the Cross
and is risen;
to mortal souls has he graciously
granted luminous life.

Now has the appointed time
returned once more;
the day of salvation comes now
again into view,
that day when the world,
because of the Lamb's shed blood,
shone forth now once more,
and darkness was left behind.

That renowned death,
mortal flesh's grim dissolution,
is what brings
fell fault's full forgiveness:
power unbesmirched stands firm,
and the conquered one
bestows victory most glorious.

A foretaste it was of our present hope,
that faithful souls should believe
that they could later arise once more,
and enter into blessed life.
[continued]

Laetare, Caelum, Desuper / Rejoice, O Heaven
[concluded]

And so let us all,
with eagerness unbounded,
filled as we are with a gift so great,
honor our magnificent,
our shining Pasch,
whence come such benefits,
such huge gifts to us.

Jesus Lord, be thou
our souls' constant paschal joy,
and so join us, too,
in our rebirth unto grace,
to the glorious victories
you have already won.

Jesus, to you be all glory,
for you surpass all
by the death you have overcome,
with the Father and the kindly Spirit
for ages e'er yet to run.
Amen.

EASTER (A): MORNING PRAYER (Sundays and Ferial Days)
Aurora Lucis Rutilat / Light's Dawning Rays Glow Bright Red

Aurora lucis rutilat,
caelum resultat laudibus,
mundus exsultans iubilat,
gemens infernus ululat,

Light's dawning rays glow bright red;
heaven echoes far and wide
in cries of praise.
The world rejoices in gladness sheer,
but hell moans and wails
in forlorn grief.

Cum rex ille fortissimus
mortis confractis viribus,
pede conculcans tartara
solvit catena miseros.

For that renowned King,
with courage full,
has shattered the power
death used to have,
has trod underfoot
hell's dusky realms, and
released wretched humankind
from the chains
they had worn so long.

Ille, quem clausum lapide
miles custodit acriter,
triumphans pompa nobili
victor surgit de funere.

Inferni iam gemitibus
solutis et doloribus,
quia surrexit Dominus
resplendens clamat angelus.

That very one whom
a soldier guarded so carefully,
once burial stone was rolled in place
to shut him in:
exultant now in regal splendor
does that conquering king arise
from shattered bonds of death.

Esto perenne mentibus,
paschale, Iesu, gaudium,
et nos renatos gratiae
tuis triumphis aggrega.

The groans and sorrows
of death's once grim realm
are now laid full to rest,
for an angel,
in glory resplendent
and with thundering voice, proclaims:
The Lord has risen!

Iesu, tibi sit gloria,
qui morte victa praenites,
cum Patre et almo Spiritu
in sempiterna saecula.
Amen.

[continued]

Aurora Lucis Rutilat / Light's Dawning Rays Glow Bright Red
[concluded]

Jesus Lord, be thou
our souls' constant paschal joy,
and so join us, too,
in our rebirth unto grace,
to the glorious victories
you have already won.

Jesus, to you be all glory,
for you surpass all
by the death you have overcome:
with the Father and the kindly Spirit
for ages e'er yet to run.
Amen.

EASTER (A): MORNING PRAYER (Ferial Days)
Chorus Novae Ierusalem / Let the Choir of the Heavenly Jerusalem

Chorus novae Ierusalem
hymni novam dulcedinem
promat, colens cum sobriis
paschale festum gaudiis.

Quo Christus invictus leo,
dracone surgens obruto,
dum voce viva personat,
a morte functos excitat.

Quam devorarat improbus,
praedam refundit tartarus;
captivitate libera
Iesum sequuntur agmina.

Triumphat ille splendide
et dignus amplitudine,
soli polique patriam
unam facit rem publicam.

Ipsum canendo supplices
Regem precemur milites,
ut in suo clarissimo
nos ordinet palatio.

Esto perenne mentibus
paschale, Iesu, gaudium,
et nos renatos gratiae
tuis triumphis aggrega.

Iesu, tibi sit gloria,
qui morte victa praenites,
cum Patre et almo Spiritu
in sempiterna saecula.
Amen.

Let the choir
of the heavenly Jerusalem
break forth into a new
and glorious song,
and with solemn joy
celebrate the paschal feast.

This the feast when Christ,
the unconquerable lion of Judah,
by rising has overwhelmed
the ancient serpent,
and with living voice resounding clear
has summoned the dead
back unto life.

Now does hell yield up the hostages
that the wicked one
had swallowed up;
from their prison now freed,
the once captive hosts
with joy follow the Lord Jesus.

Now comes he forth,
in procession great,
and worthy of all grandeur;
one kingdom does he forge
of the realms of earth and heaven.

In song let us, his soldiers,
humbly ask him, our regal King,
to place and keep us
in his most blessed, royal home.
[continued]

Chorus Novae Ierusalem / Let the Choir of the Heavenly Jerusalem
[concluded]

Jesus Lord, be thou
our souls' constant paschal joy,
and so join us, too,
in our rebirth unto grace,
to the glorious victories
you have already won.

Jesus, to you be all glory,
for you surpass all
by the death you have overcome;
with the Father and the kindly Spirit
for ages e'er yet to run.
Amen.

EASTER (A): MIDMORNING PRAYER (Sundays and Ferial Days)
Iam Surgit Hora Tertia / Now It Springs Forth

Iam surgit hora tertia,
qua Christus ascendit crucem;
nil insolens mens cogitet,
intendat affectum precis.

Now it springs forth:
third hour of the day,
when Christ ascended
his cruciform throne.
Let haughty mind
attend to nothing else,
but pay sole heed
to the solemn, loving mood
that prayer
begets.

Qui corde Christum suscipit,
innoxium sensum gerit
votisque praestat sedulis
Sanctum mereri Spiritum.

Whosoe'er receive Christ
in their hearts
have understanding
that bears no blame;
by constant, vigilant prayer
they present themselves
as made worthy
of the Spirit's sacred Gift.

Haec hora, quae finem dedit
diri veterno criminis;
hinc iam beata tempora
coepere Christi gratia.

This is the hour,
which put final end
to the long lethargy
of the ancient crime;
from this time on arise the blessed
eras
that stem from Christ's holy favor.

Iesu, tibi sit gloria,
qui morte victa praenites,
cum Patre et almo Spiritu
in sempiterna saecula.
Amen.

Jesus, to you be all glory,
for you surpass all
by the death you have overcome;
with the Father and the kindly Spirit
for ages e'er yet to run.
Amen.

EASTER (A): MIDDAY PRAYER (Sundays and Ferial Days)
Venite, Servi, Supplices / Come, All You Servants

Venite, servi, supplices,
et mente et ore extollite
dignis beatum laudibus
nomen Dei cum cantico.

Come, all you servants
who seek the Lord's favor,
and with mind and heart lift up in song
the blessed name of God the Almighty
in solemn praisegiving.

Hoc namque tempus illud est,
quo saeculorum iudicem
iniusta morti tradidit
mortalium sententia.

For this is the time, that dreadful time,
when unjust sentence of mortal judges
handed over to death
the supreme Judge of all the ages.

Et nos amore debito
timore iusto subditi,
adversus omnes impetus
quos saevus hostis incutit,

And let us too, with love that is fitting,
yet stricken with fear
that is proper as well,
in defense against all the attacks
that the firece enemy hurls at us,

Unum rogemus et Patrem
Deum regemque Filium
simulque Sanctum Spiritum,
in Trinitate Dominum.
Amen.

Call upon the one God, the Father,
and his regal Son,
and the Holy Spirit as well:
the Lord one God in Trinity sublime.
Amen.

EASTER (A): MIDAFTERNOON PRAYER (Sundays and Ferial Days)
Haec Hora, Quae Resplenduit / This Is the Hour That Shone Forth

Haec hora, quae resplenduit
cruciosque solvit nubila,
mundum tenebris exuens,
reddens serena lumina.

This is the hour that shone forth
and melted the clouds
surrounding the Cross;
it stripped the world
of its raiment of grim darkness
and restored the calm,
clear brilliance of light.

Haec hora, qua resuscitans
Iesus sepulcris corpora,
prodire mortis libera
iussit refuso spiritu.

This is the hour when
Jesus raised the bodies in the tombs,
bidding them to come forth,
free of death,
with living spirit restored.

Novata saecla credimus
mortis solutis legibus,
vitae beatae munera
cursum perennem currere.

We believe history's eras
are now remade, are new
since death's iron law is broken,
and that the blessings of life eternal
now course along
time's perennial path.

Iesu, tibi sit gloria,
qui morte victa praenites,
cum Patre et almo Spiritu
in sempiterna saecula.
Amen.

Jesus, to you be all glory,
for you surpass all
by the death you have overcome;
with the Father and the kindly Spirit
for ages e'er yet to run.
Amen.

THE SEASON OF EASTER (B)
EVENING PRAYER
Veni, Creator Spiritus / Come to Us, Holy Spirit, Creator Blest

Veni, creator Spiritus,
mentes tuorum visita,
imple superna gratia,
quae tu creasti, pectora.

Come to us, Holy Spirit, Creator blest,
Come visit the souls of the people
who are your own.
With grace from heaven on high,
fill to satiety the hearts
which you yourself have made.

Qui diceris Paraclitus,
donum Dei altissimi,
fons vivus, ignis, caritas
et spiritalis unctio.

They call you the Advocate,
the gift of God most high;
you are the living, flowing fountain,
you are fire, you are love,
you are the very anointing of the spirit.

Tu septiformis munere,
dextrae Dei tu digitus,
tu rite promissum Patris
sermone ditans guttura.

Sevenfold are you
in the gifts that you give;
the finger of the right hand of God
are you.
You are the solemnly promised gift
of the Father,
enriching throat and voice
with the words that you inspire.

Accende lumen sensibus,
infunde amorem cordibus,
infirma nostri corporis,
virtute firmans perpeti.

Make bright light, then, shine
within our minds;
pour forth love into our hearts.
With your unfailing strength,
bring back to full health
the weaknesses
our bodies so badly show.

Hostem repellas longius
pacemque dones protinus;
ductore sic te praevio
vitemus omne noxium.

Keep full far at bay the dreaded foe;
grant us peace that does not fail.
With you as leader
at the head of our column
may we encounter nothing harmful,
no bane-bearing being.

Per te sciamus da Patrem
noscamus atque Filium,
te utriusque Spiritum
credamus omni tempore.
Amen.

Grant that, through you, we may come
to know the Father, and the Son as well;
and may our faith be ever firm in you,
Spirit blest of both Father and Son.
Amen.

EASTER (B): OFFICE OF READINGS
Aeterne Rex, Altissime / Eternal King, Ruler Most Exalted

Aeterne rex, altissime,
redemptor et fidelium,
quo mors soluta deperit,
datur triumphus gratiae,

Scandis tribunal dexterae
Patris, tibique caelitus
fertur potestas omnium,
quae non erat humanitus.

Ut trina rerum machina
caelestium, terrestrium
et infernorum condita,
flectat genu iam subdita.

Tremunt videntes angeli
versam vicem mortalium:
culpat caro, purgat caro,
regnat caro Verbum Dei.

Tu, Christe, nostrum gaudium,
manens perenne praemium,
mundi regis qui fabricam,
mundana vincens gaudia.

Hinc te precantes quaesumus,
ignosce culpis omnibus
et corda sursum subleva
ad te superna gratia,

Ut, cum rubente coeperis
clarere nube iudicis,
poenas repellas debitas,
reddas coronas perditas.

Iesu, tibi sit gloria,
qui scandis ad caelestia
cum Patre et almo Spiritu
in sempiterna saecula.
Amen.

Eternal King, Ruler most exalted,
Redeemer of those
who put their trust in you:
Through you
lies death undone, overcome;
and so through you
is the triumph of grace now won.

You now rise to claim
the judgment chair
at the Father's right hand;
unto you is delivered power over all:
a power heaven-bestowed,
a power that no wise
comes from earth below.

And so the threefold realms:
of heaven, of earth, of hell itself,
let them now be subject unto you,
now bend the obedient knee.

And the angels too:
they tremble, as they gaze
upon humankind's all-changed lot:
flesh incurred guilt, flesh cured guilt:
and flesh now reigns as Word of God.

You, O Christ, are our joy,
our lasting, ever-present reward.
Yours to rule over the world
you have made,
yours to abash what earth
had thought to be its joy.

[continued]

Aeterne Rex, Altissime / Eternal King, Ruler Most Exalted
[concluded]

And so in joyous prayer
we humbly ask you:
forgive us all our faults,
and, with your heavenly grace,
lift up our hearts to you,

So that, when you begin to appear
awesome and bright
on the shining seat
of the judge most high,
you may ward off from us
the penalties we have earned,
and restore to us
the rewards we have lost.

Jesus, to you be glory
as you ascend to the heavens on high,
and to the Father as well,
and the kindly Spirit,
for ages e'er yet to run.
Amen.

EASTER (B): MORNING PRAYER
Optatus Votis Omnium / Longed For in the Desires of All

Optatus votis omnium
sacratus illuxit dies,
quo Christus, mundi spes, Deus,
conscendit caelos arduos.

Longed for in the desires of all,
the sacred day has now shone forth
when Christ, the hope of the world,
Christ God,
ascended to the heavens high above.

Magni triumphum proelii,
mundi perempto principe,
Patri praesentans vultibus
victricis carnis gloriam,

Total triumph in a battle most dire,
which saw the prince of this world
be full o'ercome:
this He presents
to the Father on high,
this the glory the Son gives the Father
when he ascends
in triumphant flesh's form.

In nube fertur lucida
et spem facit credentibus,
iam paradisum reserans,
quem protoplasti clauserant.

O grande cunctis gaudium,
quod partus nostrae Virginis,
post dira flagra, post crucem
paternae sedi iungitur.

On a bright cloud is he carried aloft,
granting hope to those
who trust in him;
e'en now he unseals
the gates of very Paradise,
long ago slammed shut
by our first parents' fatal sin.

Agamus ergo gratias
nostrae salutis vindici,
nostrum quod corpus vexerit
sublime ad caeli regiam.

Sit nobis cum caelestibus
commune manens gaudium:
illis, quod semet obtulit,
nobis, quod se non abstulit.

O joy, immeasurable and great for all!
The offspring of a Virgin,
a Virgin one of us,
after horrific lash, after cross so stern,
is now restored,
rejoined to the throne of God.

Nunc, Christe, scandens aethera
ad te cor nostrum subleva,
tuum Patrisque Spiritum
emittens nobis caelitus.
Amen.

[continued]

Optatus Votis Omnium / Longed for in the Desires of All
[concluded]

Let us therefore render grateful song
to him who has won
our salvation for us,
and now has borne human body,
like ours, on high
to the palace of heaven itself.

And so may we feel a joy,
a joy we share with the denizens
of the realm on high:
they, that He has betaken himself there,
we, that he has not taken himself away
from us here below.

And now, O Christ,
as you ascend to the heavens on high,
raise up our hearts to you,
sending your Spirit to us
from heaven above,
your Spirit, and that of the Father too.
Amen.

NOTE: During the Season of Easter (B):
    For NIGHT PRAYER, see *Iesu, Redemptor Saeculi*, pp. 72-73
    For MIDMORNING PRAYER, see *Iam Surgit Hora Tertia*, p. 82
    For MIDDAY PRAYER, see *Veni, Servi, Supplices*, p. 83
    For MIDAFTERNOON PRAYER, see *Haec Hora, Quae Resplenduit*,
        p. 84.

THE FESTIVALS OF EASTER

EASTER SUNDAY
All from the Proper of the Season, pp. 68-84

ASCENSION
All from the Proper of the Season, pp. 85-89, except for:

EVENING PRAYER
Iesu, Nostra Redemptio / Jesus, You Are Our Savior

Iesu, nostra redemptio, amor et desiderium, Deus creator omnium, homo in fine temporum,	Jesus, you are our Savior; you are the one we love, the one we seek. You are God, almighty maker of all that is; yet you are a human, come to us in these end times.

Iesu, nostra redemptio,
 amor et desiderium,
Deus creator omnium,
homo in fine temporum,

Quae te vicit clementia,
ut ferres nostra crimina,
 crudelem mortem patiens,
ut nos a morte tolleres;

Inferni claustra penetrans,
 tuos captivos redimens;
 victor triumpho nobili
ad dextram Patris residens?

Ipsa te cogat pietas,
ut mala nostra superes
parcendo, et voti compotes
nos tuo vultu saties.

Tu esto nostrum gaudium,
qui es futurus praemium;
 sit nostra in te gloria
per cuncta semper saecula.
 Amen.

Jesus, you are our Savior;
 you are the one we love,
 the one we seek.
You are God,
almighty maker of all that is;
 yet you are a human,
come to us in these end times.

What wondrous mercy
 overpowered you,
and made you bear all our sins?
Made you endure a death most cruel,
 so that you might snatch us away
 from death's wicked snare?

Made you e'en venture
into hell's own locked domain,
so as to ransom your captive people?
Now are you to take your place
 in triumph fair
at the Father's mighty right hand?
 [continued]

Iesu, Nostra Redemptio / Jesus, You Are Our Savior
[concluded]

May that faithful kindness of yours
compel you to overcome,
by your forgiving mercy,
all the evil we have done;
and to sate, by the blissing vision
of you in heaven on high,
those of us who have share
in the longing that is ours.

Be you, O Jesus, our constant joy,
for you will be our great reward;
let all our hope for glory without end
be placed in you
now and for all ages e'er yet to come.
Amen.

THE FESTIVALS OF EASTER: PENTECOST

EVENING PRAYER
See *Veni, Creator Spiritus* / Come to Us, Holy Spirit, Creator Blest,
p. 85

OFFICE OF READINGS
Lux Iucunda, Lux Insignis / The Light Is Most Pleasant

Lux iucunda, lux insignis,
qua de throno missus ignis
in Christi discipulos,

Corda replet, linguas ditat,
ad concordes nos invitat
cordis, linguae modulos.

Consolator alme, veni,
linguas rege, corda leni;
nihil fellis aut veneni
sub tua praesentia.

Nova facti creatura,
te laudamus mente pura,
gratiae nunc, sed natura
prius irae filii.

Tu qui dator es et donum,
nostri cordis omne bonum,
cor ad laudem redde pronum,
nostrae linguae formans sonum
in tua praeconia.

Tu nos purges a peccatis,
auctor ipse pietatis,
et in Christo renovatis
da perfectae novitatis
plena nobis gaudia.
Amen.

The light is most pleasant,
the light is most renowned:
the light, that is,
whereby fire was sent down
from God's own throne
on the disciples of Christ the Lord.

It fills their hearts;
it enriches their speech.
It summons us
to having hearts like theirs,
to having voices in harmony
with those they were given.

Comforter most kindly, come unto us:
rule over our voices,
soften our hearts:
for there is bitterness none,
nor poison dire,
where'er your gracious presence be.

Now become a new creature,
we praise you,
with hearts made clean;
now children of grace, though once,
as Adam-descended,
children of wrath.
[continued]

Lux Iucunda, Lux Insignis / The Light Is Most Pleasant
[concluded]

You are both giver and gift;
you are every good
our hearts could ever hope to have.
Render those hearts ready
to give you praise;
form the sound of our voice
into an ready instrument
of song unto you.

Cleanse us, we pray, of all our sins,
for you are the source of all faithfulness;
to us, now reborn in Christ, grant
the fullest joy of perfect renewal.
Amen.

PENTECOST: MORNING PRAYER
Beata Nobis Gaudia / The Circled Track of Twelvemonth Time

Beata nobis gaudia
anni reducit orbita,
cum Spiritus Paraclitus
effulsit in discipulos.

The circled track of twelvemonth time
has returned once more to us
the days of those blessed joys
when the Spirit Advocate
shone forth in the midst
of the disciples of the Lord.

Ignis vibrante lumine
linguae figuram detulit,
verbis ut essent proflui
et caritate fervidi.

With glimmering light, fire-bright,
did the Spirit bring with him
the shapes of tongues:
thus would the disciples
be fluent in speech and burning
with charity's flashing flame.

Linguis loquuntur omnium;
turbae pavent gentilium,
musto madere deputant,
quos Spiritus repleverat.

Patrata sunt haec mystice
Paschae peracto tempore,
sacro dierum numero,
quo lege fit remissio.

They speak: in the languages of all!
The crowds around them,
from many nations drawn,
tremble in fear, tremble in dread:
those men they call
besotted with wine,
whose hearts in truth
the Spirit had filled.

Te nunc, Deus piissime,
vultu precamur cernuo:
illapsa nobis caelitus
largire dona Spiritus.

Dudum sacrata pectora
tua replesti gratia;
dimitte nunc peccamina
et da quieta tempora.

All this came to be,
in mysterious, mystic mode,
after the Paschal time had passed,
after the sacred number
of fifty jubilee days had elapsed,
when freedom was granted
the captive
from the binding bonds of the law.

Per te sciamus da Patrem
noscamus atque Filium,
te utriusque Spiritum
credamus omni tempore.
Amen.

[continued]

Beata Nobis Gaudia / The Circled Track of Twelvemonth Time
[concluded]

Now, O God most faithful,
to you we pray,
with heads bowed down low:
grant us the gifts of the Spirit
that flow down from high heaven above.

Of old you filled, with your sacred grace,
the Apostles' hearts, truly made holy.
Take away now our sins;
grant our lives the quiet of your peace.

Grant that, through you,
we may know the Father,
may know too the sole-begotten Son.
Grant that, for all time to come,
we may believe in you,
the Spirit of Father and Son.
Amen.

PENTECOST: MIDMORNING PRAYER
Iam Christus Astra Ascenderat / Now Had Christ Gone Up on High

Iam Christus astra ascenderat,
regressus unde venerat,
promissa Patris munera,
Sanctum daturus Spiritum,

Now had Christ gone up on high,
returned to heaven
whence he had come;
the Spirit most High,
the promised gift of the Father,
would he now send.

Cum hora felix tertia
repente mundo intonat,
Apostolis orantibus
Deum venisse nuntians.

When the third hour— oh, happy time!
—suddenly sounded for the world,
it proclaimed to the Apostles,
rapt in prayer,
that God the Spirit had come.

De Patris ergo lumine
decorus ignus almus est,
qui fida Christi pectora
calore verbi compleat.

Thus from the light
of the Father on high
does this comely fire,
most propitius, emerge;
it comes to fill trusting hearts,
with the fervor of Christ's word.

Descende, Sancte Spiritus,
ac nostra corda altaria
orna tibi virtutibus,
tibique templa dedica.

Come down upon us, Spirit most holy;
bedeck for yourself our altar-hearts
with every virtue.
Make them dedicated temples,
consecrated unto you.

Per te sciamus da Patrem
noscamus atque Filium,
te utriusque Spiritum
credamus omni tempore.
Amen.

Grant that, through you,
we may know the Father,
may know too the sole-begotten Son.
Grant that, for all time to come,
we may believe that you are
Spirit of both Father and Son.
Amen.

ORDINARY TIME

WEEKS OF THE PSALTER I AND III

WEEKS OF THE PSALTER II AND IV

THE FESTIVALS OF ORDINARY TIME
Most Holy Trinity
Corpus Christi
Sacred Heart
Christ the King

Note: throughout all four weeks of the Psalter during Ordinary Time,
for MIDMORNING PRAYER, see *Nunc, Sancte, Nobis, Spiritus* (p. 7), OR *Certum Tenentes Ordinem* (p. 15);
for MIDDAY PRAYER, see *Rector Potens, Verax Deus* (p. 8), OR *Dicamus Laudes Domino* (p.16);
for MIDAFTERNOON PRAYER, see *Rerum, Deus, Tenax Vigor* (p.9), OR *Ternis Horarum Terminis* (p. 17);
for NIGHT PRAYER, see *Te Lucis ante Terminum* (p. 4), OR *Christe, Qui, Splendor et Dies* (p. 11).

ORDINARY TIME: PSALTER, WEEKS I AND III

SUNDAY
FIRST VESPERS
Deus, Creator Omnium / God Most High, Creator of All Things

Deus, creator omnium polique rector, vestiens diem decoro lumine, noctem soporis gratia,	God most high, Creator of all things and ruler of heaven above, you clothe the day with radiant light, and the night with the gracious favor of sleep,
Artus solutos ut quies reddat laboris usui mentesque fessas allevet luctusque solvat anxios,	So that nighttime rest might return refreshed limbs to their accustomed toil, might bring welcome cheer to weary minds, might allay anxiety and grief:
Grates peracto iam die et noctis exortu preces, voti reos ut adiuves, hymnum canentes solvimus.	With day now done, and at start of night, we sing to you our hymn and pay you our grateful prayers, that you may grant us your aid, in fulfilling our vows to you.
Te cordis ima concinant, te vox canora concrepet, te diligat castus amor, te mens adoret sobria,	Let the depth of our hearts sing in concert to you, let our voice resound in harmony to you; let chaste love embrace you, careful mind bring you homage,
Ut cum profunda clauserit diem caligo noctium, fides tenebras nesciat et nox fide reluceat.	So that when the depths of darkness shall have locked in prison the light of day, yet shall faith not know the darkness of doubt, and night itself shall shine forth with the light of faith.
Praesta, Pater piissime, Patrique compar Unice, cum Spiritu Paraclito regnans per omne saeculum. Amen.	Grant this, Father most faithful; Grant this, only begotten Son equal in being to the Father, with the Spirit Paraclete ruling throughout endless ages. Amen.

PSALTER I AND III
SUNDAY: OFFICE OF READINGS, Nighttime or Early Morning
Primo Dierum Omnium / On This First of All Days

Primo dierum omnium,
quo mundus exstat conditus
vel quo resurgens Conditor
nos, morte victa, liberat,

On this first of all days,
when the world stands forth
new-made, or when its Creator,
rising in glory, grants us freedom
(for death is now overcome),

Let us cast weariness far from us;
let us all arise in haste,
and while it is yet night,
as we have come to know the Prophet
to bid, let us seek the Faithful One,

Pulsis procul torporibus,
surgamus omnes ocius,
et nocte quaeramus pium,
sicut Prophetam novimus,

So that he might grant
gracious hearing to our prayers,
might stretch out
the right hand of his mercy to us,
and restore us, washed clear
here below of all stain,
to the abode of heaven,

Nostras preces ut audiat
suamque dextram porrigat,
et hic piatos sordibus
reddat polorum sedibus,

And so that he might gift
with his most blessed bounty
those of us who
in the most sacred time of this day,
in the quiet of the still hours,
sing our hymns to him.

Ut, quique sacratissimo
huius diei tempore
horis quietis psallimus,
donis beatis muneret.

To God the Father be glory, as also to
his sole-begotten Son,
with the Spirit Paraclete
for endless ages to come.
Amen.

Deo Patri sit gloria
eiusque soli Filio
cum Spiritu Paraclito
in sempiterna saecula.
Amen.

PSALTER I AND III
SUNDAY: OFFICE OF READINGS, during the Day
Dies Aetasque Ceteris / The Eighth Day, That Time More Sacred

Dies aetasque ceteris
octava splendet sanctior
in te quam, Iesu, consecras,
primitiae surgentium.

The eighth day, that time more sacred
than every other, shines forth, that day,
O Jesus, which you, first fruits of those
who rise from the dead,
make sacred unto yourself.

Tu tibi nostras animas
nunc primo conresuscita;
tibi consurgant corpora
secunda morte libera.

Raise now first from death
our souls unto you;
let our bodies, too,
once freed from the second death,
rise once more unto you.

Tibique mox in nubibus,
Christe, feramur obviam
tecum victuri perpetim:
tu vita, resurrectio.

O Christ, may we soon be rapt up
to meet you in the clouds of heaven,
there to share in your endless victory:
you, our life, our resurrection.

Cuius videntes faciem,
configuremur gloriae;
te cognoscamus sicut es,
lux vera et suavitas.

May we be made like unto the glory
that is yours when we look upon you
face to face; may we then
come to know you as you are,
light and sweetness most true.

Regnum, cum Patri traditos,
plenos septeno chrismate,
in temet nos laetificas,
consummet sancta Trinitas.
Amen.

When you have filled us
with your sevenfold anointing,
and when you have given us over
to the Father, may the blessed Trinity
bring your Kingdom to full completion,
and may you fill us with the joy
that is you yourself.
Amen.

PSALTER I AND III
SUNDAY: MORNING PRAYER
Aeterne Rerum Conditor / Eternal Creator of All That Is

Aeterne rerum conditor,
noctem diemque qui regis,
et temporum das tempora
ut alleves fastidium.

Eternal Creator of all that is,
you rule over both night and day;
you grant times and seasons
to keep your children's
dreary weariness at bay.

Praeco diei iam sonat,
noctis profundae pervigil,
noctura lux viantibus
a nocte noctem segregans.

Lo, the herald of the day,
now cries out, e'er-watchful over
the deepest night,
nighttime light for travelers,
divider of the parts of the night.

Hoc excitatus lucifer
solvit polum caligine;
hoc omnis erronum chorus
vias nocendi deserit.

Herald-roused, the daystar
wipes the heavens
clean of darkness;
herald-stricken, whole bands
of wandervagrants flee
their harmdoing ways.

Hoc nauta vires colligit
pontique mitescunt freta;
hoc, ipse Petra Ecclesiae,
canente, culpam diluit.

Herald-encouraged,
the sailor gathers up his strength,
and the billowings of the sea
become calm; herald-sound inspired,
the very Rock of the Church laves
clean its faults.

Iesu, labantes respice
et nos videndo corrige:
si respicis, lapsus cadunt
fletuque culpa solvitur.

Tu, lux, refulge sensibus
mentisque somnum discute;
te nostra vox primum sonet
et vota solvamus tibi.

Jesus Lord, look upon us
in our wavering, and by your gaze
correct us in our faltering.
If your gaze be upon us,
our transgressions collapse,
and guilt is dissolved
in penitent tears.

Sit, Christe, rex piissime,
tibi Patrique gloria
cum Spiritu Paraclito,
in sempiterna saecula.
Amen.

[continued]

Aeterne Rerum Conditor / Eternal Creator of All That Is
[concluded]

O Light Eternal, shine upon our senses,
and strike asunder the sloth
that grips our minds.
Let our voice first sound unto you,
and let us pay our vows to you.

O Christ, King most faithful,
may glory be given to you,
and to the Father,
with the Spirit Paraclete,
for ages without end.
Amen.

PSALTER I AND III
SUNDAY: EVENING PRAYER II
Lucis Creator Optime / Creator Most Excellent of Life So Fine

Lucis Creator optime,
lucem dierum proferens,
primordiis lucis novae
mundi parans originem;

Creator most excellent of light so fine,
you bring forth
the very light of day, of time;
at the first beginnings of light itself
you forged the start of our world.

You command that the time
till morn reaches out to eve
be called the day;
then the night slides
into fell darkness:
hear the sobs, see the tears
with which we pray.

Qui mane iunctum vesperi
diem vocari praecipis:
taetrum chaos illabitur;
audi preces cum fletibus.

Let not our soul,
with guilt weighed down,
be exile-banned from reward of life,
doomed not to think of aught
of heaven's concerns,
but able only to tangle itself
in guilt's chains
and bonded strife.

Ne mens gravata crimine
vitae sit exsul munere,
dum nil perenne cogitat
seseque culpis illigat.

Nay; but may that soul knock
on inmost door of heaven above;
and bear away the prize
even of very life itself;
shun we now all that is shameful,
cleanse we ourselves
of everything stainful.

Caelorum pulset intimum,
vitale tollat premium;
vitemus omne noxium,
purgemus omne pessimum.

Grant this, Father most faithful;
grant it, sole-begotten
Father's Son,
with the Spirit Advocate
ruling for ages to come.
Amen.

Praesta, Pater piissime,
Patrique compar Unice,
cum Spiritu Paraclito
regnans per omne saeculum.
Amen.

PSALTER I AND III
MONDAY: OFFICE OF READINGS, Nighttime or Early Morning
Somno Refectis Artubus / With Limbs Sleep-Freshed We Rise

Somno refectis artubus
spreto cubili, surgimus:
nobis, Pater, canentibus
adesse te deposcimus.

With limbs sleep-freshed we rise,
disdaining the bed;
we beg you, O Father, to be with us
as we chant our praises unto you.

Te lingua primum concinat,
te mentis ardor ambiat,
ut actuum sequentium
tu, sancte, sis exordium.

Let our tongue sing first of you;
let our ardent desire be to gain you,
so that, O Holy One, you might be
the source of all else we do.

Cedant tenebrae lumini
et nox diurno sideri,
ut culpa, quam nox intulit,
lucis labascat munere.

Let darkness yield to light,
and night to the star of day,
that the faults which night
has brought upon us
may give way to the power of light.

Precamur idem supplices
noxas ut omnes amputes,
et ore te canentium
lauderis in perpetuum.

We ask too, in suppliant prayer,
that you cut away from us
every evil act that we might do,
and that you may forever be praised
by the lips of those who sing to you.

Praesta, Pater piissime,
Patrique compar Unice,
cum Spiritu Paraclito
regnans per omne saeculum.
Amen.

Grant this, Father most faithful;
grant it, co-equal to the Father
and, as well, only Son,
who with the Spirit Paraclete
live and reign for endless ages to come.
Amen.

PSALTER I AND III
MONDAY, OFFICE OF READINGS, during the Day
Aeterna Lux, Divinitas / Light Never-Failing, Godhead Most True

Aeterna lux, divinitas,
in unitate Trinitas,
te confitemur debiles,
te deprecamur supplices.

Light never failing,
Godhead most true,
Threesome amidst unity,
we proclaim your glory,
weak though we are,
and call upon you in trustful prayer.

Summum Parentem credimus
Natumque Patris unicum,
et caritatis vinculum
qui iungit illos Spiritum.

In a Father most high
we place our faith,
and in a Son sole-born
of the Father supreme,
And in a bond of blazing love,
the Spirit, who unites Father, Son,
and Self in Divinity sublime.

O veritas, o caritas,
o finis et felicitas,
sperare fac et credere,
amare fac et consequi.

Qui finis et exordium
rerumque fons es omnium,
tu sola es solacium,
tu certa spes credentium.

O triune Truth, O triune Love,
goal of your creatures,
bliss for them true,
Make us hope, make us believe,
make us love and follow you.

Qui cuncta solus efficis
cunctisque solus sufficis,
tu sola lux es omnibus
et praemium sperantibus.

Christum rogamus et Patrem,
Christi Patrisque Spiritum;
unum potens per omnia,
fove precantes, Trinitas.
Amen.

The ending, the beginning,
the source are you
of creatures one and all;
You alone are their comfort,
alone the certain hope
of all believers true.

[continued]

Aeterna Lux, Divinitas / Light Never Failing, Godhead Most True
[concluded]

By yourself you bring all things
into being; and you alone make all
continue to be.
You alone are light for all creatures,
and reward most perfect
for those who hope in you.

To Christ do we pray,
and to the Father as well,
And to the Spirit
of Christ and the Father:
O Trinity, O Unity, O Tri-unity,
omnipotent over all,
have care for those who pray to you.
Amen.

PSALTER I AND III
MONDAY, MORNING PRAYER
Splendor Paternae Gloriae / Splendor of the Father's Glory

Splendor paternae gloriae,
de luce lucem proferens,
lux lucis et fons luminis,
diem dies illuminans,

Verusque sol, illabere
micans nitore perpeti,
iubarque Sancti Spiritus
infunde nostris sensibus.

Votis vocemus et Patrem,
Patrem perennis gloriae,
Patrem potentis gratiae,
culpam releget lubricam.

Informet actus strenuos,
dentem retundat invidi,
casus secundet asperos,
donet gerendi gratiam.

Mentem gubernet et regat
casto, fideli corpore;
fides calore ferveat,
fraudis venena nesciat.

Christusque nobis sit cibus,
potusque noster sit fides;
laeti bibamus sobriam
ebrietatem Spiritus.

Laetus dies hic transeat;
pudor sit ut diluculum
fides velut meridies,
crepusculum mens nesciat.

Aurora cursus provehit;
Aurora totus prodeat,
in Patre totus Filius
et totus in Verbo Pater.
Amen.

Brilliance of the Father's glory,
gleaning light from light itself,
brightness of brightness are you,
font of brilliance daylight-granting,
daylight itself are you,
giving light to day itself.

You are truly the very sun;
come down upon us,
gleaming with shimmering,
boundless brilliance;
pour out the sanctifying radiance
of the Holy Spirit
upon our needsome hearts.

With vows true paid
let us call upon the Father as well,
the Father of endless glory,
the Father of grace most powerful:
to banish all fall-causing faults
far from us,

To mold and shape
our restless deeds,
to blunt the jealous serpent's bite,
to lessen harsh failure's sting,
to grant us grace to bear calmly
our failures drear.

May he govern our spirits,
and establish his rule
over our bodies when
they are rendered chaste and true;
may faith grow hot with holy heat,
and never know the poisoned drug
of foul deceit.

[continued]

Splendor Paternae Gloriae / Splendor of the Father's Glory
[concluded]

And may Christ be our food,
and faith our drink;
in bliss may we partake
of the mild but curesome wine
of the Spirit Blest.

May this day pass by in joy;
let modesty be as our daybreak,
fidelity as our noontime;
and may our minds know
no dusky dimness
of twilight or of eve.

The dawn comes forth, its course to run;
may total, true Dawn come forth as well:
the Son, wholly in the Father,
and the Father wholly in the Son.
Amen.

PSALTER I AND III
MONDAY, EVENING PRAYER
Immense Caeli Conditor / Boundless Creator of the Heavens Above

Immense caeli conditor,
qui, mixta ne confunderent,
aquae fluenta dividens,
caelum dedisti limitem,

Boundless Creator
of the heavens above,
you parted the flowing waters
and set for them a boundary sky,
lest, commingling, they chaos bring.

You set a place for the heavenly flows,
a place as well
for the streams of earth,
so that water might keep in check
fell fire, lest it put to dusty flight
even the earthground itself.

Firmans locum caelestibus
simulque terrae rivulis,
ut unda flammas temperet,
terrae solum ne dissipet:

Infunde nunc, piissime,
donum perennis gratiae,
fraudis novae ne casibus
nos error atterat vetus.

Gift out upon us now,
Most Faithful One,
your endless grace,
lest the ancient error-maker
in like way destroy us
with stumbling snares
of newfound deceit.

May faith discover how best
to light the way,
and bring for us
the glow of brilliant guide-beam;
let it cast into terror-state
all false cares and deceit,
and let no untruths
restrain its guardian flight.

Lucem fides inveniat,
sic luminis iubar ferat;
haec vana cuncta terreat,
hanc falsa nulla comprimant.

Grant this, Father most loving;
grant it, Father's sole-begotten Son,
with Advocate Spirit reigning
for endless ages to come.
Amen.

Praesta, Pater piissime,
Patrique compar Unice,
cum Spiritu Paraclito
regnans per omne saeculum.
Amen.

PSALTER I AND III
TUESDAY, OFFICE OF READINGS, Nighttime or Early Morning
Consors Paterni Luminis / Sharer in the Father's Own Light

Consors paterni luminis,
lux ipse lucis et dies,
noctem canendo rumpimus:
assiste postulantibus.

Sharer in the Father's own light,
Light of Light yourself,
and daylight strong,
through night's darkness
we burst in song:
aid us as we call on you.

Aufer tenebras mentium,
fuga catervas daemonum,
expelle somnolentiam
ne pigritantes obruat.

Snatch darkness from our hearts;
put to flight the demon horde.
Drive away dull drowsiness,
lest it bury us in somnolent slumber.

Sic, Christe, nobis omnibus
indulgeas credentibus,
ut prosit exorantibus
quod praecinentes psallimus.

Christ Lord, on your believers
so bestow your forgiving boon
that our psalm chant
may profit us as we pray.

Sit, Christe, rex piissime,
tibi Patrique gloria
cum Spiritu Paraclito,
in sempiterna saecula.
Amen.

Christ God, King most loving,
to you be glory,
and to your Father most high,
with the Spirit Advocate
reigning eternally.
Amen

PSALTER I AND III
TUESDAY, OFFICE OF READINGS, during the Day
O Sacrosancta Trinitas / Godhead Most Holy, Triune Yet One

O sacrosancta Trinitas,
quae cuncta condens ordinas,
diem labori deputans
noctem quieti dedicas,

Godhead most holy, triune yet one,
you place in due order
all you have made;
the daytime you assign fo work,
but the nighttime you give over
to gentle rest.

Te mane, simul vespere,
te nocte ac die canimus;
in tua nos tu gloria
per cuncta serva tempora.

At morning time, at time of eve too,
in night's dark shadows
and in day's bright light
we sing our prayers to you;
keep us in the safety
of your power's glory
whate'er the hour may be.

Nos adsumus te cernui
en adorantes famuli;
vota precesque supplicum
hymnis adiunge caelitum.

Lo, with heads bowed low
your people come
in adoration of you.
Join our pleading prayers and
offerings with the hymns
that are sung in heaven on high.

Praesta, Pater piissime,
Patrique compar Unice,
cum Spiritu Paraclito
regnans per omne saeculum.
Amen.

Grant this, Father most faithful;
grant it, Son, sole-begotten,
Father-equal one,
reigning with the Spirit Advocate
while e'er eternity shall run.
Amen.

PSALTER I AND III
TUESDAY, MORNING PRAYER
Pergrata Mundo Nuntiat / The Dawn, The Sunbeam's First Ray

Pergrata mundo nuntiat
aurora solis spicula,
res et colore vestiens
iam cuncta dat nitescere.

Qui sol per aevum praenites,
O Christe, nobis vividus,
ad te canentes vertimur,
te gestientes perfrui.

Tu Patris es scientia
Verbumque per quod omnia
miro refulgent ordine
mentesque nostras attrahunt.

Da lucis ut nos filii
sic ambulemus impigri,
ut Patris usque gratiam
mores et actus exprimant.

Sincera praesta ut profluant
ex ore nostro iugiter,
et veritatis dulcibus
ut excitemur gaudiis.

Sit, Christe, rex piissime,
tibi Patrique gloria
cum Spiritu Paraclito,
in sempiterna saecula.
Amen.

The dawn, the sunbeam's first ray,
plays welcome herald to the world,
garbing things in brilliant hue
and now granting everything
a ruddy glow.

But, Christ our Lord, you outshine
the sun itself throughout the ages,
giving very life to us;
we turn to you with songs of praise,
eager to bask in your presence.

You are the Father's wisdom,
the Word by which
all things shine forth in marvelous array
and draw our minds to you.

Grant that we may be children of light,
and with eager tread so walk
the path of life that
what we are and what we do
will show forth
the Father's gracious kindliness.

Grant that none but honest words
may ever come forth from our mouths,
and that we may be set afire
by the pleasant joys of truth.

Christ, King most gracious,
may glory be given to you
and to the Father
with the Spirit Advocate
for ages without end.
Amen.

PSALTER I AND III
TUESDAY, EVENING PRAYER
Telluris Ingens Conditor / Creator Most Magnificent of Earth Itself

Telluris ingens conditor,
mundi solum qui eruens,
pulsis aquae molestiis,
terram dedist*i* immobilem,

Creator most magnificent
of earth itself, you raised up
the landed part of the world,
banishing the troublesome sea;
the dry land you established
will not be moved:

Ut germen aptum proferens,
fulvis decora floribus,
fecunda fructu sisteret
pastumque gratum redderet:

This so that,
as it sprouted forth suitable seed,
and, garbed with tawny blossoms,
was enriched with bountiful fruit,
it might be fecund-fair
with humankind's food:

Mentis perustae vulnera
munda virore gratiae,
ut facta fletu diluat
motusque pravos atterat,

By the green growth of your grace,
cleanse the wounds
of a spirit fire-plumed,
so that it can purge its deeds
with sorrow
and sand down smooth its evil ways,

Iussis tuis obtemperet,
nullis malis approximet,
bonis repleri gaudeat
et mortis actum nesciat.

And might, indeed,
obey your commands,
drawing nigh to no evil,
but rejoicing at being filled with good,
knowing no deed of death.

Praesta, Pater piissime,
Patrique compar Unice,
cum Spiritu Paraclito
regnans per omne saeculum.
Amen.

Grant this, Father most faithful;
grant it, only-begotten One,
to the Father most equal,
with the Spirit Advocate reigning
for endless ages to come.
Amen.

PSALTER I AND III
WEDNESDAY, OFFICE OF READINGS, Nighttime or Early Morning
Rerum Creator Optime / Most Excellent Maker of All That Is

Rerum creator optime
rectorque noster, respice;
nos a quiete noxia
mersos sopore libera.

Most excellent maker of all that is,
and our kingly ruler as well,
look upon us, free us,
though enwrapped in sleep,
from rest that would do us harm.

You, Christ most holy, we implore:
forgive us the sinful deeds
we have done.
We rise to profess your holy name,
and we break asunder
the quiet watches of the night.

Te, sancte Christe, poscimus;
ignosce tu criminibus,
ad confitendum surgimus
morasque noctis rumpimus.

Mentes manusque tollimus,
Propheta sicut noctibus
nobis gerendum praecipit
Paulusque gestis censuit.

Our minds we lift up to you,
and our hands as well,
just as the prophet bade us do
at nighttime, and Paul confirmed
by his prayerful deeds.

You see well what ill we have done;
and we bring to your sight
what elsewise we try
to keep secret as well.
We pour out our weeping prayers;
forgive us our sinful deeds.

Vides malum quod gessimus;
occulta nostra pandimus,
preces gementes fundimus;
dimitte quod peccavimus.

Christ, king most faithful,
be glory given to you,
and to the Father
and the Spirit advocate true,
for endless ages to come.
Amen.

Sit, Christe, rex piissime,
tibi Patrique gloria
cum Spiritu Paraclito,
in sempiterna saecula.
Amen.

WEDNESDAY, PSALTER I AND III
OFFICE OF READINGS, During the Day
Scientiarum Domino / To You, Lord of Wisdom Most High

Scientiarum Domino,
sit tibi iubilatio,
qui nostra vides intima
tuaque foves gratia.

To you, Lord of wisdom most high,
may joyful praise be given:
you see into the secret depths
of our hearts
and nourish them with your grace.

Shepherd most excellent,
you seek the lost,
while also guarding the unstraying:
in richest pastures grant us
a place with your faithful flock.

Qui bonum, pastor optime,
dum servas, quaeris perditum,
in pascuis uberrimis
nos iunge piis gregibus.

Let not dread fear of the angry judge
make us a part
of despairing goatly herd;
nay rather, by your kindly decree,
may we be sheep
of your eternal flock.

Ne terror irae iudicis
nos haedis iungat reprobis,
sed simus temet iudice
oves aeternae pascuae.

To you, Redeemer most high,
may glory be given,
honor too, power and victory as well,
as you rule over all things
for all ages to come.
Amen.

Tibi, Redemptor, gloria,
honor, virtus, victoria,
regnanti super omnia
per saeculorum saecula.
Amen.

WEDNESDAY, PSALTER I AND III
MORNING PRAYER
Nox et Tenebrae et Nubila / Nightsomeness, Shadows Fell

Nox et tenebrae et nubila,
confusa mundi et turbida,
lux intrat, albescit polus:
Christus venit: discedite.

Nightsomeness, shadows fell,
clouds stirred up and stormy drear,
things baffling and unordered
in our world here,
light is breaking upon us,
the heaven grows bright:
Christ is coming, begone, one and all,
ye darknesses of night!

Caligo terrae scinditur
percussa solis spiculo,
rebusque iam color redit
vultu nitentis sideris.

Earth's blackness is rent in twain,
by sun's bright light-beam smitten;
shades of brilliant hue return now
to creatures, at unflinching gaze of
bright and shining sun.

Sic nostra mox obscuritas
fraudisque pectus conscium,
ruptis retectum nubibus,
regnante pallescet Deo.

And so will our own dim darknesses,
our hearts well aware of our deceits,
be soon uncovered
by the rending of the dark clouds
and glow pale bright,
secure in the kingship of God.

Te, Christe, solum novimus,
te mente pura et simplici
rogare curvato genu
flendo et canendo discimus.

You, O Christ, alone do we know;
only to you, with pure and
single-hearted minds,
with knee full bent, do we learn to make
our prayers in tearful song.

Intende nostris sensibus
vitamque totam dispice:
sunt multa fucis illita
quae luce purgentur tua.

Look thou upon our thoughts;
test thou our whole lives:
much is there with dross besmeared:
let it all be cleansed
by your bright dawn-light.

Sit, Christe, rex piissime,
tibi Patrique gloria
cum Spiritu Paraclito
in sempiterna saecula.
Amen.

And thus, Christ most faithful,
may glory be given to thee,
to the Father as well,
with the Spirit Advocate
for endless ages to come.
Amen.

WEDNESDAY, PSALTER I AND III
EVENING PRAYER
Caeli Deus Sanctissime / Most Holy God of Heaven Above

Caeli Deus sanctissime,
qui lucidum centrum poli
candore pignis igneo
augens decori lumina,

Most holy God of heaven above,
with blazing color
you paint the bright apex of the skies:
you add brilliance to beauty.

On creation's fourth day you form
the flaming orb of the sun;
you entrust to
the ordered routes of the moon the
care of the wide-ranging
roamings of the stars.

Quarto die qui flammeam
solis rotam constituens,
lunae ministras ordini
vagos recursus siderum,

Ut noctibus vel lumini
diremptionis terminum,
primordiis et mensium
signum dares notissimum:

And so, whether to darkness
or to light, you give clear sign
of proper boundaries and limits,
limits too
of months' beginnings and ends.

Illumine human hearts;
wipe away sin's dregs
from humankind's mind.
Break human bonds, guilt-forged;
upend crushing stone of guilty deeds.

Illumina cor hominum,
absterge sordes mentium,
resolve culpae vinculum,
everte moles criminum.

Grant this, Father most faithful;
grant it, O only-begotten
and co-equal Son,
with the Spirit Advocate
ruling while e'er the ages run.
Amen.

Praesta, Pater piissime,
Patrique compar Unice,
cum Spiritu Paraclito
regnans per omne saeculum.
Amen.

THURSDAY, PSALTER I AND III
OFFICE OF READINGS, Nighttime or Early Morning
Nox Atra Rerum Contegit / Lusterless Night Conceals

Nox atra rerum contegit
terrae colores omnium:
nos confitentes poscimus
te, iuste iudex cordium,

Lusterless night conceals
the earthly hues of all that is:
as we proclaim your holy name,
O most just judge of human hearts,
we beg

Ut auferas piacula
sordesque mentis abluas,
donesque, Christe, gratiam
ut arceantur crimina.

That you will wipe away
whate'er earns punishing wrath,
will wash away
whate'er defiles our minds,
and, O Christ,
will bestow your gracious help
to ward far away our guilt and fault.

Mens, ecce, torpet impia,
quam culpa mordet noxia;
obscura gestit tollere
et te, Redemptor, quaerere.

Lo, the wicked mind lies stunned,
that very mind
which hurting guilt bites deep:
it yearns to put away hidden ill
and, O Redeemer, to seek out you.

Drive far away, to remotest place,
the darkness
from furthest inmost mind;
let it rejoice in being set
in beatific light.

Repelle tu caliginem
intrinsecus quam maxime,
ut in beato gaudeat
se collocari lumine.

Christ most holy, to you be glory,
and to the Father as well,
with the Spirit Advocate
for endless ages to tell.
Amen.

Sit, Christe, rex piissime,
tibi Patrique gloria,
cum Spiritu Paraclito,
in sempiterna saecula.
Amen.

THURSDAY, PSALTER I AND III
OFFICE OF READINGS, during the Day
Christe, Precamur Adnuas / Christ, Lord, We Humbly Beg

Christe, precamur adnuas
orantibus servis tuis,
iniquitas haec saeculi
ne nostram captivet fidem.

Christ, Lord, we humbly beg:
look with favor on your servants
as we pray to you.
Let not the wickedness
of this our age
bind down our faith in trammel fell.

Non cogitemus impie,
invideamus nemini,
laesi non reddamus vicem,
vincamus in bono malum.

Let us ponder nothing wickedly;
let us envy no one.
If we are injured,
let us not return hurt for hurt,
but rather
let us conquer evil in good.

Absit nostris e cordibus
ira, dolus, superbia;
absistat avaritia,
malorum radix omnium.

Far from our hearts
be all taint of anger, trickery, pride;
let greedy avarice depart,
avarice, of all evil
the root and the cause.

Let love unfeigned preserve
the covenants peace has forged;
let chastity remain untrammeled
through faith that has no end.

Conservet pacis foedera
non simulata caritas;
sit illibata castitas
credulitate perpeti.

To you, Christ Lord, King most faithful,
may glory by us be given,
with the Father too,
and the Spirit Advocate
for ages e'er yet to come.
Amen.

Sit, Christe, rex piissime,
tibi Patrique gloria
cum Spiritu Paraclito,
in sempiterna saecula.
Amen.

THURSDAY, PSALTER I AND III
MORNING PRAYER
Sol Ecce Surgit Igneus / Lo, Fiery Sun Arises

Sol ecce surgit igneus:
piget, pudescit, paenitet,
nec teste quisquam lumine
peccare constanter potest.

Tandem facessat caecitas,
quae nosmet in praeceps diu
lapsos sinistris gressibus
errore traxit devio.

Haec lux serenum conferat
purosque nos praestet sibi;
nihil loquamur subdolum,
volvamus obscurum nihil.

Sic tota decurrat dies,
ne lingua mendax, ne manus
oculive peccent lubrici,
ne noxa corpus inquinet.

Speculator astat desuper,
qui nos diebus omnibus
actusque nostros prospicit
a luce prima in vesperum.

Deo Patri sit gloria
eiusque soli Filio
cum Spiritu Paraclito,
in sempiterna saecula.
Amen.

Lo, fiery sun arises,
sorrifying, shaming, shriving;
nor while light tells all can anyone
be at ease in sin's dark grip.

At long last sad sightlessness
slinks away, long-time thrall
that dragged us, in error's full folly,
by fatal footfall headlong into ruin.

May this light bring us peaceful joy
and purify us for itself;
let our lips speak no cunning deception,
nor our minds so much as consider
aught darkling unseen.

May this whole day so run its course
that not lying tongue,
nor deceitful hand or eye
may yield to sin,
nor yet crime-filled deed
befoul our body.

May the Recorder Angel
be present from on high,
who each day without fail,
from light's first glimmer
till e'en's last fleeting shade,
gazes upon us and all we do.

To God the Father be endless praise,
and to his only Son as well,
with the Spirit Advocate,
while e'er the ages shall run.
Amen.

THURSDAY, PSALTER I AND III
EVENING PRAYER
Magnae Deus Potentiae / Lord God of Massive Power

Magnae Deus potentiae,
qui ex aquis ortum genus
partim remittis gurgiti,
partim levas in aera,

Lord God of massive power,
of creatures from primal waters risen
you send some back
to dwell in watery depths,
but others you raise up
into earth's bright air.

Demersa lymphis imprimens,
subvecta caelis irrogans,
ut, stirpe una prodita,
diversa repleant loca:

You press down firmly
into murky depths
those you have assigned there,
and you ordain the place to dwell
for those elevated in the skies:
thus, though sprung
from a single root, they might serve
you alike in filling all locales.

Largire cunctis servulis,
quos mundat unda sanguinis,
nescire lapsus criminum
nec ferre mortis taedium,

Grant that all your servant children,
whom the flood of the Lord's blood
has cleansed,
may know no sin or fault,
nor may bear upon themselves
the loathsome sentence of death.

Ut culpa nullum deprimat,
nullum levet iactantia,
elisa mens ne concidat,
elata mens ne corruat.

Grant that guilt may none o'ercome,
nor yet in vain boasting any stray soul
itself exalt;
let no humbled soul stumble and fall,
nor let even haughty soul
tumble down in o'erweening pride.

Grant this, Father most faithful;
grant it, Son to the Father most equal,
with the Spirit Advocate:
Trinity ruling for endless ages to be.
Amen.

Praesta, Pater piissime,
Patrique compar Unice,
cum Spiritu Paraclito
regnans per omne saeculum.
Amen.

FRIDAY, PSALTER I AND III
OFFICE OF READINGS, Nighttime or Early Morning
Tu, Trinitatis Unitas / You, O God, Are Unity in Trinity

Tu, Trinitatis Unitas,
orbem potenter qui regis,
attende laudum cantica
quae excubantes psallimus.

You, O God, are Unity
in Trinity mysterious;
mightily do you rule the earth
spread out beneath you.
Listen, we pray, to the hymns of praise
that we rise from our beds
and sing unto you.

Nam lectulo consurgimus
noctis quieto tempore,
ut flagitemus vulnerum
a te medelam omnium,

For pallet and bed we leave behind
in the still hour of the night,
that we may beg of you
a healing cure for all that wounds,

And at the same time, beg that,
whatever fault by demon deceit
we have committed in darkness time,
your glorious power may come
from heaven's height
and wipe full clean.

Quo, fraude quicquid dæmonum
in noctibus deliquimus,
abstergat illud caelitus
tuae potestas gloriae.

With trusting heart we ask of you:
fill us with your divine light;
through it may we not stumble and fall
in whate'er we do
in the course of our allotted days.

Te corde fido quaesumus,
reple tuo nos lumine,
per quod dierum circulis
nullis ruamus actibus.

Grant this, Father most faithful;
grant it, only-begotten one,
to the Father equal in all, God the Son,
ruling with the Spirit Advocate
while e'er the ages run.
Amen.

Praesta, Pater piissime,
Patrique compar Unice,
cum Spiritu Paraclito
regnans per omne saeculum.
Amen.

FRIDAY, PSALTER I AND III
OFFICE OF READINGS, during the Day
Adesto, Christe, Cordibus / Be Present, O Christ, to Our Hearts

Adesto, Christe, cordibus,
celsa redemptis caritas;
infunde nostris fervidos
fletus, rogamus, vocibus.

Be present, O Christ, to our hearts;
it was your great love
that redeemed them.
Fill our prayerful song, we beg,
with heartfelt, burning sorrow.

Ad te preces, piissime
Iesu, fide profundimus;
dimitte, Christe, quaesumus,
factis malum quod fecimus.

Jesus most faithful, in trusting faith
do we pour out our prayers;
we beg of you, Christ Lord:
forgive the evil deeds
that we have done.

Sanctae crucis signaculo,
tuo sacrato corpore,
defende nos ut filios
omnes, rogamus, undique.

Under the banner of the sacred cross,
sanctified by your own precious blood,
defend us all as your children,
we beg, throughout
the whole world's length and breadth.

Sit, Christe, rex piissime,
tibi Patrique gloria
cum Spiritu Paraclito,
in sempiterna saecula.
Amen.

Christ God, King most faithful,
may glory be given to you,
and to the Father most high,
as also to the Spirit Advocate
for ages ne'er to end.
Amen.

FRIDAY, PSALTER I AND III
MORNING PRAYER
Aeterna Caeli Gloria / Ceaseless Splendor of the Heavens Above

Aeterna caeli gloria,
beata spes mortalium,
celsi Parentis Unice
castaeque proles Virginis,

Ceaseless splendor
of the heavens above,
most blest hope of mortal race,
sole-begotten of the Father on high,
offspring of the virgin most chaste,

Da dexteram surgentibus,
exsurgat et mens sobria
flagrans et in laudem Dei
grates rependat debitas.

Stretch forth your strong right hand
to us as we arise.
Sober in mind may we come forth
from sleep, and return
ardent, fitting thanks in praise of you,
our God most high.

Ortus refulget lucifer
ipsamque lucem nuntiat,
cadit caligo noctium,
lux sancta nos illuminet,

The day star rises, brightly gleams,
proclaims the brightness of light itself;
the darkness of night falters,
all overcome.
May this most sacred light
shine full upon us,

Manensque nostris sensibus
noctem repellat saeculi
omnique fine temporis
purgata servet pectora.

Remain unwavering in our minds,
repulse the darkness of the world, and,
for every limiting measure of time,
keep safe our hearts when once
they are cleaned of sin's foul stain.

Quaesita iam primum fides
radicet altis sensibus,
secunda spes congaudeat;
tunc maior exstat caritas.

May long-sought faith root itself
deep in our hearts;
may hope, second in rank,
rejoice to be there as well;
and then may charity,
greatest of the three,
shine forth in brilliance rare.

Sit, Christe, rex piissime,
tibi Patrique gloria
cum Spiritu Paraclito,
in sempiterna saecula.
Amen.

To you, O Christ, King most faithful,
and to your Father on high,
may endless glory be accorded,
with the Spirit Advocate,
for all scope of ages
e'er to be recorded.
Amen.

FRIDAY, PSALTER I AND III
EVENING PRAYER
Plasmator Hominis, Deus / Fashioner Most Blessed

Plasmator hominis, Deus,	Fashioner most blessed
qui, cuncta solus ordinans,	of the human race,
humum iubes producere	God of power, God most high,
reptantis et ferae genus;	with none to assist, you have made
	fast the rank and order of all things.
	You bid the ground to bring forth
	crawling beasts,
	yea, and wild, fierce ones as well.
Qui magna rerum corpora,	The massive forms of creaturehood,
dictu iubentis vivida,	enquickened by your commanding
ut serviant per ordinem	word, you have presented
subdens dedisti homini:	to humankind,
	so that to man and woman they might
	render subservient service
	each according to its kind.
Repelle a servis tuis	Far from those who serve you, drive
quicquid per immunditiam	whatever evil,
aut moribus se suggerit,	through uncleanness' bane,
aut actibus se interserit.	suggests itself to them
	by custom's rote,
	whatever ill insinuates itself
	in whate'er their actions may be.
	Grant them joy's great rewards,
	grant them grace's holy gifts.
Da gaudiorum praemia,	Rend apart the bonds of strife;
da gratiarum munera;	knit close together
dissolve litis vincula,	the promises and pledges
astringe pacis foedera.	of blessed peace.
	Grant this, Father most faithful;
	grant it, only Son,
Praesta, Pater piissime,	to the Father most akin,
Patrique compar Unice,	with the Spirit Paraclete ruling
cum Spiritu Paraclito	for endless ages, e'er going out, e'er
regnans per omne saeculum.	coming in.
Amen.	Amen.

SATURDAY, PSALTER I AND III
OFFICE OF READINGS, Nighttime or Early Morning
Summae Deus Clementiae / God of Mercy Unsurpassed

Summae Deus clementiae
mundique factor machinae,
qui trinus almo numine
unusque firmas omnia,

God of mercy unsurpassed,
maker of the wondrous work
that is our world,
with nurturing godhead,
triune but also one,
you keep all things in being.

Nostros piis cum canticis
fletus benigne suscipe,
quo corde puro sordibus
te perfruamur largius.

In your gracious kindness,
receive our tearful prayers,
offered with grateful hymns;
may we thus,
with hearts cleansed of all stain,
enjoy your company ever more fully.

Lumbos adure congruis
tu caritatis ignibus,
accincti ut adsint perpetim
tuisque prompti adventibus,

Set our inmost selves aflame
with the fires that belong to sacred love,
so that they may ever be girt
and stand prepared,
alert to whene'er you come,

Ut, quique horas noctium
nunc concinendo rumpimus,
donis beatae patriae
ditemur omnes affatim.

So that we who now break
the stillness of nights' hours
with joyful song of praise
may all be made rich
with the gifts of our heavenly home
in measure full unbounded.

Praesta, Pater piissime,
Patrique compar Unice,
cum Spiritu Paraclito
regnans per omne saeculum.
Amen.

Grant this, Father most faithful;
grant it, only-begotten Son,
to the Father equal in all,
ruling with the Spirit Advocate
through all ages to come.
Amen.

SATURDAY, PSALTER I AND III
OFFICE OF READINGS, during the Day
Auctor Perennis Gloriae / Source of Ne'er-Failing Splendor

Auctor perennis gloriae,
qui septiformis gratiae
das Spiritum credentibus,
assiste mitis omnibus.

Source of ne'er-failing splendor,
to your believers you grant your Spirit,
with sevenfold grace;
come gently to the aid of us all.

Expelle morbos corporum,
mentis repelle scandalum,
exscinde vires criminum,
fuga dolores cordium.

Drive far from us
whate'er would hurt our bodies,
turn aside
whate'er would tempt
our mind toward ill.
Root out the power of sin,
put to flight
the sorrows our hearts bear.

Serenas mentes effice,
opus honestum perfice,
preces orantum accipe,
vitam perennem tribue.

Make tranquil our minds;
make worthy the work that we do.
Receive the prayers
of those who pray to you;
grant them life without end.

Septem dierum cursibus
nunc tempus omne ducitur;
octavus ille ultimus
dies erit iudicii,

On the turnings of seven days
is now all time reckoned;
that last, eighth day,
will be the day of judgment

in quo, Redemptor, quaesumus,
ne nos in ira arguas,
sed a sinistra libera,
ad dexteram nos colloca,

On which, O Redeemer, we beg
that you will not reprove us in wrath;
nay, free us from that dread place
at your left hand,
and station us on your right,

Ut, cum preces susceperis
clemens tuarum plebium,
reddamus omnes gloriam
trino Deo per saecula.
Amen.

So that, when in your mercy
you receive the prayers
of your faithful people,
we may all give glory to you,
our triune God, for ages endless.
Amen.

SATURDAY, PSALTER I AND III
MORNING PRAYER
Aurora Iam Spargit Polum / Now Does Dawn Besprinkle the Heavens

Aurora iam spargit polum,
terris dies illabitur,
lucis resultat spiculum:
discedat omne lubricum.

Now does dawn besprinkle the heavens;
daylight flows down upon the earth.
Light's sharp shaft springs forth:
let all deceit take flight.

Iam vana noctis decidant,
mentis reatus subruat,
quicquid tenebris horridum
nox attulit culpae, cadat,

Let darkness' deceptions
depart in haste,
and mind's guilts pass now far from us;
let whatever savage fault
night has brought in darkness
now fall full away.

Ut mane illud ultimum,
quod praestolamur cernui,
in lucem nobis effluat,
dum hoc canore concrepat.

Thus may that final judgment morn,
which, with heads bowed low,
we now await,
flow forth into full brightness for us,
even as this, our present home,
collapses in noisy ruin.

Deo Patri sit gloria
eiusque soli Filio
cum Spiritu Paraclito,
in sempiterna saecula.
Amen.

To God the Father be glory given,
and to his sole-begotten Son,
with the Spirit Advocate
for eons forever yet to come.
Amen.

ORDINARY TIME: PSALTER, WEEKS II AND IV

SUNDAY
FIRST VESPERS
Rerum, Deus, Fons Omnium / God Our Father, Source of All That Is

Rerum, Deus, fons omnium,
qui, rebus actis omnibus,
totius orbis ambitum
censu replesti munerum,

God our Father, source of all that is,
the great task of creation
is now finished:
you have filled the length and breadth
of the entire world
with the riches of your gifts.

Ac, mole tanta condita,
tandem quietem diceris
sumpsisse, dans laboribus
ut nos levemur gratius:

Once such a measureless mass
of good is now firmly in place,
you are said to have taken,
at last, your rest,
granting thus that we too might
more readily find
relief from the labors that are ours.

Concede nunc mortalibus
deflere vitae crimina,
instare iam virtutibus
et munerari prosperis,

Grant now to us mortal beings
the grace to bewail
the sins of our lives,
to devote ourselves
to the practice of virtue,
to find reward in your good favor,

Ut cum tremendi iudicis
horror supremus coeperit,
laetemur omnes invicem
pacis repleti munere.

So that when the ultimate terror
of the fearsome judge shall have
begun its course,
we may all rejoice together,
filled as we are
with the gift of confident peace.

Praesta, Pater piissime,
Patrique compar Unice,
cum Spiritu Paraclito
regnans per omne saeculum.
Amen.

Grant this, Father most faithful;
grant this, only-begotten one,
to the Father akin,
with the Spirit Advocate
ruling through eon and age alike.
Amen.

SUNDAY, PSALTER II AND IV
OFFICE OF READINGS, Nighttime or Early Morning
Mediae Noctis Tempus Est / Now Has Midnight's Hour Come

Mediae noctis tempus est;
prophetica vox admonet
dicamus laudes ut Deo
Patri semper ac Filio,

Now has midnight's hour come;
the seer's voice warns us to render
ceaselessly our hymns of praise
to God the Father, God the Son,

And God the Spirit as well:
for perfect Trinity, yet godhead of
but a single substance
must we always praise.

Sancto quoque Spiritui:
perfecta enim Trinitas
uniusque substantiae
laudanda nobis semper est.

This hour brings terror: it is
the hour when the destroying angel
brought death to the Egyptian,
snatched away
the lives of the firstborn.

Terrorem tempus hoc habet,
quo, cum vastator angelus
Aegypto mortem intulit,
delevit primogenita.

But for the righteous,
this hour brings salvation,
those righteous whom,
likewise in Egypt land,
the destroying angel
dared not afflict,
knowing full well the warning
of the blood-sign's dreaded ban.

Haec iustis hora salus est,
quos tunc ibidem angelus
ausus punire non erat,
signum formidans sanguinis.

Egypt wept bitterly:
so many died so awfully!
Israel alone rejoiced, safe
behind the rampart
of the blood of the lamb.

Aegyptus flebat fortiter
tantorum diro funere;
solus gaudebat Israel
agni protectus sanguine.

But we are the true Israel:
we rejoice in you, O Lord, even as
we spurn the enemy most evil,
and are guarded
by the blood of Christ.

Nos verus Israel sumus:
laetamur in te, Domine,
hostem spernentes et malum,
Christi defensi sanguine.

Lord most excellent, make us
worthy of the glory
of the kingdom to come.
Thus may we be made fit
to sing praises to you
with songs unceasing.
Amen.

Dignos nos fac, rex optime,
futuri regni gloria,
ut mereamur laudibus
aeternis te concinere.
Amen.

SUNDAY, PSALTER II AND IV
OFFICE OF READINGS, during the Day
Salve Dies, Dierum Gloria / Hail to You, Wondrous Day!

Salve dies, dierum gloria,
dies felix Christi victoria,
dies digna iugi laetitia,
    dies prima.

Lux divina caecis irradiat,
in qua Christus infernum spoliat,
mortem vincit et reconciliat
    summis ima.

Sempiterni regis sententia
sub peccato inclusit omnia;
ut infirmis superna gratia
    subveniret,

Dei virtus et sapientia
temperavit iram clementia,
cum iam mundus in praecipita
    totus iret.

Resurrexit liber ab inferis
restaurator humani generis,
ovem suam reportans umeris
    ad superna.

Angelorum pax fit et hominum,
plenitudo succrescit ordinum,
triumphantem laus decet
    Dominum,
    laus aeterna.

Harmoniae caelestis patriae
vox concordet matris Ecclesiae,
"Alleluia" frequentet hodie
    plebs fidelis.

Triumphato mortis imperio,
triumphali fruamur gaudio;
in terra pax, et iubilatio
    sit in caelis.
    Amen.

Hail to you, wondrous day!
The boast of all days,
day exultant in Christ's victory,
day worthy of lasting joy:
first day, week-start day.

On you, this day, divine light
shatters blindness of heart:
divine light in which
Christ robs hell of its spoils,
snatches victory
from the hands of death,
reunites created with supreme.

Stern decree of deathless Sovereign
imprisoned all under thrall of sin.
But so that heaven's grace
might rescue the sore-afflicted,

God-power, God-wisdom
reined in wrath with mercy fair,
while yet the entire world
was plunging headlong into ruin.

He has risen, freed of death's fetters!
He has risen, the redeemer
of the human race;
he carries back
on triumphant shoulders
his errant sheep,
returning now
to his eternal pasture-home.

[continued]

Salve Dies, Dierum Gloria / Hail to You, Wondrous Day!
[concluded]

Peace is come to angels,
to humankind as well;
righteous order springs forth
in measure full.
Praise is well due the triumphant Lord,
praise never-ending.

With the song of our heavenly home
blends the voice
of Mother Church this day:
"Alleluia!" now repeats with joy
the militant faithful band.

Now the rule of death is conquered well.
So let us enjoy
triumph's holy bliss now nigh;
let there be peace on earth,
let joy be exultant in heaven on high.
Amen.

SUNDAY, PSALTER II AND IV
MORNING PRAYER
Ecce Iam Noctis Tenuatur Umbra / Lo, Night's Shadowy Dark

Ecce iam noctis tenuatur umbra,
lucis aurora rutilans coruscat;
nisibus totis rogitemus omnes
cunctipotentem,

Lo, night's shadowy dark
begins to wane;
light's dawn reddens,
then flashes forth:
with all our strength,
let each of us eagerly beseech
the all-powerful One,

Ut Deus, nostri miseratus,
omnem pellat angorem,
tribuat salutem,
donet et nobis pietate patris
regna polorum.

And ask that our God have pity on us,
drive away from us
every anxious care,
grant us safe health and grant us,
with a Father's loving faithfulness,
the kingdom of the skies as well.

Praestet hoc nobis Deitas beata,
Patris ac Nati, pariterque Sancti
Spiritus, cuius resonat per
omnem
gloria mundum.
Amen.

May the Godhead blessed
grant this to us:
God Father, God Son,
likewise God Holy Spirit,
whose triune praise resounds
throughout the entire world.
Amen.

SUNDAY, PSALTER II AND IV
EVENING PRAYER II
O Lux, Beata Trinitas / Light Eternal, Blessed Trinity

O lux, beata Trinitas
et principalis Unitas,
iam sol recedit igneus:
infunde lumen cordibus.

Light eternal, blessed Trinity
yet paradigm of Unity,
the fiery sun has now sought its rest:
pour now your own light
into our darkling hearts.

Te mane laudum carmine,
te deprecemur vespere;
te nostra supplex gloria
per cuncta laudet saecula.

As at break of day,
so at end of dusky eve,
let us call upon you with song of laud;
may our prostrate praise
render you honor
for ages endless yet to come.

Christum rogamus et Patrem,
Christi Patrisque Spiritum;
unum potens per omnia,
fove precantes, Trinitas.
Amen.

This of Christ we ask, of the Father too,
and of the Spirit of Son and Parent true;
ever one in power, grant favor,
O Triune God, to those who cry to you.
Amen.

MONDAY, PSALTER II AND IV
OFFICE OF READINGS, Nighttime or Early Morning
Ipsum Nunc Nobis Tempus Est / Now Is That Hour Come for Us

Ipsum nunc nobis tempus est
quo voce evangelica
venturus sponsus creditur,
regni caelestis conditor.

Now is that hour come for us
when, in Gospel lore,
he is thought to be nigh:
the bridegroom,
the founder of the kingdom on high.

Occurrunt sanctae virgines
obviam tunc adventui,
gestantes claras lampades,
magno laetantes gaudio.

At this very hour rush the holy virgins
to meet his spousal coming,
carrying their lamps bright with flame,
exultant in boundless joy.

Stultae vero quae remanent
exstinctas habent lampadas,
frustra pulsantes ianuam,
clausa iam regni regia.

But the foolish ones,
who remain behind,
hold lamps that no longer burn;
in vain do they knock upon the door,
for the portal of the kingdom
stands closed and firm.

Nunc vigilemus sobrii
gestantes mentes splendidas,
ut venienti Domino
digni curramus obviam.

And so let us now,
bearing minds aflame,
keep careful watch,
so that we may be fit and swift
to meet the Lord when He shall come.

Dignos nos fac, rex optime,
futuri regni gloria,
ut mereamur laudibus
aeternis te concinere.
Amen.

King most blessed, make us worthy
of that kingdom which shall yet come,
so that we may be privileged
to sing your praises
for ages that shall not end.
Amen.

MONDAY, PSALTER II AND IV
OFFICE OF READINGS, during the Day
Vita Sanctorum, Via, Spes Salusque / Christ, Lord, Life of Your Saints

Vita sanctorum, via, spes
salusque,
Christe, largitor probitatis atque
conditor pacis, tibi voce, sensu
pangimus hymnum:

Christ, Lord, life of your saints,
Way of way, truth, and life,
hope, salvation:
grantor of righteousness
and founder of peace,
with ardent voice and burning heart
do we come to sing our hymn to you.

Cuius est virtus manifesta totum
quod pii possunt, quod habent,
quod ore,
corde vel factis cupiunt, amoris
igne flagrantes.

Clear your task, clear your power:
to tell full well whate'er,
when inflamed with the fire of your love,
your faithful people can do:
make clear too
whate'er they hold as theirs
and whate'er in speech
or heart or deed they fondly seek.

Temporum pacem, fidei tenorem,
languidis curam veniamque lapsis,
omnibus praesta pariter beatae
munera vitae.

Grant peace to our times,
grant steady faith;
grant remedy for the sluggish,
pardon for the fallen.
And to all alike,
grant the gifts of a blessed life.

Aequa laus summum celebret
Parentem
teque, Salvator, pie rex, per aevum:
Spiritus Sancti resonet per
omnem
gloria mundum.
Amen.

Let equal praise proclaim the Father,
and you also, Redeemer faithful king,
for ever:
Let praise for the Holy Spirit too
resound throughout the universe
without end.
Amen.

MONDAY, PSALTER II AND IV
MORNING PRAYER
Lucis Largitor Splendide / Most Brilliant Bestower of Luminous Light

Lucis largitor splendide,
cuius sereno lumine
post lapsa noctis tempora
dies refusus panditur,

Most brilliant bestower
of luminous light,
nighttime has now run its course;
through your tranquil radiance
the day pours forth,
spreads out before us.

Tu verus mundi lucifer,
non is qui parvi sideris
venturae lucis nuntius
angusto fulget lumine,

You are the true light-bearer
of the world,
you, not the one who, messenger
of the light to come
from a small star
that shines forth with crabbed gleam,

Sed toto sole clarior,
lux ipse totus et dies,
interna nostri pectoris
illuminans praecordia.

But rather you, more brilliant
than the sun in all its glory,
you yourself, light essential
and daylight most pure,
you who light up
the inmost depths of our hearts.

Evincat mentis castitas
quae caro cupit arrogans,
sanctumque puri corporis
delubrum servet Spiritus.

May purity of mind overcome
what arrogant flesh demands;
may it guard, as a sacred shrine
of the Spirit blest,
a body undefiled.

Sit, Christe, rex piissime,
tibi Patrique gloria
cum Spiritu Paraclito
in sempiterna saecula.
Amen.

O Christ, King most faithful,
may glory be given you,
given to the Father too,
with the Spirit Advocate
true for ages ever yet to run.
Amen.

MONDAY, PSALTER II AND IV
EVENING PRAYER
Luminis Fons, Lux et Origo Lucis / Font of Brilliance Most High

Luminis fons, lux et origo lucis,
tu pius nostris precibus faveto,
luxque, peccati tenebris fugatis,
nos tua adornet.

Font of brilliance most high,
light, yea, very source of light,
in your gracious kindness
listen with favor to our prayers;
once sin's black darkness
is full routed,
let your own pure light surround
and adorn us.

Ecce transactus labor est diei,
teque nos tuti sumus adnuente;
en tibi grates agimus libentes
tempus in omne.

Lo: now is the work of the day
all done;
under your gracious grant,
we are safe at eventide.
See: readily do we give you thanks
now and for all times to come.

The sun departs, and so brings back
darkness' grim shadows:
but may that true and blazing sun
gleam forth for us
with all its brilliance,
that sun which with its golden beam
graces even the sacred ranks of the
angel hosts.

Solis abscessus tenebras reduxit:
ille sol nobis radiet coruscus
luce qui fulva fovet angelorum
agmina sancta.

Whate'er hidden faults this present day
holds concealed,
O Christ most faithful,
Christ most meek,
wipe thou firmly away;
at time of night, may our hearts glow
brilliant with brightness pure and clean.

Quas dies culpas hodierna texit,
Christus deleto pius atque mitis,
pectus et puro rutilet nitore
tempore noctis.

Praise to you, O Father!
Glory also to the Son!
Equal dominion be
to the Sacred Spirit too:
for with supreme and triune power
you rule all through ages yet to come.
Amen.

Laus tibi Patri, decus atque Nato,
Flamini Sancto parilis potestas,
cuncta qui sceptro regitis supremo
omne per aevum.
Amen.

TUESDAY, PSALTER II AND IV
OFFICE OF READINGS, Nighttime or Early Morning
Nocte Surgentes Vigilemus Omnes / E'en Yet in Darkness' Gloom

Nocte surgentes vigilemus omnes,
  semper in psalmis meditemur
    atque
viribus totis Domino canamus
  dulciter hymnos.

E'en yet in darkness' gloom,
  let us rise, one and all;
  let us ever be prayerful
    in psalm chant,
and with all our strength
sing tuneful hymns to the Lord,

Ut, pio regi pariter canentes,
cum suis sanctis mereamur aulam
ingredi caeli, simul et beatam
  ducere vitam.

So that, as to our faithful king
  we sing our hymns apace,
  we may be found worthy
  to accompany his saints
into the courtyard of heaven,
and live therein a life ever blessed.

Praestet hoc nobis Deitas beata
Patris ac Nati, pariterque Sancti
Spiritus, cuius resonet per omnem
  gloria mundum.
    Amen.

May the gracious Godhead, Father,
Son, and Holy Spirit likewise,
  grant this to us:
  may the Trinity's glory
    resound
throughout the entire world.
    Amen.

TUESDAY, PSALTER II AND IV
OFFICE OF READINGS, during the Day
Ad Preces Nostras Deitatis Aures / To Our Humble Prayers

Ad preces nostras deitatis aures,
Deus, inclina pietate sola;
supplicum vota suscipe, precamur
famuli tui.

To our humble prayers, O God,
given just your faithful love alone,
grant godhead's gracious ear.
Accept the vows of those
who call upon you,
we, your chosen ones, now pray.

Respice clemens solio de sancto
vultu sereno, lampadas illustra
olei nostri, tenebras depelle
pectore cunctas.

From your heavenly throne look down
with kindly mercy and favorable mien.
Light up the lamps we fill with oil;
put to distant flight all darkness
from our hearts.

Crimina laxa pietate multa,
ablue sordes, vincula disrumpe,
parce peccatis, revela iacentes
dextera tua.

In your loving kindness
loose the many bonds
our sins have forged;
wash away the stains we bear,
shatter the chains that bind us,
forgive our sins, and bring
to your own light those
who by their own doing
lie hidden in darkness drear.

Gloria Deo sit aeterno Patri,
sit tibi semper, Genitoris Nate,
cum quo per saecula Spiritus
aequalis
saecula regnat.
Amen.

Glory be given to God
the eternal Father;
glory be ever given to you,
God the Father's Son,
with whom the Spirit, divine and equal,
reigns for ages ne'er to end.
Amen.

TUESDAY, PSALTER II AND IV
MORNING PRAYER
Aeterne Lucis Conditor / Light's Own Eternal Maker

Aeterne lucis conditor,
lux ipse totus et dies,
noctem nec ullam sentiens
　　natura lucis perpeti,

Iam cedit pallens proximo
diei nox adventui,
obtundens lumen siderum
　　adest et clarus lucifer.

Iam stratis laeti surgimus
grates canentes et tuas,
quod caecam noctem vicerit
revectans rursus sol diem.

Te nunc, ne carnis gaudia
blandis subrepant aestibus,
　　dolis ne cedat saeculi
mens nostra, sancte, quae-
　　　　sumus.

Ira ne rixas provocet,
gulam ne venter incitet,
opum pervertat ne famis,
turpis ne luxus occupet,

Sed firma mente sobrii,
casto manentes corpore
　　totum fideli spiritu
Christo ducamus hunc diem.

Praesta, Pater piissime,
Patrique compar Unice,
　　cum Spiritu Paraclito
regnans per omne saeculum.
　　　　Amen.

Light's own eternal maker,
complete light are you yourself,
　　complete daybright;
nor, given what light unchangeably is,
　　is there any darkness
　　that you undergo.

Now does darkling night give way
to nearby-lurking onrush of day;
　　now is come
the shimmering lightbearer itself,
to dim the very light of the stars.

Now with joy do we rise
　　from slumber deep,
to sing your grateful praises,
for the sun has now overcome
sightless night and brought back,
once more, daytime bright.

You, most holy one, we now beg:
let not carnal pleasure steal upon us
　　with enticing warmth
　　nor let our minds yield
to the wiles the world holds forth.

Let wrath stir up
neither dispute nor strife
nor let unfed maw inflame
gluttony's stinging pangs;
let not paucity of assets turn us
　　astray,
nor shameful excess
engross our minds.

[continued]

Aeterne Lucis Conditor / Light's Own Eternal Maker
[concluded]

Nay: but let us be
firm-minded, temperate;
with chaste bodies let us go forward
and spend this entire day with a spirit
faithful to Christ our Lord.

Grant this, Father most faithful;
grant it, Only-begotten one,
to the Father most alike,
Ruling with the Spirit Advocate
for ages ever yet to come.
Amen.

TUESDAY, PSALTER II AND IV
EVENING PRAYER
Sator Princepsque Temporum / Sower and Reaper of Time's Wise
Divisions

Sator princepsque temporum,
clarum diem laboribus
noctemque qui soporibus
fixo distinguis ordine,

Sower and reaper
of time's wise divisions,
with steadfast rule you mark off
bright-sunshined day with its labors
from shadowy night
and its slumbers due.

Mentem tu castam dirige,
obscura ne silentia
ad dira cordis vulnera
telis patescant invidi.

Guide you the chaste heart,
lest darksome repose begin
to make possible
harsh wound of heart
by dint of stinging arrows
of the envious one.

Vacent ardore pectora,
faces nec ullas perferant,
quae nostro haerentes sensui
mentis vigorem saucient.

Let our hearts be void of sinful fire;
let them bear no stinging firebrand
to cling to perception,
to blur our vision, and so
to wound thought's full clear might.

Praesta, Pater piissime,
Patrique compar Unice,
cum Spiritu Paraclito
regnans per omne saeculum.
Amen.

Grant this, Father most faithful;
grant it, only-begotten One,
to the Father full alike;
ruling with the Spirit Advocate
for ages e'er to come.
Amen.

WEDNESDAY, PSALTER II AND IV
OFFICE OF READINGS, Nighttime or Early Morning
O Sator Rerum, Reparator Aevi / Sower-Father of All Creation

O Sator rerum, reparator aevi,
Christe, rex regum, metuende
censor,
tu preces nostras pariterque
laudes
suscipe clemens.

Sower-Father of all creation,
re-giver of eternity sublime
Christ, King of Kings,
Judge most fearsome,
in your mercy divine receive our prayers,
likewise our praises true.

Lo, during night's dark course
we bring you our votive praises;
grant that they may be deemed
worthy in your sight;
and may you, author of light itself,
comfort us by the endless song
of this, your heavenly throng.

Noctis en cursu tibi vota laudum
pangimus; praesta tibi sint
ut apta,
nosque concentu refove perenni,
luminis auctor.

Da dies nobis probitate faustos
mortis ignaram tribuendo vitam,
semper ut nostros tua sit per
actus
gloria perpes.

Grant us days auspicious in goodness
by bestowing on us a life
that knows no death;
thus, throughout whate'er we do,
may your glory be e'er endless-sung.

Enblaze our hearts; in your faithful love
set our inmost selves on fire
with flame divine.
Make us watchful, that in our hands
we may ever hold lanterns bright
with faithful gleam.

Ure cor nostrum, pius ure lumbos
igne divino vigilesque nos fac,
semper ardentes manibus
lucernas
ut teneamus.

May equal praise give glory
to the Father eternal,
as well as to you, Savior, kindly King,
for ages to come:
let too the praise of the Holy Spirit
resound throughout the length and
breadth of the world.
Amen.

Aequa laus summum celebret
Parentem
teque, Salvator, pie rex, per
aevum:
Spiritus Sancti resonet per
omnem
gloria mundum.
Amen.

WEDNESDAY, PSALTER II AND IV
OFFICE OF READINGS, during the Day
Christe, Lux Vera, Bonitas et Vita / Christ Lord, You Are Light Unfailing

Christe, lux vera, bonitas et vita,
gaudium mundi, pietas immensa,
Qui nos a morte vivido salvasti
sanguine tuo,

Christ Lord, you are light unfailing,
goodness and life;
you are the world's joy,
faithful love beyond measure.
By your own life-giving blood
you have rescued us
from the toils of death.

Insere tuum, petimus, amorem
mentibus nostris, fidei refunde
lumen aeternum, caritatis auge
dilectionem.

Implant your love into our hearts,
we pray;
pour forth faith's unending glow,
increase charity's ardent love.

Procul a nobis perfidus absistat
Satan, a tuis viribus confractus;
Sanctus assistat Spiritus, a tua
sede demissus.

Let treacherous Satan depart
far from us,
his power shattered by your might;
let the Holy Spirit come to our aid,
sent from your heavenly home.

Gloria Deo sit aeterno Patri,
sit tibi semper, Genitoris Nate,
cum quo per cuncta Spiritus
aequalis
saecula regnat.
Amen.

Glory be given to God, Eternal Father;
glory also to you, Only Son
of the Maker of All,
with whom the Spirit, equal in divinity,
rules for ages uncountable.
Amen.

WEDNESDAY, PSALTER II AND IV
MORNING PRAYER
Fulgentis Auctor Aetheris / Maker of the Flashing Skies Above

Fulgentis auctor aetheris,
qui lunam lumen noctibus,
solem dierum cursibus
certo fundasti tramite,

Nox atra iam depellitur,
mundi nitor renascitur,
novusque iam mentis vigor
dulces in actus erigit.

Laudes sonare iam tuas
dies relatus admonet,
vultusque caeli blandior
nostra serena pectora.

Vitemus omne lubricum,
declinet prava spiritus,
vitam facta non inquinent,
linguam culpa non implicet;

Sed, sol diem dum conficit,
fides profunda ferveat,
spes ad promissa provocet,
Christo coniungat caritas.

Praesta, Pater piissime,
Patrique compar Unice,
cum Spiritu Paraclito
regnans per omne saeculum.
Amen.

Maker of the flashing skies above,
in manner most certain
have you appointed
the moon as light for nighttime,
and the sun is given
a certain path to follow,
as it courses through the days.

Now is dusky night put to flight,
now is earth's splendor full renewed;
a new energy of spirit
lifts us up to doing wondrous deeds.

Daylight, now brought back to us,
warns us to pour forth your praise;
heaven's own alluring face
renders our hearts
both calm and serene.

So let us shun every deceit,
let our spirit turn away from any evil.
Let our deeds bring no stain to our life;
let no guilt entangle whate'er we say.

No: but when the sun uses up the day,
let faith profound burn deep and bright.
Let hope call us forth
to what you have promised;
let charity yoke us firmly
to Christ the Lord.

Grant this, Father most faithful;
grant it, Only-begotten One,
to the Father entirely equal,
ruling with the Spirit Paraclete
for ages and ages e'ermore to run.
Amen.

WEDNESDAY, PSALTER II AND IV
EVENING PRAYER
Sol, Ecce, Lentus Occidens / Lo, Lingering Sun in Its Departure

Sol, ecce, lentus occidens
montes et arva et aequora
maestus relinquit, innovat
sed lucis omen crastinae,

Lo, lingering sun in its departure
sadly leaves behind
mountains and fields and oceans.
No matter; it renews the assurance of
tomorrow's clear light.

Mirantibus mortalibus
sic te, Creator provide,
leges vicesque temporum
umbris dedisse et lumini.

We humans gaze on in wonder:
most prudent Creator, you have thus
given rules and assignments of time
to both shadow and light.

Ac dum, tenebris aethera
silentio prementibus,
vigor laborum deficit,
quies cupita quaeritur.

And so while, as darkness surrounds
the heavens with silence,
Work's stern labor wanes, and
the rest the workers crave
is now being sought.

Spe nos fideque divites
tui beamur lumine
Verbi, quod est a saeculis
splendor paternae gloriae.

Enriched and blessed are we by hope
and faith in the light of your Word,
which, from ages of yore
is the brilliance of the Father's glory.

Est ille sol qui nesciat
ortum vel unquam vesperum;
quo terra gestit contegi,
quo caeli in aevum iubilant.

He is that Sun who knows no rising
nor e'er a setting;
by him the earth strives
to be protected, be preserved,
by him the heavens rejoice
for ages to come.

Hac nos serena perpetim
da luce tandem perfrui,
cum Nato et almo Spiritu
tibi novantes cantica.
Amen.

At long last grant, Father most holy,
that we may ever enjoy peaceful light;
with the Son and the faithful Spirit
do we ever sing renewed praises
to you.
Amen.

THURSDAY, PSALTER II AND IV
OFFICE OF READINGS, Nighttime or Early Morning
Ales Diei Nuntius / The Crow of the Cock

Ales diei nuntius
lucem propinquam praecinit;
nos excitator mentium
iam Christus ad vitam vocat.

The crow of the cock,
messenger of daystart's gleam,
gives omen that light is near.
Now does Christ the Lord,
arouser true of minds and hearts,
summon us to wakefulness,
summon us to life.

"Auferte,"— clamat— "lectulos
aegros, sopores, desides;
castique, rec*ti* ac sobrii
*vigi*late; iam sum proximus."

His hail: "Away with slumber that
sickens, that stultifies, that slothifies!
Keep ye watch, rather; be ye pure,
righteous, and clear-minded:
for I am now nigh!"

Ut, cum coruscis flatibus
aurora caelum sparserit,
omnes labore exercitos
confirmet ad spem luminis,

And so, when dawn shall bedew
the heavens with its flaming breath,
may it strengthen all who in labor toil
with the hope bright of light unending.

Iesum ciamus vocibus
flentes, precantes, sobrii;
intenta supplicatio
dormire cor mundum vetat.

Let us then call upon Jesus
with our cries, sorrowful, prayerful,
clear of mind; for attentive prayer
forbids a purified heart
to stumble into dreamy slumber-rest.

Tu, Christe, somnum disice,
tu rumpe noctis vincula,
tu solve peccatum vetus
novumque lumen ingere.

Christ Lord, to you we pray:
drive sleep far away;
to you we pray, shatter the chains
that night has woven;
to you we pray, unbind us from
the ancient sin, and pour forth
your new light into our darkened hearts.

Sit, Christe, rex piissime,
tibi Patrique gloria
cum Spiritu Paraclito,
in sempiterna saecula.
Amen.

Christ, King most faithful,
may glory be given to you,
and to the Father as well,
in union with the Spirit Advocate
for ages uncountable yet to come.
Amen.

THURSDAY, PSALTER II AND IV
OFFICE OF READINGS, during the Day
Amoris Sensus Erige / Granter of Pardon Sublime

Amoris sensus erige
ad te, largitor veniae,
ut fias clemens cordibus
purgatis inde sordibus.

Granter of pardon sublime,
direct our feelings of love to you,
so that you may show mercy
to hearts
that are cleansed thereby from sin.

As aliens do we come here,
as exiles do we sigh
and sound our plea;
you are safe harbor,
you are fatherland beloved:
lead us to the mansions
of life eternal.

Externi huc advenimus
et exsules ingemimus;
tu portus es et patria.
Ad vitae duc nos atria.

Felix quae sitit caritas
te fontem vitae, o Veritas;
beati valde oculi
te speculantis populi.

Happy that love which thirsts for you,
O fountain of life, O truth supernal;
happy beyond imagining the eyes
of those who in fact
do gaze upon you.

To be mindful of your praise
is itself great glory given you,
a glory
in which those rejoice without end
who raise their hearts
from the depths below.

Grandis est tibi gloria
tuae laudis memoria,
quam sine fine celebrant
qui cor ab imis elevant.

Grant this, Father most faithful;
grant it, Only-born one,
equal to the Father,
ruling for endless ages
with the Spirit Advocate.
Amen.

Praesta, Pater piissime,
Patrique compar Unice,
cum Spiritu Paraclito
regnans per omne saeculum.
Amen.

THURSDAY, PSALTER II AND IV
MORNING PRAYER
Iam Lucis Orto Sidere / The Light Star Has Now Risen in the Sky

Iam lucis orto sidere Deum precemur supplices, ut in diurnis actibus nos servet a nocentibus.	The light-star has now risen in the sky, and so to God almighty let us come to petition, to pray, to ask that, in whatever we do in the course of the day, He may preserve us from whatever is harmful, is baneful, is danger-filled.
Linguam refrenans temperet, ne litis horror insonet; visum fovendo contegat, ne vanitates hauriat.	May he restrain and guide our tongue, lest dread strife sound forth full shrill; may his gentle care cover and guard our sight, lest it admit into itself the fickle, the foolish, the false.
Sint pura cordis intima, absistat et vecordia; carnis terat superbiam potus cibique parcitas;	Let the depth of our hearts be pure; let folly depart far away. Let temperance in what we eat and drink wear down the o'erweening pride of vaunting flesh.
Ut, cum dies abscesserit noctemque sors reduxerit, mundi per abstinentiam ipsi canamus gloriam.	And so, when day will have finished its span, and due course shall have brought back the hours of night, may we sing glorious praise to him by abstaining from the world's allures.
Deo Patri sit gloria eiusque soli Filio cum Spiritu Paraclito, in sempiterna saecula. Amen.	To God the Father be glory given, and to his only Son as well, as also to the Spirit Advocate for ages fore'er to run. Amen.

THURSDAY, PSALTER II AND IV
EVENING PRAYER
Deus, Qui Claro Lumine / Lord God, with Light Most Brilliant

Deus, qui claro lumine
diem fecisti, Domine,
tuam rogamus gloriam
dum pronus dies volvitur.

Lord God, with light most brilliant
have you fashioned the shining day.
Now, as that day begins
to fail and finish its course,
we ask for your glorious presence.

Iam sol urgente vespero
occasum suum graditur,
mundum concludens tenebris,
suum observans ordinem.

For now the sun,
at stern behest of eventide,
moves toward its rest,
wrapping up the world in shadow,
doing what it is commanded to do.

Tu vero,
excelse Domine,
precantes tuos famulos
diurno lassos opere
ne sinas umbris opprimi,

But you, Lord most exalted,
let not your suppliant children,
wearied with the labor of the day,
be overcome by shadows' gloom,

Nor let the world's daylight
depart from us
while our minds lie darkened;
rather, guarded by your own grace,
may we be bathed in favoring light.

Ut non fuscatis mentibus
dies abscedat saeculi,
sed tua tecti gratia
cernamus lucem prosperam.

Grant this, Father most faithful;
Grant it, Only Son,
to the Father all-equal,
ruling with the Spirit Advocate
for endless ages to come.
Amen.

Praesta, Pater piissime,
Patrique compar Unice,
cum Spiritu Paraclito
regnans per omne saeculum.
Amen.

FRIDAY, PSALTER II AND IV
OFFICE OF READINGS, Nighttime or Early Morning
Galli Cantu Mediante / The Song of the Cock Now Halves in Twain

Galli cantu mediante
noctis iam caliginem
et profundae noctis atram
levante formidinem,
Deus alme, te rogamus
supplicesque poscimus.

The song of the cock
now halves in twain
the inky blackness of the night
and assuages the stark fear
we have of the deep-measured dark:
therefore, God most faithful,
we bring our prayers to you
and suppliantly make our plea.

Vigil, potens, lux venisti
atque custos hominum
dum tenerent simul cuncta
medium silentium,
redderent necnon mortalem
mortui effigiem,

As powerful have you come,
as watchful light,
and as guardian of the human race,
while now too all things as one embrace
night's mid-point silence
and take unto themselves
the pallid likeness of the dead.

Excitares quo nos, Christe,
de somno malitiae,
atque gratis liberares
nocturno de carcere,
redderesque nobis lucem
vitae semper comitem.

Therefore, O Christ, may you arouse us
from the malice deep sleep brings;
freely may you rescue us
from nighttime's prison fell
and bring back for us day's shining light,
the constant companion of our life.

Honor Patri sit ac tibi,
Sancto sit Spiritui,
Deo trino sed et uni,
paci, vitae, lumini,
nomini prae cunctis dulci
divinoque numini.
Amen.

Praise to the Father ever be,
as also, Father's only Son, to thee;
and to the Blessed Spirit as well:
to the God who is three, who yet is one,
who is peace, is life, is light,
whose name is blessed above all others
and who is the godhead divine.
Amen.

FRIDAY, PSALTER II AND IV
OFFICE OF READINGS, during the Day
Adesto, Rerum Conditor / Be Present to Us, Creator of All That Is

Adesto, rerum conditor,
paternae lucis gloria,
cuius amota gratia
nostra pavescunt pectora,

Be present to us, Creator of all that is;
you are the splendor
of the Father's own brilliant light.
If your grace be taken away from us,
our hearts are filled with fear.

But if our hearts be filled
with your sacred Spirit,
and bear within themselves
the very Godhead itself,
then to none of the dreadful deceits
of the ravaging evil one
may they lie open.

Tuoque plena Spiritu,
secum Deum gestantia,
nil rapientis perfidi
diris patescant fraudibus,

And thus, amidst all the worldly deeds
which we must do, things
which the exercise of life
demands be endured,
may we be innocent of any crime,
and live according to the laws
you have set.

Ut inter actus saeculi,
vitae quos usus exigit,
omni carentes crimine
tuis vivamus legibus.

To you, Christ, King most faithful,
may glory be given,
And to your Father as well,
along with the Spirit Advocate,
for ages e'er yet to come.
Amen.

Sit, Christe, rex piissime,
tibi Patrique gloria
cum Spiritu Paraclito,
in sempiterna saecula.
Amen.

FRIDAY, PSALTER II AND IV
MORNING PRAYER
Deus, Qui Caeli Lumen Es / Lord Our God, You Are the Very Brilliance

Deus, qui caeli lumen es
satorque lucis, qui polum
paterno fultum bracchio
praeclara pandis dextera,

Lord our God, you are the very brilliance
that gleams forth in the skies above;
you are the source of light itself.
With a Father's strong arm
do you sustain the heavens;
and with your glorious right hand
you stretch them forth.

Aurora stellas iam tegit
rubrum sustollens gurgitem,
umectis atque flatibus
terram baptizans roribus.

Bright dawn now hides the stars,
flinging its bright red foamy spume
up into the sky;
with cool-damp breezes
it washes over the earth
with dewy touch.

Now does the shadow of night depart,
now does darkness flee
from the heavens on high;

Iam noctis umbra linquitur,
polum caligo deserit,
typusque Christi, lucifer
diem sopitum suscitat.

The morning-star, the image of Christ,
summons to full awakeness
the sleep-sodden day.

God almighty,
the day of all days are you,
and the very light of light itself:

Dies dierum tu, Deus,
lucisque lumen ipse es,
Unum potens per omnia,
potens in unum Trinitas.

powerful in all things
as one in Godhead,
powerful in all things
as Three in One.

And now, O Savior, we bring our prayer
and humbly bend our knee to you,
the Father too

Te nunc, Salvator, quaesumus
tibique genu flectimus
Patrem cum Sancto Spiritu
totis laudantes vocibus.
Amen.

with the Sacred Spirit as well
do we laud
with full-throated cries of praise.
Amen.

FRIDAY, PSALTER II AND IV
EVENING PRAYER
Horis Peractis Undecim / Now Are Eleven Hours Full Spent

Horis peractis undecim
ruit dies in vesperum;
solvamus omnes debitum
mentis libenter canticum.

Now are eleven hours full spent,
and the day rushes forward
to meet evening time:
let us all, with full and ready will,
sing as is our duty
the song that reason demands.

Labor diurnus transiit
quo, Christe, nos conduxeras;
da iam colonis vineae
promissa dona gloriae.

The work of the day has now passed,
that work, O Christ,
for which you have hired us;
grant now to those
who cultivate your vineyard
the promised gift of bless'd bliss.

Mercede quos nunc advocas,
quos ad futurum muneras,
nos in labore adiuva
et post laborem recrea.

For those of us you summon
through boon to be gained,
and whom you reward
with gifts that to future look:
grant us your help in our toils;
grant us calm renewal
after that work is done.

Sit, Christe, rex piissime,
tibi Patrique gloria
cum Spiritu Paraclito,
in sempiterna saecula.
Amen.

O Christ, King most faithful,
may glory be given to you,
and to the Father as well,
as to the Spirit Advocate too,
for ages e'er to come.
Amen.

SATURDAY, PSALTER II AND IV
OFFICE OF READINGS, Nighttime or Early Morning
Lux Aeterna, Lumen Potens / Light Eternal, Brilliance Most Powerful

Lux aeterna, lumen potens,
dies indeficiens,
debellator atrae noctis,
reparator luminis,
destructorque tenebrarum,
illustrator mentium:

Light eternal, brilliance most powerful,
unfailing glow of day,
conqueror of night's inky hue:
renewer of daytime are you,
destroyer of darkness,
enlightener of minds that seek to know:

Quo nascente suscitamur,
quo vocante surgimus;
faciente quo beati,
quo linquente miseri;
quo a morte liberati,
quo sumus perlucidi;

When you rise, we are awakened,
and at your summons we too arise;
when you act among us,
we are blessed,
when you abandon us our joy departs.
By you are we freed from death,
by you made radiant in vibrant life.

Mortis quo victores facti,
noctis atque saeculi;
ergo nobis, rex aeterne,
lucem illam tribue,
quae fuscatur nulla nocte,
solo gaudens lumine.

You make us conquerors of death,
of night, of the world's allure.
And so, King immortal, we beg:
grant us that wondrous light
which no night dims,
which knows none
but brightness ever blessed.

Honor Patri sit ac tibi,
Sancto sit Spiritui,
Deo trino sed et uni,
paci, vitae, lumini,
nomini prae cunctis dulci
divinoque numini.
Amen.

Let greatest praise be given
to the Father, to you,
and to the Spirit blest:
Godhead triune while yet one,
Godhead who are peace,
and life, and light,
Name most precious above all others,
Godhead full divine.
Amen.

SATURDAY, PSALTER II AND IV
OFFICE OF READINGS, during the Day
Deus de Nullo Veniens / Great God the Father

Deus de nullo veniens,
Deus de Deo prodiens,
Deus ab his progrediens,
in nos veni subveniens.

Great God the Father,
from no source derived;
Great God the Son,
the Father God's sole-begotten one,
Great God the Spirit,
from Father and Son alike proceeding:
come to us
with your help from on high.

Tu nostrum desiderium,
tu sis amor et gaudium;
in te nostra cupiditas
et sit in te iucunditas.

May you be all we desire;
may you be what we love
and what makes us glad.
In you may all our wants be centered,
all our happiness find its home.

Pater, cunctorum Domine,
cum Genito de Virgine,
intus et in circuitu
nos rege Sancto Spiritu.

Memento, sancta Trinitas,
quod tua fecit bonitas,
creando prius hominem,
recreando per sanguinem.

O Father, Lord of all that is,
rule over us:
with the One who was born
of the Virgin,
and with the Holy Spirit as well,
rule our inmost being
and all that takes place around us.

Nam quos creavit Unitas,
redemit Christi caritas;
patiendo tunc diligens,
nunc diligat nos eligens.

Be mindful, O Trinity most holy,
of what your own goodness
has wrought,
first in creating the human race,
then in re-creating it
by the blood of the Son.

Triadi sanctae gaudium,
pax, virtus, et imperium,
decus, omnipotentia,
laus, honor, reverentia.
Amen.

[continued]

Deus de Nullo Veniens / Great God the Father
[concluded]

For those whom
the Divine Unity created,
the love of the Christ
has now redeemed:
may he who then suffered in his love
now love us by
choosing us to be his own.

To the sacred Trinity be joy,
peace, strength, and rule;
as also glory, supreme power,
praise, honor, and adoration due.
Amen.

SATURDAY, PSALTER II AND IV
MORNING PRAYER
Diei Luce Reddita / Now That Light Has Come Back to Daylight

Diei luce reddita,
laetis gratisque vocibus
Dei canamus gloriam,
Christi fatentes gratiam.

Now that the light of day
has returned to us,
with happy and grateful song
let us sing God's glory
and proclaim Christ's kindly favor.

Per quem creator omnium
diem noctemque condidit,
aeterna lege sanciens
ut semper succedant sibi.

Through the Christ
the Creator of all that is
established day, established night,
and with ordinance eternal
ordained that forever
each should follow the other in turn.

Tu vera lux fidelium,
quem lex veterna non tenet,
noctis nec ortu succidens,
aeterno fulgens lumine.

True light are you of those
whose faith rests firmly in you;
precepts of the ancient law
bind you not at all.
Nor are you overcome by rise of night,
for you shine forth
with brilliance total and eternal.

Praesta, Pater ingenite,
totum ducamus iugiter
Christo placentes hunc diem
Sancto repleti Spiritu.
Amen.

O Father, from no source arisen,
grant that we may ever spend
this entire day in pleasing Christ
filled as we are with the Holy Spirit.
Amen.

THE FESTIVALS OF ORDINARY TIME

THE SUNDAY AFTER PENTECOST: MOST HOLY TRINITY
EVENING PRAYER I AND II
Immensa et Una, Trinitas / All-Encompassing Are You, O Sacred Trinity

Immensa et una, Trinitas,
cuius potestas omnia
facit regitque tempora
et exstat ante saecula,

All-encompassing are you,
O Sacred Trinity,
yet one are you, not many or all.
Your power brings all things into being;
it rules over all the ages;
it ruled supreme e'en before
those ages began.

Tu sola pleno sufficis
tibi beata gaudio;
tu pura, simplex, provida
caelos et orbem contines.

You alone, three-in-one,
are all that you need
for your own happiness sublime;
you alone, as one-in-three, take care
for the heavens and for the earth,
indeed, contain
the heavens and the earth.

Omnis, Pater, fons gratiae,
Lumen paternae gloriae,
Sancte utriusque Spiritus
interminata caritas,

God Father, you are the source
of all grace that we have;
God Son, you are the Father's own light;
and you, God Spirit
of both Father and Son,
are burning love without any end.

Ex te suprema origine,
Trias benigna, profluit
creata quicquid sustinet,
quicquid decore perficit.

Ultimate, yea primal font were you,
O Trinity most kindly,
from whom poured forth
whatever sustains creation,
whatever with beauty adorns it.

Quos et corona muneras
adoptionis intimae,
nos templa fac nitentia
tibi placere iugiter.

On us you bestow a crown
of fond sonship, of loving adoption.
Make us shining,
bright-glowing temples,
pleasing to you for ever.

O viva lux, nos angelis
da iungi in aula caelica,
ut grati amoris laudibus
te concinamus perpetim.
Amen.

O triune living light,
grant that we may be conjoined to
the angels in high heaven's holy halls.
And thus may we ever sing to you
the praises of a grateful and loving
heart. Amen.

TRINITY SUNDAY: OFFICE OF READINGS
Te Patrem Summum Genitumque Verbum / Our Faith in You, O Father

Te Patrem summum genitumque
Verbum
Flamen et Sanctum Dominum
fatentur
unicum, quotquot paradisi amoenus
hortus adunat.

Our faith in you, O Father most high,
and in you, Word sole-begotten,
and in you, Spirit most holy,
God, only Lord, they firmly profess:
all of those whom
the wondrous garden
of Paradise blest
draws together into one.

In how wondrous a fashion you live,
O faithful Trinity, no one sees;
yet even unto eternity
you sate heaven's denizens
with the vision of your glory,
as with joyous voices they chant
your praises on high.

Quam modis miris, Trias alma, vivas
percipit nemo, tamen usque in
aevum
caelites vultu satias, alacri
voce canentes.

Their song proclaims
that you have established
the massive body
that is the world,
that you rule over the universe
with ne'er failing light,
and that, with the fire
of a love from on high,
you rekindle the hearts
of your faithful.

Te canunt mundi statuissse molem,
Lumine aeterno regere universa,
ignibus celsi refovere Amoris
corda tuorum.

We blend our thoughts with those
of your flock from on high;
now let us join
our hymnsongs with theirs:
we hope that we may be blessed
by your everlasting peace
for ages that do not end.
Amen.

Mente permisti superum catervis,
iam choris illis sociamus hymnos,
qui tua optamus fore sempiterna
pace beati.
Amen.

TRINITY SUNDAY: MORNING PRAYER

Trinitas, Summo Solio Coruscans / O Trinity Blest, Resplendent

Trinitas, summo solio coruscans,
gloriae carmen tibi sit perenne,
quae tenes nostri vehementi
amore
pectoris ima.

O Trinity blest,
resplendent on your throne
in heaven's glorious heights,
let a song of praise that does not end
be chanted unto you,
for you hold firm to our hearts,
at their deepest point,
in strongest love.

Conditor rerum, Pater, alma virtus,
quos tuae vitae facis atque formae
esse consortes, fidei fac usque
dona mereri.

Creator of all, O Father majestic,
faithful are you, kindly and strong.
Make those whom you bring to share
in your life and in your likeness
to be worthy too of the gifts
that faith brings in its train,
trusting and true.

Candor aeterne speculumque
lucis,
Nate, quos dicis sociasque fratres,
palmites viti tibi nos inesse
da viridantes.

Radiance eternal, imager of light itself,
Grant, O God-Son most holy,
that we whom you call,
whom you join close to yourself
as companions true,
may be verdant branches
firmly implanted in the vine that is you.

Caritas, ignis, pietas, potenti
lumine ac blando moderans
creata,
Spiritus, mentem renova, foveto
intima cordis.

Charity are you, fire, fidelity too,
guardian as well of all creation
with your powerful yet beguiling light,
O Holy Spirit: renew our spirits;
foster fully what you have graven
deep in the hearts that are ours.

Hospes o dulcis, Trias obsecranda,
nos tibi iugi fac amore nexos,
perpetes donec modulemur
hymnos
teque fruamur.
Amen.

O Guest so wondrous to entertain,
O blessed Trinity, so willingly implored:
join us to you
in firmest bond of faithful love,
until the day comes
when we can sing to you
our unending songs,
and be blessed and blissed
in your company forever. Amen.

THURSDAY (or Sunday, in some places) AFTER TRINITY SUNDAY
THE MOST PRECIOUS BODY AND BLOOD OF CHRIST
EVENING PRAYER I AND II
Pange, Lingua, Gloriosi Corporis / Sing, O Tongue of Mine!

Pange, lingua, gloriosi
corporis mysterium,
sanguinisque pretiosi,
quem in mundi pretium
fructus ventris generosi
Rex effudit gentium.

Sing, o tongue of mine!
Tell of the mystery
of that glorious body,
of that priceless blood,
which the King of Heaven,
offspring of a womb most excellent,
a womb most noble, has poured forth:
ransom it is for our entire world.

Nobis datus, nobis natus
ex intacta Virgine,
et in mundo conversatus,
sparso verbi semine,
sui moras incolatus
miro clausit ordine.

Bestowed upon us,
born unto us of a Virgin most pure,
he dwelt with us
in this world and then,
once the seeds of his message
had been full sown,
finished the days of his stay among us
in fashion most wonderful to behold.

In supremae nocte cenae
recumbens cum fratribus,
observata lege plene
cibis in legalibus,
cibum turbae duodenae
se dat suis manibus.

For on the night when he ate
his final meal in the world,
at table with his companions,
he did all the law had prescribed
as to food, and then,
with his own hands,
gave his very self as food
to the group of twelve
he had gathered around him.
[continued]

Verbum caro panem verum
verbo carnem efficit,
fitque sanguis Christi merum,
et, si sensus deficit,
ad firmandum cor sincerum
sola fides sufficit.
[continued]

Pange, Lingua, Gloriosi Corporis / Sing, O Tongue of Mine!
[concluded]

Tantum ergo sacramentum
veneremur cernui,
et antiquum documentum
novi cedat ritui;
praestet fides supplementum
sensuum defectui.

By the word that he did utter,
the Word that had been made flesh
makes bread become in truth
his very own flesh;
rich and undiluted the wine
that becomes the blood of Christ
and, should human senses
fail to perceive it,
faith is enough to confirm
the loyal heart's belief.

Genitori Genitoque
laus et iubilatio,
salus, honor, virtus quoque
sit et benedictio;
procedenti ab utroque
compar sit laudatio.
Amen.

Such an unspeakable holy sign:
let us adore it, bowed down low;
let what was a rite prescribed of old
now give way to a rite prescribed anew;
and let faith grant help
for when the senses fail.

To the Father, to the Son,
be praise and happiness full;
to them be well-being, honor, and power
as well, and blessing too:
and to the one who proceeds
from both Father and Son
be equal glory ever given.
Amen.

THE BODY AND BLOOD OF CHRIST
OFFICE OF READINGS
Sacris Sollemniis Iuncta Sint Gaudia / Let Joy Be Paired

Sacris sollemniis
iuncta sint gaudia,
et ex praecordiis
sonent praeconia;
recedant vetera, nova sint omnia,
corda, voces, et opera.

Noctis recolitur cena novissima,
qua Christus creditur
agnum et azyma dedisse
fratribus iuxta legitima
priscis indulta patribus.

Dedit fragilibus corporis ferculum,
dedit et tristibus
sanguinis poculum,
dicens: "Accipite
quod trado vasculum;
omnes ex eo bibite."

Sic sacrificium istud instituit,
cuius officium committi voluit
solis presbyteris,
quibus sic congruit,
ut sumant et dent ceteris.

Panis angelicus
fit panis hominum;
dat panis caelicus
figuris terminum.
O res mirabilis:
manducat Dominum
servus pauper et humilis.

Te, trina Deitas
unaque, poscimus;
sic nos tu visitas sicut te colimus:
per tuas semitas
duc nos quo tendimus
ad lucem quam inhabitas.
Amen.

Let joy be paired to these sacred rites;
and, from the depths of their hearts,
let the people sing
their hymns of praise.
Let things from of old
pass from the scene;
let all things—
hearts and voices and deeds—
now be made new.

To mind there comes
that night's final supper,
where faith tells us
that Christ the Lord
gave his companions
both paschal lamb
and bread unleavened,
following the rites handed down
by the ancients of old.

But then to weak men he gave
the dish that held his own body;
to sorrowing men he gave
the cup of his blood,
saying as he did,
"Accept this cup
that I give you;
from it drink you, one and all."

And so he began that sacrifice,
whose continuation he willed should
be entrusted to priests alone.
Thus it is fitting
that they first receive it,
and then give it to others.

[continued]

Sacris Sollemniis Iuncta Sint Gaudia / Let Joy Be Paired
[concluded]

The bread of angels becomes
the bread of humankind;
heavenly bread brings an end
to the symbols of old.
Unheard of, marvelous event!
A slave, poor and lowly,
consumes his own Master!

You, Godhead triune, yet Godhead one,
do we implore:
in the way that we worship you,
so be present unto us.
By your holy paths lead us
to the goal that we seek:
to the light
where you dwell forever.
Amen.

THE BODY AND BLOOD OF CHRIST
MORNING PRAYER
Verbum Supernum Prodiens nec Patris / The Word Comes Forth

Verbum supernum prodiens
nec Patris linquens dexteram,
ad opus suum exiens
venit ad vitae vesperam.

The Word comes forth
from heaven on high,
yet ne'er leaves
the Almighty Father's right hand:
as he went forth to fulfill
the task that is his,
he arrived at the evening of his life.

In mortem a discipulo
suis tradendus aemulis,
prius in vitae ferculo
se tradidit discipulis.

He is about to be handed over
to his enemies,
and that by a disciple-friend;
he is about to be handed over to die.
But first he handed himself over
to his disciples and to his friends
in the food of eternal life.

Quibus sub bina specie
carnem dedit et sanguinem,
ut duplicis substantiae
totum cibaret hominem.

His flesh and his blood he gave them,
and that in double guise,
so that he might tend
to all their human needs,
needs the body shows
needs for which the spirit cries.

Se nascens dedit socium,
convescens in edulium,
se moriens in pretium,
se regnans dat in praemium.

O salutaris hostia,
quae caeli pandis ostium,
bella premunt hostilia:
da robur; fer auxilium.

At his birth,
he gave himself as comrade;
at his table,
he gave himself as food;
at his death,
he gave himself as ransom-price;
in his rule as king,
he gives himself as reward supreme.

Uni trinoque Domino
sit sempiterna gloria,
qui vitam sine termino
nobis donet in patria.
Amen.

[continued]

Verbum Supernum Prodiens Nec Patris / The Word Comes Forth
[concluded]

O saving victim, you fling open wide
the gate of heaven.
Wars oppress us;
enemies besiege us:
give us strength,
grant us aid.

To the God who is one and three
be glory everlasting given;
may our triune God grant us
life with no end
in our blessed fatherland on high.
Amen.

FRIDAY AFTER THE SECOND SUNDAY AFTER PENTECOST
MOST SACRED HEART OF JESUS
EVENING PRAYER I AND II
Auctor Beati Saeculi / Blest Creator of the Ages' Long Span

Auctor beate saeculi,
Christe, Redemptor omnium,
lumen Patris de lumine
Deusque verus de Deo:

Blest Creator of the ages' long span,
Christ, holy Redeemer of all,
Light of the Father,
coming forth from the Father,
true God from true God,

Amor coegit te tuus
mortale corpus sumere,
ut, novus Adam, redderes
quod vetus ille abstulerat:

Your love it was that made you
take to yourself a human frame:
as new Adam, you might thus restore
what Adam of old
had sinfully stolen away.

Ille amor, almus artifex
terrae marisque et siderum,
errata patrum miserans
et nostra rumpens vincula.

That same love it was,
a love that was kindly Maker
of earth, of oceans, of stars,
that took pity
on the mistakes our elders had made,
that broke the bonds
our own sins had forged.

Non corde discedat tuo
vis illa amoris incliti:
hoc fonte gentes hauriant
remissionis gratiam.

Ad hoc acerbam lanceam
passumque ad hoc est vulnera,
ut nos lavaret sordibus
unda fluente et sanguine.

May the strong power
of your wondrous love
ne'er depart from your sacred heart:
nay, rather, let it be that
from that sacred font
all peoples may drink deep
of the flavor, of the favor
of forgiveness full.

Iesu, tibi sit gloria,
qui cordis fundis gratiam,
cum Patre et almo Spiritu
in sempiterna saecula.
Amen.

[continued]

Auctor Beati Saeculi / Blest Creator of the Ages' Long Span
[concluded]

For that was why
your heart suffered
that sharp lance,
those dire wounds:
so that it might wash us
clean of sin
by its streaming bath
of blood and water clear.

Jesus, to you be great glory,
as you pour forth
the favors of your heart.
Glory too be to the Father
and the kindly Spirit,
for all ages e'er yet to come.
Amen.

MOST SACRED HEART OF JESUS
OFFICE OF READINGS
Cor, Arca Legem Continens / Heart of Christ, Strong and Safe Shelter

Cor, arca legem continens,
non servitutis veteris,
sed gratiae, sed veniae,
sed et misericordiae;

Heart of Christ,
strong and safe shelter for the law:
not the law of the ancient slavery,
but the law of grace, of pardon,
the law of mercy mild;

Cor, sanctuarium novi
intemeratum foederis,
templum vetusto sanctius
velumque scisso utilius:

Heart of Christ,
inviolable home of the new covenant
temple more holy
than the ancient temple,
veil more useful
than the veil once rent of old:

Te vulneratum caritas
ictu patenti voluit,
amoris invisibilis
ut veneremur vulnera.

God's love did decree
that you be struck by rending blow,
so that we could pay honor
to the visible wounds
of the love we could not see.

Hoc sub amoris symbolo
passus cruenta et mystica,
utrumque sacrificium
Christus sacerdos obtulit.

Quis non amantem redamet?
quis non redemptus diligat
et caritate iugiter
haerere Christo gestiat?

Beneath this symbol
of his great love for us,
Christ the High Priest
suffered cruel wounds, but also
wounds mystical and mysterious,
and so offered for us
his twofold sacrifice:
a sacrifice of body,
but a sacrifice of spirit too.

Iesu, tibi sit gloria,
qui corde fundis gratiam,
cum Patre et almo Spiritu
in sempiterna saecula. Amen.

[continued]

Cor, Arca Legem Continens / Heart of Christ, Strong and Safe Shelter
[concluded]

Who is there who would not return love
to one who loves so much?
Who among the redeemed
would not love him,
yea, would not fore'er strive
in love to cling
to Christ the Redeemer King?

Jesus, to you be great glory,
as you pour forth
the favors of your heart.
Glory too be given the Father
and the kindly Spirit,
for all ages e'er to come.
Amen.

MOST SACRED HEART OF JESUS
MORNING PRAYER
Iesu, Auctor Clementiae / Jesus Lord, Source of Mercy Mild

Iesu, auctor clementiae,
totius spes laetitiae,
dulcoris fons et gratiae,
verae cordis deliciae:

Jesus Lord, source of mercy mild,
our hope for fullest joy,
fountain of sweetest favor,
truest delight of all our hearts:

Iesu, spes paenitentibus,
quam pius es petentibus,
quam bonus te quaerentibus;
sed quid invenientibus?

Jesus, you are the hope
the repentant have.
How faithful you are
to those who seek you,
how good to those who search for you;
what must you be
to those who find you?

Tua, Iesu, dilectio,
grata mentis refectio,
replet sine fastidio,
dans famem desiderio.

O Iesu dilectissime,
spes suspirantis animae,
te quaerunt piae lacrimae,
te clamor mentis intimae.

Your love, Jesus Lord,
is the food fulfilling for our spirits.
It feeds them,
but does not over-sate them,
for it gives them hunger
to desire yet more.

Mane nobiscum, Domine,
mane novum cum lumine,
pulsa noctis caligine
mundum replens dulcedine.

Jesus most beloved,
you are the hope of the longing soul;
its faithful tears pursue you,
its inmost spirit cries after you.

Iesu, summa benignitas,
mira cordis iucunditas,
incomprehensa bonitas,
tua nos stringit caritas.

Iesu, flos Matris virginis,
amor nostrae dulcedinis,
laus tibi sine terminis,
regnum beatitudinis.
Amen.

Lord, remain with us;
you are the new morn
with its bright light.
Once night's deep darkness
is driven into full flight,
fill the world with your sweet delight.
[continued]

Iesu, Auctor Clementiae / Jesus Lord, Source of Mercy Mild
[concluded]

Jesus Lord, you are supreme kindliness,
the heart's wondrous joy;
you are goodness immeasurable;
your love binds us together as one.

Jesus, offspring of Mary the Virgin,
loving cause of our delight,
praise be to you, and kingship in bliss,
for ages without end.
Amen.

34th SUNDAY OF THE YEAR: CHRIST THE KING
EVENING PRAYER I AND II
Te Saeculorum Principem / You, O Christ, We Profess to Be

Te saeculorum principem,
te, Christe, regem gentium,
te mentium, te cordium
unum fatemur arbitrum.

You, O Christ, we profess to be
ruler of all ages, king of all peoples;
you are the judge supreme
of minds and hearts,
you and you alone.

Quem prona adorant agmina
hymnisque laudant caelitum,
te nos ovantes omnium
regem supremum dicimus.

You are the one whom
the prostrate throngs on high adore;
they worship you in song
in high heaven above.
With ovation full and clear
we too name you
king most high
of peoples one and all.

O Christe, princeps pacifer,
mentes rebelles subice,
tuoque amore devios
ovile in unum congrega.

Ad hoc cruenta ab arbore
pendes apertis brachiis,
diraque fossum cuspide
cor igne flagrans exhibes.

O Christ, princely maker of peace,
make rebellious minds
be subject unto you;
by your great love
bring those who have wandered away
back into a single flock once more.

Ad hoc in aris abderis
vini dapisque imagine,
fundens salutem filiis
transverberato pectore.

Iesu, tibi sit gloria,
qui cuncta amore temperas,
cum Patre et almo Spiritu
in sempiterna saecula.
Amen.

This was why
you hang from a bloody tree,
with arms outstretched full wide,
and this is why
you show forth your heart,
full ablaze and wounded
by the soldier's sharp spear.
[continued]

Te Saeculorum Principem / You, O Christ, We Profess To Be
[concluded]

This is why
you conceal yourself on our altars
under species of wine to drink
and bread to eat;
from your pierced heart you pour forth
graced salvation for your children.

Jesus, to you be glory without measure;
you rule all things in boundless love.
Glory too be to the Father given,
and the kindly Spirit as well,
for all ages e'er yet to come.
Amen.

CHRIST THE KING
OFFICE OF READINGS
Iesu, Rex Admirabilis / Jesus You Are the King Most Venerable

Iesu, rex admirabilis,
et triumphator nobilis,
dulcedo ineffabilis,
totus desiderabilis:

Jesus, you are King most venerable;
you are conqueror most renowned.
You are sweetness indescribable;
entirely does one love you.

Rex virtutum, rex gloriae,
rex insignis victoriae,
Iesu, largitor gratiae,
honor caelestis curiae:

King are you of all virtue,
King of all glory,
King of victory shining bright.
Jesus, you grant us the boon of grace;
you are the supreme honor
of your heavenly court.

Te caeli chorus praedicat
et tuas laudes replicat.
Iesus orbem laetificat
et nos Deo pacificat.

The choirs of heaven
proclaim your name,
and chant your praises
again and again.
Jesus gives joy to the world,
and makes peace 'twixt us and God.

Iesus in pace imperat,
quae omnem sensum superat,
hanc semper mens desiderat
et illo frui properat.

Iam prosequamur laudibus
Iesum, hymnis et precibus,
ut nos donet caelestibus
cum ipso frui sedibus.

The commands of Jesus
are given in peace,
a peace that surpasses
all sight and sound;
a peace our mind e'er yearns for,
and hastens to make its own.

Iesu, flos matris virginis,
amor nostrae dulcedinis,
laus tibi sine terminis,
regnum beatitudinis.
Amen.

[continued]

Iesu, Rex Admirabilis / Jesus, You Are the King Most Valuable
[concluded]

Now let us honor Jesus
with our hymns and prayers of praise,
so that he may grant
that, in his blessed company,
we might rejoice
in heaven's bright halls.

Jesus, offspring of Mary the Virgin,
loving cause of our delight,
praise be to you, and kingship in bliss,
for ages without end.
Amen.

CHRIST THE KING
MORNING PRAYER
Aeterna Imago Altissimi / Eternal Image of the Father Most High

Aeterna imago Altissimi,
Lumen, Deus, de Lumine,
tibi, Redemptor, gloria,
honor, potestas regia.

Eternal Image
of the Father most high,
Light from Light, true God indeed:
to you, Redeemer blest,
be glory, honor, and kingly rule.

Tu solus ante saecula
spes atque centrum temporum;
tibi volentes subdimur,
qui iure cunctis imperas.

Before the ages began,
you alone were their hope;
you are the centerpoint of time.
Willingly do we
subject ourselves to you,
for by truest right do you rule over all.

Tu flos pudicae Virginis,
nostrae caput propaginis,
lapis caducus vertice
ac mole terras occupans.

You are the offspring
of a Virgin most chaste,
the regal head of our human race,
the stone falling
from the mountain height
and, with its mass,
claiming all the space of the earth.

Diro tyranno subdita,
damnata stirps mortalium
per te refregit vincula
sibique caelum vindicat.

Doctor, sacerdos, legifer,
praefers notatum sanguine
in veste "Princeps principum
regumque rex altissimus."

Of old under thrall
of the tyrant-chief of hell,
the doomed race of humankind,
by sole means of you,
shattered its bonds
and lays claim for itself
to heaven once more.

Patri, tibi, Paraclito
sit, Christe, perpes gloria,
qui nos redemptos sanguine
ad regna caeli pertrahis.
Amen.

[continued]

Aeterna Imago Altissimi / Eternal Image of the Father Most High
[concluded]

Teacher, priest, solon wise,
you bear before you,
on your garment inscribed,
the caption blood-written,
"Prince of Princes,
and most high King of Kings."

To the Father, to the Spirit blest,
and to you, O Christ,
be glory never-ending,
for you have redeemed us
with your blood
and brought us finally
to the kingdom of heaven.
Amen.

PROPER OF THE SAINTS

Note: throughout Ordinary Time:

for MIDMORNING PRAYER, see *Nunc, Sancte, Nobis, Spiritus* (p. 7) or *Certum Tenentes Ordinem* (p. 15);

for MIDDAY PRAYER, see *Rector Potens, Verax Deus* (p. 8), or *Dicamus Laudes Domino* (p. 16);

for MIDAFTERNOON PRAYER, see *Rerum, Deus, Tenax Vigor* (p. 9), or *Ternis Horarum Terminis* (p. 17).

for NIGHT PRAYER, see *Te Lucis ante Terminum* (p. 4), or *Christe, Qui Splendor* (p. 11).

For the Office of Readings, Morning Prayer, and Evening Prayer: if no specific hymn is assigned for a particular celebration, then see the Commons, pp. 313ff below.

JANUARY 21: ST. AGNES
OFFICE OF READINGS
Igne Divini Radians Amoris / Stunning in the Flashing, Flaming Beams

Igne divini radians amoris
corporis sexum superavit Agnes,
et super carnem potuere carnis
claustra pudicae.

Stunning in the flashing, flaming beams
of her love divine,
Agnes has overcome whatever feminine
frailty her body entailed:
the safeguards adopted by a flesh that
is chaste
have truly been able to conquer
what flesh might elsewise demand.

Spiritum celsae capiunt cohortes
candidum, caeli super astra
tollunt;
iungitur Sponsi thalamis pudica
sponsa beatis.

The heavenly throngs welcome
her blessed spirit;
they raise her on high,
above the very stars of heaven.
The chaste bride is united with her
Beloved in the marriage chamber
of heaven above.

Virgo, nunc nostrae miserere
sortis
et, tuum quisquis celebrat
tropaeum,
impetret sibi veniam reatus
atque salutem.

O virgin blest, take pity now
on our wretched lot;
and let whoever shall celebrate
your triumph
obtain the forgiveness of guilt incurred,
obtain salvation as well.

Redde pacatum populo precanti
principem caeli dominumque
terrae,
donet ut pacem pius et quietae
tempora vitae.

For your people who make fervent plea,
make placated once more
the Lord of heaven,
the very ruler of earth itself:
in his faithful kindness may he bestow
upon us freedom from turmoil,
and a time of calm, tranquil life.

Laudibus mitem celebremus
Agnum,
casta quem sponsum sibi legit
Agnes,
astra qui caeli moderatur atque
cuncta gubernat.
Amen.

Let us celebrate with praiseful song
the gentle Lamb,
whom Agnes, chaste Lady,
has chosen as spouse for herself:
the Lamb who guides
the stars of heaven,
and rules all creation
without limit or end.
Amen.

JANUARY 21: ST. AGNES
MORNING AND EVENING PRAYERS
Agnes Beatae Virginis / This Is the Birthday of Agnes

Agnes beatae virginis
natalis est, quo spiritum
caelo refudit debitum,
pio sacrata sanguine.

This is the birthday of Agnes,
the holy virgin.
This is the day when
she returned her sacred spirit
to heaven, where it belonged:
Agnes, sanctified by the shedding
of her own brave and holy blood.

Matura martyrio fuit
matura nondum nuptiis;
prodire quis nuptum putet,
sic laeta vultu ducitur.

She was, surely, old enough
for martyrdom,
though not yet old enough
for a marriage bond.
But one might well think
that her husband was approaching,
so joyous was her face
as she was led off to death.

Aras nefandi numinis
adolere taedis cogitur;
respondet: "Haud tales faces
sumpsere Christi virgines.

They try to force her to honor the altars
of a false and dreadful deity
with sprigs of pitch and pine;
her answer comes true:
"It is not firebrands such as these
that the virgins of Christ
have grasped in their hands.

"Hic ignis exstinguit fidem,
haec flamma lumen eripit;
hic, hic ferite, ut profluo
cruore restringuam focos."

"A fire like this snuffs out faith;
a flame of this sort takes away light.
Smite me here, here in this place,
so that I might rein in this fire-hearth,
might contain it
with this outflow of my blood."
[continued]

Percussa quam pompam tulit!
Nunc veste se totam tegens,
terram genu flexo petit
lapsu verecundo cadens.

Iesu, tibi sit gloria,
qui natus es de Virgine,
cum Patre et almo Spiritu
in sempiterna saecula.
Amen.

Agnes Beatae Virginis / This Is the Birthday of Agnes
[concluded]

As she was here stricken,
magnificent the courage she did
display;
but now, covering her whole body
with a garment blest,
she seeks the earth in her fall,
her knees full bent,
most modest of mien.

Jesus, you are born of the Virgin;
to you be glory on high,
with the Father and the kindly Spirit,
for ages without end.
Amen.

JANUARY 25: CONVERSION OF SAINT PAUL
OFFICE OF READINGS
Pressi Malorum Pondere / Burdened Full with Evil's Pond'rous Weight

Pressi malorum pondere
te, Paule, adimus supplices,
qui certa largus desuper
dabis salutis pignora.

Burdened full
with evil's pond'rous weight,
we come to you, St. Paul,
to bring our plea,
for in your generous goodness
you will grant us from on high
the clear and certain promises
of salvation bright.

Nam tu beato concitus
divini amoris impetu,
quos insecutor oderas,
defensor inde amplecteris.

For you yourself were summoned
by the blesseding blow
of God's own burning love;
and those you hated
as their persecutor,
as their protector
you now embrace.

Amoris, eia, pristini
ne sis, precamur, immemor,
et nos supernae languidos
in spem reducas gratiae.

Lo! be not forgetful
of that ancient love you had,
we pray;
lead us, too, in our weakness
back into the firm hope
of heavenly favor,
of heavenly grace.

Te deprecante floreat
ignara damni caritas,
quam nulla turbent iurgia
nec ullus error sauciet.

O grata caelo victima,
te, lux amorque Gentium,
o Paule, clarum vindicem,
nos te patronum poscimus.

At your plea, let charity blaze forth,
that charity
that knows not how to wreak harm,
which no quarrel dast disturb,
which no error make bold
to wound or hurt.

Laus, Trinitati, cantica
sint sempiternae gloriae,
quae nos boni certaminis
tecum coronet praemiis.
Amen.

[continued]

Pressi Malorum Pondere / Burdened Full with Evil's Pond'rous Weight
[concluded]

A victim you were,
pleasing to heaven above.
We beg you, St. Paul,
as the beloved teacher
of gentiles one and all,
as avenger, defender,
protector renowned,
we call upon you: be our patron
strong and true.

Let praise,
let a song of eternal jubilation
be rendered to the Trinity on high;
in your company
may Father, Son, and Spirit
crown us, as they have crowned you,
with the bright rewards of a struggle
e'er faithful to our God one in three.
Amen.

JANUARY 25: CONVERSION OF SAINT PAUL
MORNING PRAYER
Doctor Egregie, Paule / Teacher So Renowned, O Paul

Doctor egregie, Paule,
mores instrue et mente polum
nos transferre satage,
donec perfectum
largiatur plenius,
evacuato quod ex parte gerimus.

Teacher so renowned, O Paul,
guide our words and deeds,
and strive to direct us
in our minds, to heaven above,
until that full enjoyment of heaven
be granted us
and that which we know but in part
shall have passed away.

Sit Trinitati sempiterna gloria,
honor, potestas atque iubilatio,
in unitate, cui manet imperium
ex tunc et modo
per aeterna saecula.
Amen.

To the Trinity, one in three,
be glory without end,
be honor, power, and joy e'erlasting;
for kingly rule remains the Lord's,
now indeed,
but as well for all ages ere yet to come.
Amen.

JANUARY 25: CONVERSION OF SAINT PAUL
EVENING PRAYER
Excelsam Pauli Gloriam / Let All the Members of Christ's Church

Excelsam Pauli gloriam
concelebret Ecclesia,
quem mire sibi apostolum
ex hoste fecit Dominus.

Let all the members
of Christ's Church together rejoice
at the shining glory of Saint Paul;
in manner wondrous did
the Lord Jesus snatch him
from enmity, and make him
an apostle eminent
for his own glorious name.

Quibus succensus aestibus
in Christi nomen saeviit,
exarsit his impensius
amorem Christi praedicans.

Inflamed with burning zeal,
he raged against Christ's name;
on fire yet more with love for Christ
did he Christ's love e'en yet more fervently proclaim.

O magnum Pauli meritum!
Caelum conscendit tertium,
audit verba mysterii
quae nullis audet eloqui.

Such great things did Paul deserve!
To the third heaven he was taken;
he heard mysterious words
he later dared to repeat
to no one at all.

Dum verbi spargit semina,
seges surgit uberrima;
sic caeli replent horreum
bonorum fruges operum.

When he sowed the seed
that was the Word,
a rich crop sprang up;
thus do the fruits of holy works
replenish the granaries
of heaven above.

Micantis more lampadis
perfundit orbem radiis;
fugat errorum tenebras,
ut sola regnet veritas.

Like a lamp flashing brilliant
does he pour out his light
upon the earth;
the darkness of error he puts to flight,
so that nothing but Christ's truth
may now prevail.

Christo sit omnis gloria,
cum Patre et almo Spiritu,
qui dedit vas tam fulgidum
electionis gentibus.
Amen.

To Christ be the whole of glory,
as to the Father and kindly Spirit
as well, the God who granted
to the gentile races
a vessel of choice so shining bright.
Amen.

FEBRUARY 2: PRESENTATION OF THE LORD
EVENING PRAYER I AND II
Quod Chorus Vatum Venerandus Olim / Lo, It Is Now Clear

Quod chorus vatum venerandus
ollim
Spiritu Sancto cecinit repletus,
in Dei factum genetrice constat
esse Maria.

Lo, now it is certain:
what the ancient choir of prophets,
filled with the Holy Spirit, once sang,
has now come to pass
in the mother of God, Mary most holy.

Haec Deum caeli Dominumque
terrae
virgo concepit peperitque virgo,
atque post partum meruit manere
inviolata.

For now has Mary the virgin
conceived in her womb
the God of heaven
and the Lord of earth,
and has borne him,
while yet remaining a virgin pure.
For even after his birth
did she deserve to remain
untouched, inviolate, undefiled.

Quem senex iustus Simeon in
ulnis
in domo sumpsit Domini, gavisus
ob quod optatum proprio videret
lumine Christum.

That very God and Lord
did the holy old man, Simeon,
take into his arms
within the temple of the Lord,
rejoicing to be able to see the Christ,
as he had longed,
with his very own eyes.

Tu libens votis, petimus,
precantum,
regis aeterni genetrix, faveto,
clara quae fundis Geniti benigni
munera lucis.

O mother of the eternal King, we pray:
lend kindly ear to the prayers
of those who cry to you,
for you are the one who pours forth
the radiant favors of your kindly Son.

Christe, qui lumen Patris es
superni,
qui Patris nobis reseras profunda,
nos fac aeternae tibi ferre laudes
lucis in aula.
Amen.

Christ Lord, you are the light
of the eternal Father,
and you make known unto us
his hidden mysteries.
Grant that we may bring you our praises
in the place where shines eternal light.
Amen.

FEBRUARY 2: PRESENTATION OF THE LORD
OFFICE OF READINGS
Legis Sacratae Sanctis Caeremoniis / By the Holy Rites
of the Sacred Law

Legis sacratae sanctis
caeremoniis
subiectus omnis calamo Mosaico
dignatur esse, qui regit perfulgidos
in arce Patris ordines angelicos,
caelumque, terram fundavit ac
maria.

By the holy rites of the sacred law
to the Mosaic rule full subject
does he deign to be,
though he rules supreme
o'er the shining ranks
of the angels in his Father's realm,
though he is maker most high
of heavens, of land, of seas.

His mother blest, in chaste embrace,
carries God, under humankind veil;
with lips pressed close does she place
kisses most tender upon the face
of him who is true God
and yet true man:
for he so bids,
he who is the one whereby
all other things have come to be.

Mater beata carnis sub velamine
Deum ferebat umeris castissimis,
dulcia strictis oscula sub labiis
Deique veri hominisque
impresserat
ori, iubente quo sunt cuncta
condita.

Here truly there is a light
for the gentiles, shining in his eyes;
here is the glory of the stock
born to the Israelic twelve.
Set is he to be the cause
of scandal's stunning stumble,
but the cause too
of the salvation of all people,
till the time comes when the secrets
of men's and women's hearts
are made full plain for all to see.

Hic lumen ardens gentium in
oculis,
gloria plebis Israelis germinis;
positus hic est in ruinam scandali
et in salutem populorum omnium,
donec secreta revelentur cordium.

Glory be given the Father
through ages without measure;
let honor and power
be yours as well, Divine Son.
To the Holy Spirit, too, be power
without end.
To the Trinity be, one in three,
blessed acknowledgement,
glory, and laud for each,
through the endless roll of the ages.
Amen.

Gloria Patri per immensa saecula,
sit tibi, Nate, decus et imperium,
honor, potestas Sanctoque Spiritui;
sit Trinitati salus individua
per infinita saeculorum saecula.
Amen.

FEBRUARY 2: PRESENTATION OF THE LORD
MORNING PRAYER
Adorna, Sion, Thalamum / Make Ready and Regal, O Sion

Adorna, Sion, thalamum
quae praestolaris Dominum;
sponsum et sponsam suscipe
vigil fidei lumine.

Make ready and regal, O Sion,
the wedding chamber,
as now you await the Lord:
be watchful
by means of the light of faith,
and receive
the bridegroom and his bride.

Beate senex, propera,
promissa comple gaudia
et revelandum gentibus
revela lumen omnibus.

Hasten, old man most blessed;
come, bring to fulfillment the joys
that were promised you,
and make known
the light which now is to be revealed
to all races of humankind.

Parentes Christum deferunt,
in templo templum offerunt;
legi parere voluit
qui legi nihil debuit.

His parents bring him hither, the Christ:
in earthly temple,
they offer the temple divine.
He would fain obey the law,
who owes no fealty to that law.

Offer, beata, parvulum,
tuum et Patris unicum;
offer per quem offerimur,
pretium quo redimimur.

Blessed lady, offer now the child
the soleborn of you,
the soleborn of the Father, too.
Offer him through whom
we ourselves are offered,
offer him who is the price
for our redemption to be paid.

Procede, virgo regia,
profer Natum cum hostia;
monet omnes ad gaudium
qui venit salus omnium.

Come then, queenly virgin:
bring in your son,
along with your offering.
He apprises us all of very great joys,
for he comes as the savior of us all.

Iesu, tibi sit gloria,
qui te revelas gentibus,
cum Patre et almo Spiritu
in sempiterna saecula.
Amen.

Jesus, to you be glory,
as you make yourself known
to the tribes of humankind;
glory as well to the Father
and the kindly Spirit
for ages ere yet to run. Amen.

FEBRUARY 22: CHAIR OF SAINT PETER
OFFICE OF READINGS

Iam, Bone Pastor, Petre / And Now, Good and Kindly Shepherd Peter

Iam, bone pastor, Petre,
clemens accipe
vota precantum,
et peccati vincula
resolve, tibi potestate tradita
qua cunctis caelum
verbo claudis, aperis.

And now,
good and kindly shepherd Peter,
receive the prayers of those
who call upon you,
and shatter their sin-forged bonds
by that power
which the Lord gave to you:
the power that lets you open or shut
heaven for everyone
by whichever command
you deign to give.

Sit Trinitati sempiterna gloria,
honor, potestas atque iubilatio,
in unitate, cui manet imperium
ex tunc et modo
per aeterna saecula.
Amen.

Let everlasting glory be given the Trinity,
as also honor, power, and gladness true:
to the Three-in-One, the God for whom
royal rule awaits both now, and, indeed,
through the eternal ages as well.
Amen.

FEBRUARY 22: CHAIR OF SAINT PETER
MORNING PRAYER
Petrus Beatus Catenarum Laqueos / Blessed Be Peter! He Shatters, in Fashion Most Marvelous

Petrus beatus catenarum laqueos
  Christo iubente rupit mirabiliter,
  custos ovilis et doctor Ecclesiae,
  pastorque gregis, conservator
      ovium
  arcet luporum truculentam
      rabiem.

Blessed be Peter! He shatters,
  in fashion most marvelous,
  our chains' thick snares,
  at Christ's behest.
  Guardian of the flock,
  teacher of the Church,
  shepherd of the sheep,
  guardian of the fold:
  he wards off full well
the fierce savagery of the wolves so wild.

Quodcumque vinclis super terram
      strinxerit,
  erit in astris religatum fortiter,
  et quod resolvit in terris arbitrio,
  erit solutum super caeli radium;
  in fine mundi iudex erit saeculi.

Whatever on earth he shall have bound
  with chain so stern,
  that shall in heaven be held tight
  and equally firm;
  whate'er on earth
  he may choose to loose,
  that shall in freedom full be
  e'en over the expanse
  of heaven itself.
  And when this world
  shall draw to its chose,
judge will he be of the years it has had.

Gloria Patri per immensa saecula,
  sit tibi, Nate, decus et imperium,
  honor, potestas Sanctoque
      Spiritui,
  sit Trinitati salus individua
  per infinita saeculorum saecula.
      Amen.

Through the immeasurable ages,
  let glory be given to the Father;
  to you, holy Son,
  let there be praise and kingly rule.
  Let honor and power be given
  the Holy Spirit;
  and in the each of the Trinity,
  three in one,
  through countless ages to come,
let bliss eternal be, now and for eternity.
      Amen.

FEBRUARY 22: CHAIR OF SAINT PETER
EVENING PRAYER
Divina Vox Te Deligit / The Voice of God Chooses You, O Fisherman!

Divina vox te deligit,
piscator, ac pro retibus
remisque qua tu gloria
caeli refulges clavibus!

The voice of God chooses you,
O fisherman!
instead of having grip on nets and oars,
with what splendor do you shine forth
in having in your hands
the very keys of heaven itself!

Tenax amoris proferens
ac dulce testimonium,
omnes amor quos laverat
oves regendas accipis.

Once, twice, thrice,
and most pleasingly to the Lord,
do you profess your steadfast love,
and so receive into your ruling care
all those whom Love himself
has washed full clean:
his own sheep, to be guarded well,
guided well, governed well.

Lapsus, superno robore
tu petra stas Ecclesiae,
qua splendet illa saeculis
nullis subacta viribus.

Once you fell; now,
with heavenly strength you stand firm
as the Church's foundation stone,
whence its light shines forth
to the ages,
unconquerable by gates of hell
or, indeed, all else.

Tu, Petre, Christi oraculo
luces magister omnium,
fratresque firmas, providus
tu verba vitae nuntias.

You, O Peter, by Christ's divine decree,
shine forth as teacher of all;
you confirm those who share your task,
and in watchful care
you proclaim the words of life.

Gregem fac unum, prospera
laetis in aevum fructibus,
salvumque ab hostis impetu
ad lucis adduc pabula.

Make your flock to be one;
foster it with joyous fruitfulness
for ages to come; and lead it,
safe from foul enemy's fell snares,
to blessed pasture
in the fields of eternal light.

Sit summa Christo gloria,
qui nos tuis suffragiis
intrare caeli ianuam
det in superna gaudia.
Amen.

Let highest praise be given
to Christ the Lord!
Through your intercession, O Peter,
may He grant that we may enter
through the gate of heaven
into joy everlasting. Amen.

MARCH 19: SAINT JOSEPH
EVENING PRAYER I AND II
Te, Joseph, Celebrent / Let the Heavenly Throng, O Joseph

Te, Joseph, celebrent agmina caelitum,
te cuncti resonent christiadum
chori,
qui, clarus meritis, iunctus es
inclitae
casto foedere Virgini.

Let the heavenly throng, O Joseph,
shout forth your glorious praises;
let all the choirs of Christfollowers
sing out to you in joy,
for, in merits rich, you are joined,
in chastest bond,
to the Virgin most renowned.

Almo cum tumidam germine
coniugem
admirans, dubio tangeris anxius,
afflatu superi Flaminis angelus
conceptum puerum docet.

Gazing in wonder
at your beloved spouse,
now grown great with blessed child,
you are troubled, you are doubt-beset.
But then the angel tells you
that this child has been begotten
by the breath of the Spirit most high.

Tu natum Dominum stringis,
ad exteras
Aegypti profugum tu sequeris
plagas;
amissum Solymis quaeris
et invenis
miscens gaudia fletibus.

You hold the newborn Lord close to you;
but soon you go with him
as an infant becomes a fugitive,
as you take him to far-off Egypt land.
You seek him and find him
when he is lost in Jerusalem
seeking with tears, finding with joy.

Electos reliquos mors pia
consecrat
palamque emeritos gloria suscipit;
tu vivens, superis par, frueris Deo
mira sorte beatior.

A holy death is needed to make blessed
all else who are joined
to the ranks of the chosen;
only then does glory visibly extend its
hand
to welcome the elect.
But you are blessed
with a more glorious lot:
while yet alive, you enjoy,
like unto the dwellers in heaven above,
the very presence of God.

Nobis, summa Trias, parce
precantibus;
da Ioseph meritis sidera scandere,
ut tandem liceat nos tibi perpetim
gratum promere canticum.
Amen.

Trinity most blessed,
spare us who pray to you.
Through blessed Joseph's prayers
grant that we may scale the stars
to heaven on high,
and so at last be allowed to offer you
a hymn worthy and without end. Amen.

MARCH 19: SAINT JOSEPH
OFFICE OF READINGS
Iste, Quem Laeti Colimus, Fideles / Joseph It Is to Whom We Faithful

Iste, quem laeti colimus, fideles,
cuius excelsos canimus triumphos,
hac die Ioseph meruit perennis
gaudia vitae.

Joseph it is to whom we faithful people,
in our joy, pay honor today;
we proclaim in song his triumphs,
exalted to heaven above.
On this, his festal day,
has he proven himself worthy
of the joys of everlasting life.

O nimis felix, nimis o beatus,
cuius extremam vigiles ad horam
Christus et Virgo simul astiterunt
ore sereno.

Happy is he beyond measure;
blessed beyond anyone's dreams,
for at his last earthly hour
there stood faithful vigil,
with countenance serene,
Christ his son, and Mary likewise,
the Virgin Wife sublime.

Iustus insignis, laqueo solutus
carnis, ad sedes placido sopore
migrat aeternas, rutilisque cingit
tempora sertis.

Just man, outstanding man,
freed now from the bondage
of the flesh,
does he, in happy repose,
press on to the eternal halls of heaven,
his forehead garlanded
in flowers red and gold.

Ergo regnantem flagitemus omnes,
adsit ut nobis, veniamque nostris
obtinens culpis, tribuat supernae
munera pacis.

And so let all of us entreat him,
as he reigns glorious on high,
so that he may be present to help us,
so that he may obtain for us
forgiveness of our sins,
and may grant us the great gift
of heavenly peace.

Sint tibi plausus, tibi sint honores,
trine qui regnas Deus, et coronas
aureas servo tribuis fideli
omne per aevum.
Amen.

Let fervent applause be given you,
every honor too, O God our Lord,
who as one and triune rule,
and who grant crowns of gold to one
who is your faithful servant
for ages without end. Amen

MARCH 19: SAINT JOSEPH
MORNING PRAYER

Caelitum, Ioseph, Decus atque Nostrae / Heaven-sent Splendor Are
You, O Joseph

Caelitum, Ioseph, decus atque
nostrae
certa spes vitae columenque
mundi,
quas tibi laeti canimus, benignus
suscipe laudes.

Heaven-sent splendor are you,
O Joseph, sure hope of our lives,
and sturdy pillar shoring up
this world of ours.
In your kindness, receive the praises
which, in our joy, we sing out unto you.

You, O Son of David,
did the Creator choose
to be the husband of the Virgin;
he willed that you be called
the father of the Word;
he gave you to us
to aid and abet our eternal salvation.

Te, satum David, statuit Creator
Virginis sponsum, voluitque Verbi
te patrem dici, dedit et ministrum
esse salutis.

In joy, you look upon your Redeemer,
lying helpless in a manger;
he is the one
whom the company of prophets
foretold would come.
To you is it given to be first
to adore him, in company with
his Mother, for you are her
companion and her beloved spouse.

Tu Redemptorem stabulo
iacentem,
quem chorus vatum cecinit
futurum,
aspicis gaudens, sociusque matris
primus adoras.

Rex Deus regum, dominator orbis,
cuius ad nutum tremit infernorum
turba, cui pronus famulatur aether,
se tibi subdit.

God himself, the King of Kings,
the Ruler of the universe,
at whose nod hell's fell hordes
tremble in terror,
whom the heavens themselves
fall down and serve:
that very God
makes himself subject to you.

Laus sit excelsae Triadi perennis,
quae, tib*i* insignes tribuens
honores,
det tuis nobis meritis beatae
gaudia vitae.
Amen.

To the Trinity most high
be endless praise;
just as God grants you
honors rare and sublime,
so may he, by your merits and prayers,
grant us the joys of blessed life. Amen.

MARCH 25: ANNUNCIATION
EVENING PRAYER I
Agnoscat Omne Saeculum / Let the Ages, One and All, Know It Well

Agnoscat omne saeculum venisse vitae praemium; post hostis asperi iugum apparuit redemptio.	Let the ages, one and all, know it well: life's full recompense has appeared on earth. Once we endured the yoke of the enemy most foul; but now has our redemption dawned.
Isaias quae praecinit completa sunt in Virgine; annuntiavit Angelus, Sanctus replevit Spiritus.	What Isaiah sang, as prophet of old, has now come to pass in the Virgin blest. The archangel's message she has heard, and the Spirit most holy has come upon her to make her fruitful with child divine.
Maria ventre concepit verbi fidelis semine; quem totus orbis non capit, portant puellae viscera.	Mary has conceived in her womb by the seed of the truth-telling word: now the one whom the universe with all its parts could not contain a young girl's flesh does carry within.
Adam vetus quod polluit, Adam novus hoc abluit; tumens quod ille deicit, humillimus hic erigit.	What Adam the Old besmirched, Adam the New washes clean; what Adam the old in pride cast away, Adam the New, in humility great, summons back and fully restores.
Christo sit omnis gloria, Dei Parentis Filio, quem Virgo felix concipit Sancti sub umbra Spiritus. Amen.	To Christ be every glory, Christ, the Son of the Father on high, whom the blessed Virgin has conceived 'neath the overshadow of the Spirit blest. Amen.

MARCH 25: ANNUNCIATION
OFFICE OF READINGS
Iam Caeca Vis Mortalium / Once Did Blinded Nature of Humankind

Iam caeca vis mortalium
venerans inanes naenias,
vel aera vel saxa algida
vel ligna credebat Deum.

Haec dum sequuntur perfidi,
praedonis in ius venerant
et mancipatam fumido
vitam baratho immiserant.

Stragem sed istam non tulit
Christus cadentum gentium;
impune ne forsan sui
Patris periret fabrica,

Mortale corpus induit
ut, excitato corpore,
mortis catenam frangeret
*homin*emque portaret Patri.

Hic ille natalis dies,
quo te Creator arduus
spirivat et limo indidit,
Sermone carnem glutinans.

O quanta rerum gaudia
alvus pudica continet,
ex qua novellum saeculum
procedit et lux aurea!

Iesu, tibi sit gloria,
qui natus es de Virgine,
cum Patre et almo Spiritu
in sempiterna saecula.
Amen.

Once did blinded nature
of humankind sing
an empty worship-song:
sky had it chosen,
or cold, lifeless stone,
or earthborn wood
to be its god.

Treading such foolish paths,
poor faithless souls,
they had come under the sway
of the betrayer of all, and
had plunged the soul-lives
they had enslaved and sold
into a bottomless, smoke-filled pit.

But such a disaster
for fallen tribes and races
Christ the Lord would not permit,
lest perchance
the heavenly handiwork
of his Father on high should perish
without hindrance or let.

Unto himself he therefore took
a mortal frame,
so that with body risen
and full again alive
he might break the chains
death had forged,
and restore humankind
to the Father once more.

[continued]

Iam Caeca Vis Mortalium / Once Did Blinded Nature of Humankind
[concluded]

This is the day your birth began,
that day when the Creator most high
breathed upon you, O Christ,
and garbed you
with earthly body new-made,
stitching flesh together
by the force of his word.

O how great a joy for creaturekind
does that chaste womb contain!
From it shall come an age renewed,
and a light gleaming with purest gold.

Jesus, born of the Virgin,
to you be all glory,
in company with the Father
and the gentle Spirit
for ages without end.
Amen.

MARCH 25: ANNUNCIATION
MORNING PRAYER
O Lux, Salutis Nuntia / O Day So Bright

O lux, salutis nuntia,
qua Virgini fert Angelus
complenda mox oracula
et cara terris gaudia.

O day so bright,
herald of salvation's coming,
day whereon Gabriel the Angel
brought to the Virgin declaration divine
of what would soon happen,
would soon be fulfilled,
would be a joy most cherished
by the entire wide world.

Qui Patris aeterno sinu
aeterna proles nascitur,
obnoxius fit tempori
matremque in orbe seligit.

The one who was born eternal offspring
on the eternal breast
of the Father most high:
now is he subject to base time,
now has he chosen a mother
in this world here so far below.

Nobis piandis victima
nostros se in artus colligit,
ut innocenti sanguine
scelus nocentum diluat.

A victim now for expiating our crimes,
he takes upon himself
our flesh, our limbs,
that thereby, by innocent blood,
he might cleanse the guilty
from all the sins that are theirs.

Concepta carne Veritas,
umbrata velo Virginis,
puris videnda mentibus,
imple tuo nos lumine.

Et quae modesto pectore
te dicis ancillam Dei,
regina nunc caelestium,
patrona sis fidelium.

Truth sublime,
you are conceived into flesh,
shadowed over
by the Virgin's veiling body,
to be known by stainless minds:
fill us, we pray,
with your revealing light.

Iesu, tibi sit gloria,
qui natus es de Virgine,
cum Patre et almo Spiritu,
in sempiterna saecula.
Amen.

[continued]

O Lux, Salutis Nuntia / O Day So Bright
[concluded]

Virgin blest, with modest mien
you term yourself
the handmaiden of God.
Now are you
the queen of heaven above;
be advocate and intercessor most fair
for all your faithful people.

Jesus, born of the Virgin,
to you be all glory,
in company with the Father
and the gentle Spirit
for ages without end.
Amen.

APRIL 25: SAINT MARK
OFFICE OF READINGS
O Vir Beate, Apostolis / O Blessed Man, Companion of the Apostles

O vir beate, Apostolis
comes laborum dedite
adiutor atque muneris,
laudes precesque suscipe.

O blessed man, dedicated companion
of the Apostles in their labors,
their helper in the works
they were chosen to do:
accept our humble praises,
receive our fervent prayers.

Christi per illos nuntios
exorta sunt laetissima
et veritatis saecula
et pacis atque gaudii.

Through these apostolic messengers
of Christ have there sprung forth
most blessed eras
of truth, of peace, of joy.

By heaven above have you been
chosen to be
partner in a work so important to see.
You shine forth in our sight
as equal sharer in apostolic glory,
prominent wielder of power so great.

Assumptus es tu caelitus
ad tanta consors pondera,
compar nitescis gloria
potentiaque promines.

Tu, seminator luminis,
fac sole Christi vivido
virere ubique germina
caeli replenda ad horrea.

A source of light are you:
make it be
that under the blazing sun of Christ
there may everywhere bud forth
verdant and glorious plants,
to make brimful the storehouses
that heaven so happily has.

In company with the first apostles
you are about to stand
before the Judge: dreadful, supreme.
Grant that our debts may be forgiven;
grant that we may be embraced
by the glorious grasp
of God's merciful grace.

Simulque cum primoribus
summo astiturus Iudici,
da nostra solvi debita,
nos da foveri gratia.

Christo sit omnis gloria
cum Patre et almo Spiritu,
quorum beati lumine
simul fruemur gaudiis.
Amen.

To Christ be every meed of glory,
and to the Father
and kindly Spirit as well.
Made blessed by their heavenly glory,
may we likewise enjoy the joys
they bestow. Amen.

APRIL 25: SAINT MARK
MORNING PRAYER AND EVENING PRAYER
Mentibus Laetis Tua Festa, Marce / Joyful Are our Thoughts

Mentibus laetis tua festa, Marce,
atque pergratis celebramus
omnes,
magna qui Christi tribuisse plebi
te memoramus.

Joyful are our thoughts; grateful too,
O blessed Saint Mark,
as one and all
we celebrate your festal day.
For we recall full well that it was you
who handed on to the Christian people
the record of the marvelous deeds
of Christ.

Matris exemplis, venerans amore
fervido Petrum, sequeris fidelis,
verba de Christi labiis ab ipso
hausta recondis.

With fervor, indeed with love
you admired Saint Peter,
and with full fidelity followed him true;
like Mary, the Mother most holy,
you stored deep in your heart
the words of which Peter had drunk fully
from the lips of the Lord.

Spiritu accensus, modico libello
mira tu summi reseras Magistri
gesta, tu narras quibus et loquelis
instruat orbem.

Inspired by the Holy Spirit,
in a book that was brief and small
you made full known
the marvelous deeds
of the Master sublime, and you tell
with what words as well he instructed
the whole wide world.

Carus et Paulo, studiosus eius
cordis ardores imitans, laboras,
multa pro Iesu pateris, cruorem
fundis amanter.

Beloved were you of Paul, eager
to imitate the fiery zeal of his heart.
You labor, you suffer much for Jesus,
you pour out your blood in love.

Laus, honor Christo, decus atque
virtus
cuius et testes valeamus esse,
ac, tuis escis recreati, in aevum
cernere vultum.
Amen.

Praise and honor be to Christ,
glory and power as well;
may we too be his witnesses true.
Renewed by your heavenly food,
may we gaze upon him, face to face,
for ages without end.
Amen.

APRIL 29: SAINT CATHERINE OF SIENA
OFFICE OF READINGS
Virgo Prudentum Comitata Coetum / A Virgin Blest with a Group of Wise Companions

Virgo prudentum comitata coetum
obviam sponso veniens parata,
noctis horrendae
removet tenebras
lampade pura.

A virgin blest
has joined a group of wise
companions, and
comes prepared to meet her spouse;
with the limpid light
of her blazing torch
she takes away the darkness
of fearful, frightful night.

Ille fulgentem nitidis lapillis
anulum miri tribuit decoris
virgini dicens, "Tibi trado sancti
pignus amoris."

To the virgin the spouse gives
a signet ring of singular beauty,
agleam with polished,
precious stones;
he says, "To you do I give
my pledge of sacred love."

Mota flagrantis stimulo caloris
mentis excessu rapitur frequenti,
fixa dum portat Catharina membris
vulnera Christi.

Struck by the force
of that blazing love,
Catherine is overcome
by oft-repeated rapture of soul,
as now she bears
in her limbs implanted
the sacred but hidden wounds
of Christ the Lord.

Unde ter felix quater et beata
in sinu sponsi requievit almi,
inter illustres animas relata
lux nova caeli.

And so, thrice happy,
four times blessed,
has she come to rest
on the bosom of her beloved Spouse:
a brand new light proclaimed
in the heavens,
midst so many
bright and shining souls.

Sit Deus caeli residens in arce,
trinus et simplex benedictus ille,
qui potens totum stabili gubernat
ordine mundum.
Amen.

Let the God of heaven,
seated on his throne,
the God one in three:
let him be blessed forever,
for to him it belongs
to rule the entire world
with firm, unchanging hand. Amen.

APRIL 29: SAINT CATHERINA OF SIENA
MORNING PRAYER
Te, Catharina, Maximis / And Now, O Blessed Catherine

Te, Catharina, maximis
nunc veneramur laudibus,
cunctae lumen Ecclesiae,
sertis ornata plurimis.

And now, O blessed Catherine,
with greatest praise we honor you:
shining light for the entire holy Church,
saintly soul bedecked
with flower-wreathes
no one has counted,
flower-wreathes no one can count.

Magnis aucta virtutibus
et vita florens inclita,
humili mente ac strenua
per crucis pergis tramitem.

Great have you grown
with virtues sublime;
you bear the fruit of a glorious life.
With a spirit humble and yet nimble
you press forward
on the path of the Cross.

Stella videris populis
salubris pacis nuntia;
mores restauras optimos,
feroces mulces animos.

A heavenly star you seem
to God's holy people,
announcing the good news
of salutary peace.
Good morals, good habits
you bring back to them,
softening hearts
that are grown harsh and fierce.

Sancto compulsa Spiritu,
ignita verba loqueris,
quae lucem sapientiae,
aestus amoris ingerunt.

Inspired by the Holy Spirit,
you speak words that become fire;
they bring to the people
the light of wisdom
and the ardor of love.

Tuis confisos precibus,
virgo dilecta Domino,
nos caritate concitos
fac Sponsi regna quaerere.

O virgin beloved of the Lord,
make us who trust in your prayers
be stirred up by charity's force
and so seek the kingdom
of your heavenly Spouse.

Iesu, tibi sit gloria,
qui natus es de Virgine,
cum Patre et almo Spiritu
in sempiterna saecula.
Amen.

Jesus, you are born of the Virgin blest;
to you be all glory,
in union with the Father
and the gentle Spirit
for all ages ere yet to come. Amen.

MAY 1: SAINT JOSEPH THE WORKER
OFFICE OF READINGS
Te, Pater Ioseph, Opifex Colende / With Delighted Voices, O Joseph

Te, Pater Ioseph, opifex colende,
Nazarae felix latitans in umbra,
vocibus laetis humilique cuncti
corde canamus.

Regiam stirpem tenuemque
victum
mente fers aequa tacitusque
portas,
sacra dum multo manuum labore
pignora nutris.

O faber, sanctum speculum
fabrorum,
quanta das plebi documenta
vitae,
ut labor sudans, ut et officina
sanctificetur.

Qui carent escis, miseros faveto;
tempera effrenos perimasque
lites;
mysticus Christus patriae sub
umbrae
tegmine crescat.

Qui Deus trinus simul unus exstas,
qui pater cunctis opifexque rerum,
fac patrem Ioseph imitemur actu,
morte imitemur.
Amen.

With delighted voices,
O Joseph, father most blest,
and with humble heart
do all of us sing to you.
Workman you are most imitable,
most revered,
and yet content to remain
in the small shadow of Nazareth-town.

With serene spirit do you accept,
and in holy silence bear,
both royal lineage
and humble way of life,
while all the while,
with labor unceasing
of your workman's hands,
you nurture the promised ones,
sacred and sublime.

Carpenter and worker most holy,
blessed model for workers one and all,
what great examples of how to live life
do you give the people, to show
that labor's sweat, that tasks assigned
can find themselves
with holiness blessed!

Look with kindness
on those wretched souls
who lack bare sustenance itself;
temper too human greed,
prevent conflict dire.
May the Body of Christ
in its mystic guise
grow well .neath the shelter
of his father's holy house.
[continued]

Te, Pater Ioseph, Opifex Colende / With Delighted Voices, O Joseph
[concluded]

O God, you are three, and yet are one;
you are father to all,
and creator of everything that is.
Grant that we may imitate father Joseph
in how he lived, and
may imitate him too
in how he completed his life
in holiest death. Amen.

MAY 1: SAINT JOSEPH THE WORKER
MORNING PRAYER
Aurora Solis Nuntia / The Dawn Announces the Coming of the Sun

Aurora solis nuntia,
mundi labores excitans,
fabri sonoram malleo
domum salutat Nazarae.

The dawn announces
the coming of the sun,
and calls to wakefulness clear
the labors and the laborers
of this world of ours.
It salutes the house at Nazareth,
where already there ring forth
the clash and the clang
of workman's faithful tools.

Salve, caput domesticum,
sub quo supremus Artifex,
sudore salso roridus,
exercet artem patriam.

Hail to you, O household head,
'neath whose gentle sway
the Craftsman Supreme,
glowing with salty sweat,
hones his skill
at his father's woodman's-art.

Altis locatus sedibus
celsaeque Sponsae proximus,
adesto nunc clientibus,
quos vexat indigentia.

Now have you claimed
a place on a throne high above,
near to your Spouse most high.
But be present too
to those who call upon you, those
whom stark need so sorely oppresses.

Absintque vis et iurgia,
fraus omnis a mercedibus,
victus cibique copiam
mensurat una parcitas.

Let hostile force, let contention dire
now be put far away;
let whatever or whoever
would workmen deceive
be banished for ever.
Let one, let a single,
let a moderate standard
govern what sort of life,
what sort of food
each of God's children
shall henceforth have.

Sit Trinitati gloria,
quae, te precante, iugiter
in pace nostros omnium
gressus vitamque dirigat.
Amen.

[continued]

Aurora Solis Nuntia / The Dawn Announces the Coming of the Sun
[concluded]

To our triune God be glory given!
May our God, O Joseph, at your request,
ever guide the paths and the lives
of us all into the way of peace.
Amen.

MAY 1: SAINT JOSEPH THE WORKER
EVENING PRAYER
Te, Ioseph, Celebrent / Let the Heavenly Throng, O Joseph
[see page 198]

MAY 3: SAINTS PHILIP AND JAMES
OFFICE OF READINGS
Philippe, Summae Honoris / Blessed Saint Philip

Philippe, summae honoribus
vocationis enitens,
cum cive Petro principe
qua mente Christum diligis!

At ipse amoris intima
tibi rependit pignora,
tibique Patris disserit
suaeque vitae dogmata.

Nec te minus complecitur,
Iacobe, Christi caritas,
qui frater eius diceris
sed et columna Ecclesiae.

Almae Sion qui praesides
primus gregi clarissimo,
nos usque scriptis providis
verbum salutis edoces.

O vos, beati, nobili
Iesum professi sanguine,
spe nos fideque currere
date in supernam patriam,

Ut, quando mansionibus
iam Patris immorabimur,
simul canamus perpetim
in Trinitatis gloriam.
Amen.

Blessed St. Philip, you stand out
eminent among us,
resplendent in the glory
of your calling most holy,
you, and your fellow-townsman Peter,
the leader of the Church.
With what enthusiastic hearts
do you pledge your love to Christ!

Ah, but he gives to you in return
profoundest pledges
of his own perfect love;
he makes known to you
what his Father would have you know,
what his life on earth does truly mean.

Nor in any lesser degree
does the love of Christ
embrace you, holy St. James;
you are termed his brother.
Nay more,
you are a pillar of the Church as well.

You were the first to have charge
of the most blessed flock
of exalted Jerusalem;
forever do you show your care for us
by what your letter says: by it
you bring us the word of salvation.
[continued]

Philippe, Summae Honoribus / Blessed Saint Philip
[concluded]

And so, O Philip, O James,
happy are you,
proclaiming Jesus to be Lord
by noble blood poured freely forth.
Grant to us the grace to run, with haste,
in hope and in faith,
to our home in heaven above,

So that, when it is granted us
to tarry in the houses
of the Father's holy kingdom,
we may as one chant without end
the glory of the Trinity sublime.
Amen.

MAY 14: SAINT MATTHIAS
MORNING PRAYER
Matthia, Sacratissimo / Matthias, Saint Most High

Matthia, sacratissimo
apostolorum coetui
quam miro tu consilio
ascriptus es divinitus!

Matthias, saint most high,
how wondrous was the divine decree,
that came upon you from heaven above,
and enrolled you in the sacred company
of the apostles of the Lord!

Abscesserat discipulus,
tristi miser suspendio
magni gradum fastigii
Christique amorem denigans.

For a disciple had departed,
wretched man, had hanged himself
and ended his own doleful life,
had rejected his place of highest rank,
had spurned the love of Christ the Lord.

En Christi te dilectio
ad eius transfert gloriam,
Petri movente labia
sortesque Sancto Spiritu.

Lo, the love of Christ puts you now
in the glorious place
that Judas once had:
Peter's voice decrees the deed,
and the Holy Spirit guides
the casting of the lots.

Tanto dicatus muneri,
lucem revelas gentibus
ad mortem usque, strenuus
Iesum confessus sanguine.

You gave yourself wholly
to the great task:
you showed the divine light
to the gentiles:
with constancy professing,
by shedding your blood,
e'en to the point of death itself,
Jesus Christ, the King and the Lord.

Da nos, beate apostole,
laetis promptisque cordibus
almus quascumque Spiritus
vias demonstrat, persequi.

Grant, most blessed apostle,
that with joyful and eager hearts
we too may pursue whatever paths
our loving Holy Spirit
may choose to mark out for us.

Sit Trinitati gloria
quae nobis ad caelestia
per te concedat scandere
hymnosque aeternos dicere.
Amen.

Let glory be given the Trinity,
God one in three: through your prayers,
may they allow us to rise to the heights
of heaven and to proclaim
the divine praise in hymns
that shall know no end. Amen.

MAY 31: VISITATION OF THE BLESSED VIRGIN MARY
OFFICE OF READINGS
Veni, Praecelsa Domina / Come, Be with Us O Mary

Veni, praecelsa Domina;
Maria, tu nos visita,
quae iam cognatae domui
tantum portasti gaudii.

Come, be with us,
O Mary, Lady most exalted;
come be with us, just as when
you brought joy unbounded
to the mountain home
of your cousin so dear.

Veni, iuvamen saeculi,
sordes aufer piaculi,
ac visitando populum
poenae tolle periculum.

Come, be with us;
you are the help of the ages.
Take away the stain of our sin, and
by coming to your people, take away
the peril of the punishment we deserve.

Veni, stella, lux marium,
infunde pacis radium;
rege quodcumque devium,
da vitam innocentium.

Come, be with us,
O Star, O Light of the Seas.
Pour forth among us
the radiance of peace;
set straight whate'er has gone astray,
and grant us life as holy people.

Veni, precamur, visites
nobisque vires robores
virtute sacri impetus,
ne fluctuetur animus.

Come, be with us,
we pray; be with us for all time,
and foster our strength
by the power of your own holy ardor,
lest ever our spirits falter, waver, fail.

Veni, virga regalium,
reduc fluctus errantium
ad unitatem fidei,
in qua salvantur caelici.

Come, be with us,
royal branch of heaven above.
Direct back homeward
the path of those who stray,
back to that one faith
where heavendwellers find
their salvation full and true.

Veni, tecumque Filium
laudemus in perpetuum,
cum Patre et Sancto Spiritu
qui nobis dent auxilium.
Amen.

Come, be with us.
Let us praise you and your Son
for all ages to come.
Let us praise too the Father
and the Spirit Blessed;
may they grant us
whatever aid we shall ever need. Amen.

MAY 31: VISITATION OF THE BLESSED VIRGIN MARY
MORNING PRAYER
Veniens, Mater Inclita / As You Come, O Mother Most Renowned

Veniens, mater inclita,
cum Sancti dono Spiritus,
nos ut Ioannem visita
in huius carnis sedibus.

As you come, O mother most renowned,
and bring with you the gift
that the Holy Spirit
has on you bestowed,
be amongst us,
as once you visited the infant John
in his place of human abode.

Procede, portans parvulum,
ut mundus possit credere
et tuae laudis titulum
omnes sciant extollere.

Come forward,
bearing your child most blest,
that the world might come to firm belief,
and that all people might come to know
why they should extol you in such glory.

Saluta nunc Ecclesiam,
ut tuam vocem audiens
exsurgat in laetitia,
adventum Christi sentiens.

Give greeting now to the Church,
so that when it hears your voice
it may rise up in joy, knowing
that the coming of Christ is near.

Maria, levans oculos,
vide credentes populos:
te quaerunt piis mentibus,
his opem feres omnibus.

O Mary, lift up your gaze,
look upon your believing people:
with purified minds they seek you,
and you will bring to them all
whatever aid they need.

O verae spes laetitiae,
nostrae portus miseriae,
nos iunge caeli curiae
ornatos stola gloriae.

You are our hope for joy that is true,
the safe-harbor we seek in our distress.
Join us to the court of heaven above,
when once we are given
that shining garment of glory.

Tecum, Virgo, magnificat
anima nostra Dominum,
qui laude te nobilitat
et hominum et caelitum.
Amen.

Along with you, O virgin,
may our souls glorify the Lord,
who has exalted you
full well and glorious too
by the praise of earth and heaven alike.
Amen.

MAY 31: VISITATION OF THE BLESSED VIRGIN MARY
EVENING PRAYER
Concito Gressu Petis Alta Montis / With Urgent, Eager Step

Concito gressu petis alta montis,
Virgo, quam matrem Deus ipse
fecit,
ut seni matri studiosi amoris
pignora promas.

With urgent, eager step, O Virgin pure,
you seek the mountain lands'
lofty heights. God himself
has made you a mother,
so that you might reveal to a mother
filled with years the promises
of his earnest, careful love.

Cum salutantis capit illa vocem,
abditus gestit puer exsilire,
te parens dicit dominam, salutat
teque beatam.

When that mother hears
the sound of your voice in greeting fair,
the child concealed within her
strives to leap up inside her womb;
his mother greets you
as mother of the Lord,
greets you as blessed soul.

Ipsa praedicis fore te beatam
Spiritu fervens penitus loquente,
ac Deum cantu celebras amoeno
magna operantem.

Your yourself foretell: you will indeed
be blessed; afire are you inside
as the Spirit speaks forth
clear and true,
and with a canticle most magnificent
do you give laud to God
who works such wondrous deeds.

Teque felicem populi per orbem
semper, O mater, recitant ovantes
atque te credunt Domini favorum
esse ministram.

Your people too, O holy mother,
throughout the world, joyfully and
ceaselessly proclaim you happy;
and they firmly trust
that you are the one chosen
to bestow on them
the gracious favor-gifts of the Lord.

Quae, ferens Christum, nova
semper affers
dona, tu nobis fer opes salutis,
qui pie tecum Triadem supernam
magnificamus.
Amen.

You bear the Christ:
and so you never cease
to bring us divine boons ever new.
Bring us, we pray, the riches
of salvation too, as in company
with you we faithfully proclaim
the praises of the Trinity most high.
Amen.

JUNE 11: SAINT BARNABAS
OFFICE OF READINGS
O Vir Beate, Apostolis / O Blessed Man, Dedicated Companion
[See page 206]

MORNING AND EVENING PRAYERS
Barnabae Clarum Colimus Tropaeum / Now Come We All to Celebrate

Barnabae clarum colimus
tropaeum
quo micat celsus merita corona,
multa pro Christi vehementer
usque
passus honore.

Now come we all to celebrate
the great victory-day
of Barnabas the saint;
on it he is raised up on high
and shines forth, brightly shimmering,
with well-deserved crown,
for he suffered much
with all his strength
for the honor of Christ his Lord.

Abdicans agro, generosus urget
ut, fide vivax ope caritatis,
nominis plebes nova christiani
laeta virescat.

Quam libens noscit, petit atque
defert,
maximum Paulum, socio labore
Spiritus nutu peragrans
fidelis
litora multa!

Renouncing the land that was his,
he pressed forth, generous in spirit,
so that, lavished with life in faith
through love's fond labor,
a new race might bear
the Christian name
and grow happy and strong.

Nil sibi parcit cupidusque Christo
plurimos affert, bonus atque
pascit,
donec effuso rutila probatur
sanguine palma.

How gladly did he come to know,
seek out, and bring with him
great Saint Paul, then go with him,
at the urging of the Spirit,
as faithful companion and fellow-worker
through many journeys
and journeys' end.

Da, Deus, tanto famulo rogante,
nos sequi fortes iter ad salutem,
ut domo aeterna tibi concinamus
cantica laudis.
Amen.

[continued]

Barnabae Clarum Colimus Triumphum / Now Come We All to Celebrate
[concluded]

From nothing did he spare himself;
desiring only Christ,
he gained for him many souls.
Good man that he was,
he nourished them, too,
until, by the shedding of his blood,
he won approval that
the stark red palm of victory
should crown his holy work.

Grant, O God, through the prayers
of your many holy people,
that we may bravely follow
the path that leads to salvation, and so,
in the e'erlasting home of heaven,
may sing to you our hymns of praise.
Amen.

JUNE 24: BIRTH OF SAINT JOHN THE BAPTIST
EVENING PRAYER I and II
Ut Queant Laxis Resonare Fibris / So That Your Devoted People

Ut queant laxis resonare fibris
mira gestorum famuli tuorum,
solve polluti labii reatum,
sancte Ioannes.

So that your devoted people,
with voices well-pitched, true-tuned,
may proclaim in song
the wonders of what you have done,
be pleased, O holy Saint John,
to cleanse us
from any stain of sullied lips.

Nuntius caelo veniens supremo,
te patri magnum fore
nasciturum,
nomen et vitae seriem gerendae
ordine promit.

Lo, the messenger came
from highest heaven
to say to your father,
in prophecy well ordered,
that you would be born,
a great offspring, and to foretell
both what your name would be
and what path
your life was fated to follow.

Ille promissi dubius superni
perdidit promptae modulos
loquelae;
sed reformasti genitus
peremptae
organa vocis.

But Zachary doubted
what the heavenly promise foretold,
and so lost the power to speak at will.
When once you were born, however,
you restored
the power of speech he had lost.

Ventris obstruso positus cubili
senseras regem thalamo
manentem;
hinc parens nati meritis uterque
abdita pandit.

Lying in hiding in the bed
of Elizabeth's womb,
you had sensed the presence
of the King, likewise remaining
in his own regal chamber.
And so it was that each parent,
by the merits of a son,
revealed what was to come.

Laudibus cives celebrant
superni
te, Deus simplex pariterque
trine;
supplices ac nos veniam
precamur:
parce redemptis.
Amen.

In praises resounding
do the citizens of heaven
extol your holy name,
O God equally one and equally three;
in humble petition we too beg
for forgiveness:
have pity on those
whom you have chosen to redeem.
Amen.

JUNE 24: BIRTH OF SAINT JOHN THE BAPTIST
OFFICE OF READINGS
Antra Deserti Teneris sub Annis / E'en during the Tender Years

Antra deserti teneris sub annis,
civium turmas fugiens, petisti,
ne levi saltem maculare vitam
    famine posses.

E'en during the tender years of youth,
    you sought the desert's caves,
        shunning the crowds
        of even your own people,
        lest it be possible for you
        to sully your life-course
    by even the smallest desire
        for worldly things.

Praebuit hirtum tegimen camelus
artubus sacris, strophium
    bidentes,
cui latex haustum, sociata pastum
    mella locustis.

From a humped camel,
a rough garment to clothe you;
from animals, a leather belt
to engirdle your sacred frame;
    for your drink, water,
    and for your food, honey,
mixed with locusts, lay ready at hand.

Ceteri tantum cecinere vatum
corde praesago iubar affuturum;
    tu quidem mundi scelus
        auferentem
        indice prolis.

With divining hearts,
    other prophets foretold
only that heavenly splendor
        would appear;
but you, with finger true, pointed
to the very One who would take away
        the sin of the world.

Non fuit vasti spatium per orbis
sanctior quisquam genitus Ioanne,
qui nefas saeculi meruit levantem
    tingere lymphis.

Throughout the length
and breadth of this immense world
there has been no one born more holy
than John, who deserved to baptize
    in Jordan's stream him who was,
        e'en then, taking away
            the world's guilt.

Laudibus cives celebrant superni
te, Deus simplex pariterque trine;
    supplices ac nos veniam
        precamur:
        parce redemptis.
            Amen.

In praises resounding do
    the citizens of heaven extol
your holy name, O God equally one
and equally three; in humble petition
we too beg for forgiveness: have pity
on those whom you have chosen
        to redeem. Amen.

JUNE 24: BIRTH OF SAINT JOHN THE BAPTIST
MORNING PRAYER
O Nimis Felix Meritique Celsi / All Too Blessed Are You

O nimis felix meritique celsi,
nesciens labem nivei pudoris,
praepotens martyr eremique
cultor,
maxime vatum.

All too blessed are you,
and of exceeding high merit,
knowing no stain upon your chastity,
pure as driven snow;
martyr most powerful, lover of solitude,
greatest of prophets.

Nunc potens nostri meritis opimis
pectoris duros lapides repelle,
asperum planans iter, et reflexos
dirige calles,

In your power,
mightified by your rich merits,
drive off, now,
the harsh stoniness of our hearts;
make smooth our rough ways,
make straight
our winding, uneven paths,

Ut pius mundi sator et redemptor,
mentibus pulsa macula politis,
rite dignetur veniens sacratos
ponere gressus.

So that the gracious creator
and redeemer of the world,
when he comes, may be pleased
to direct his holy footsteps
into our cleansed hearts,
once stain has been cast
into full frightened flight.

Laudibus cives celebrant superni
te, Deus simplex pariterque trine;
supplices ac nos veniam
precamur:
parce redemptis.
Amen.

In praises resounding
do the citizens of heaven
extol your holy name.
O God equally one and equally three;
in humble petition we too beg
for forgiveness:
have pity on those
whom you have chosen to redeem.
Amen.

JUNE 29: SAINTS PETER AND PAUL
EVENING PRAYER I
Aurea Luce et Decore Roseo / Golden in Your Glow

Aurea luce et decore roseo,
lux lucis,
omne perfudisti saeculum,
decorans caelos inclito martyrio
hac sacra die,
quae dat reis veniam.

Ianitor caeli, doctor orbis pariter,
iudices saecli,
vera mundi lumina,
per crucem alter,
alter ense triumphans,
vitae senatum
laureati possident.

O Roma felix,
quae tantorum principum
es purpurata pretioso sanguine,
non laude tua,
sed ipsorum meritis
excellis omnem
mundi pulchritudinem.

Olivae binae pietatis unicae,
fide devotos,
spe robustos maxime,
fonte repletos caritatis geminae
post mortem carnis
impetrate vivere.

Sit Trinitati sempiterna gloria,
honor, potestas atque iubilatio,
in unitate, cui manet imperium
ex tunc et modo
per aeterna saecula.
Amen.

Golden in your glow,
rose-hued in your beauty sublime,
Light of very light,
you have made brilliant
all ages without fail.
And now you bedeck
e'en the heavens above
with martyrdom triumphant
on this most holy day,
a day that grants the guilty
the forgiveness they so earnestly seek.

The keeper of heaven's keys,
and likewise the teacher of the world,
each a judge of the human era,
both true lights of this our world:
the one by means
of cruel cross triumphing,
the other by sharp-edged sword,
now are they with glory crowned
and take their place in the ruling band
of heaven most high.

Happy are you, O Rome, city eternal,
to have been washed
with the sacred blood
of such wondrous chieftains!
Not for reasons of what you are or do,
but rather for the merits of these two,
do you surpass whatever other beauty
is elsewhere in this world
to be sought and found.

[continued]

Aurea Luce et Decore Roseo / Golden in Your Glow
[concluded]

Twin woods of precious olive are you,
O Peter, O Paul, united in holiness true.
Obtain for us—dedicated by faith,
strengthened mightily by hope,
filled fully with the charity
possessed by each of you:
beg for us that,
when earthly life comes to its end,
we may yet live on.

To the Trinity be glory without end,
be honor, be power,
be happiness forever
as one and trine;
to God does rule pertain now,
and, yea more, for the past
and for all ages to come. Amen.

JUNE 29: SAINTS PETER AND PAUL
OFFICE OF READINGS
Felix per Omnes Festum / Now There Stands Out

Felix per omnes
festum mundi cardines
apostolorum praepollet alacriter,
Petri beati, Pauli sacratissimi,
quos Christus almo
consecravit sanguine,
ecclesiarum deputavit principes.

Now there stands out,
readily pre-eminent
throughout all the poles of the earth,
this joyous feast of the apostles,
of Peter the blessed,
of Paul the most holy,
whom Christ anointed
with his own redeeming blood
and appointed to be
heads of the churches:
of the people of old,
but of the gentiles too.

Hi sunt olivae duae
coram Domino
et candelabra luce radiantia,
praeclara caeli duo luminaria;
fortia solvunt
peccatorum vincula
portasque caeli
reserant fidelibus.

These are the two olive trees
that stand in the presence of the Lord;
they are the twin candle-stands,
gleaming with glowing flame;
they are the two brilliant, shining lights
of heaven on high.
Theirs to loose the steely bonds of sin,
theirs to fling open heaven's gates
to faithful souls.

Gloria Patri
per immensa saecula,
sit tibi, Nate, decus et imperium,
honor, potestas
Sanctoque Spiritui;
sit Trinitati salus individua
per infinita saeculorum saecula.
Amen.

Let glory be given the Father
throughout the immeasurable ages;
to you, blessed Son,
be splendor and kingly rule;
and to the Sacred Spirit
be honor and all might.
To each person of the Trinity,
may reverent salutation be given
through the endless roll
of all years and eras and eons to come.
Amen.

JUNE 29: SAINTS PETER AND PAUL
MORNING PRAYER
Apostolorum Passio / This Most Sacred Day of Days

Apostolorum passio
diem sacravit saeculi,
Petri triumphum nobilem,
Pauli coronam praeferens.

This most sacred day of days
have the sufferings of the Apostles
full hallowed,
for by them it has claimed as its own
the noble triumph of Peter,
the golden crown of Paul.

Coniunxit aequales viros
cruor triumphalis necis;
Deum secutos praesulem
Christi coronavit fides.

These two men has the blood
of a glorious death joined in equal bond;
the faith that they had in Christ the Lord
is now their crown,
for they followed loyally
their leader-God.

Primus Petrus apostolus;
nec Paulus impar gratia,
electionis vas sacrae
Petri adaequavit fidem.

Verso crucis vestigio
Simon, honorem dans Deo,
suspensus ascendit, dati
non immemor oraculi.

Peter the Apostle was the first;
but Paul was not his unequal
in the grace that he received;
as a vessel of election most sacred
he matched the faith that Peter showed.

Hinc Roma celsum verticem
devotionis extulit,
fundata tali sanguine
et vate tanto nobilis.

The cross's foot became its head,
and Simon, giving great glory to God,
was fastened to it, yea,
ascended upon it,
scarcely unmindful of the doomful omen
that had long since become his own.

Huc ire quis mundum putet,
concurrere plebem poli:
electa gentium caput,
sedes magistri gentium.

Horum, Redemptor, quaesumus,
ut principum consortio
iungas precantes servulos
in sempiterna saecula.
Amen.

And thus has Rome claimed the exalted
high point of faithful service to God,
founded as it is on such sacred blood,
benobled by such an exalted master
and such a teacher sublime.
[continued]

Apostolorum Passio / This Most Sacred of Days
[concluded]

To Rome would one think
that the world would go in haste,
that the tribes of heaven itself
might run:
here the chosen chair
of the head of the nations,
here the chosen seat
of the teacher of the nations.

O Redeemer blest, we pray:
join us, your prayerful servants,
to the company of these great leaders
for all ages to come.
Amen.

JUNE 29: SAINTS PETER AND PAUL
EVENING PRAYER II
O Roma Felix / Happy Are You, O Rome

O Roma felix,
quae tantorum principum
es purpurata pretioso sanguine!
Excellis omnem
mundi pulchritudinem
non laude tua,
sed sanctorum meritis,
quos cruentatis iugulasti gladiis.

Happy are you, O Rome, city eternal,
to have been washed
with the sacred blood
of such wondrous chieftains!
Not for reasons of what you are or do,
but rather for the merits of these saints
do you surpass whatever other beauty
is elsewhere in this world
to be sought and found:
these very saints whom,
with bloodstained sword,
you have so cruelly slain.

Vos ergo modo,
gloriosi martyres,
Petre beate, Paule, mundi lilium,
caelestis aulae
triumphales milites,
precibus almis vestris
nos ab omnibus
munite malis,
ferte super aethera.

And so now, most glorious martyrs,
Peter most blessed,
Paul fair lily of the world,
soldiers both triumphant
in heaven's own realm:
you do we beg that,
with your kindly prayers,
you guard us from all evil,
and bring us too
to those same realms on high.

Let glory be given the Father
throughout the immeasurable ages;
to you, blessed Son,
be splendor and kingly rule;
and to the Sacred Spirit
be honor and all might.
To each person of the Trinity,
be reverent salutation given
through the endless roll
of all years and eras and eons to come.
Amen.

Gloria Patri
per immensa saecula,
sit tibi, Nate, decus et imperium,
honor, potestas
Sanctoque Spiritui;
sit Trinitati salus individua
per infinita saeculorum saecula.
Amen.

JULY 3: SAINT THOMAS THE APOSTLE
MORNING PRAYER

Qui Luce Splendis Ordinis / Blessed Saint Thomas, as a Brilliant Star

Qui luce splendes ordinis
apostolorum maxima,
Thoma, benignus accipe
laudes tibi quas pangimus.

Blessed St. Thomas, as a brilliant star
you blaze forth in the bright glow
of the Apostles' twelve-fold rank;
be pleased, in your kindness,
to receive the praises
which now we pour forth to you.

Te lucidis in sedibus
amore Christus collocat;
amore promptus expetis
tu pro Magistro commori.

In his love Christ places you
in highest heaven above.
It was because of love
that you once sought,
on your Master's behalf,
to go with him, and die with him.

Te torquet et dilectio
narrantibus cum fratribus
vis certus esse, visere,
palpare Iesu vulnera.

Love it was, too, that tortured you,
after you rejoined your companions
and they told you the news; you want
to be certain: to inspect and to see
with your own eyes,
to touch with your hands
the very wounds of Jesus.

Quantoque cordis gaudio
ipsum misertum conspicis
Deumque dicis credulus,
fervore adorans pectoris.

And with what great joy of spirit
did you look upon him
as he took pity on you,
and as, full believer now,
you called him your Lord and your God,
and adored him with unreserved heart.

Nobisque qui non vidimus
per te fides sit acrior,
fit aestus et potentior
quo Christi amorem quaerimus.

And now, through your example, may we,
who have not seen him or touched
his wounds, be granted a faith
that grows ever stronger;
may it become a burning desire,
a yearning ever more powerful,
to seek the love of Christ the Lord.

Christo sit omnis gloria,
qui te rogante praebeat
nobis fide ambulantibus
ipsum videre perpetim.
Amen.

To Christ be all glory! May he,
through your intercession,
as we walk onward on this,
our journey on earth,
grant unto us the grace
to come to his unending vision. Amen.

JULY 11: SAINT BENEDICT
OFFICE OF READINGS AND EVENING PRAYER
Inter Aeternas Superum Coronas / We Venerate All Their Crowns

Inter aeternas superum coronas,
quas sacro partas colimus
triumpho,
emicas celsis meritis coruscus,
O Benedicte!

We venerate all their crowns,
the crowns of the saints in heaven,
for all were earned in sacred triumph.
But among them yours, O Benedict,
stands out, gleaming brightly
with merits supernal.

A holy maturity adorned you
when you were yet young;
pleasure won you over
by none of its allures.

Sancta te compsit puerum
senectus,
nil sibi de te rapuit voluptas,
aruit mundi tibi flos, ad alta
mente levato.

What the world had to offer
was dried up, barren in your sight:
your mind fast intent
on much higher things.

Thus in haste did you flee
from your homeland,
leaving your parents behind,
summoned to be

Hinc fuga lapsus patriam, parentes
deseris, fervens nemorum colonus;
inde conscribis documenta vitae
pulchra beatae.

an eager dweller of forest-land fair.
From there came your writings,
beauteous and stern,
on the soul-spirit's life,
so blessed, so high.

Iam docens omnes populos
subesse
legibus tandem
placitisque Christi,
fac tuis cunctos precibus petamus
caelica semper.

And now, at last, you teach all peoples
to submit themselves to the laws
and the wishes of Christ.
So too make us now,
through your powerful prayers,
ever seek the high,
holy realms of heaven above.

Brilliance eternal be ever to the Father.
and to his begotten Son most high;

Claritas Patri genitaeque Proli,
Flamini Sancto decus atque cultus,
gratia quorum tibi tanta laudis
gloria lucet.
Amen.

to the Spirit who is breathed forth
be glory and worship.
It is by their gracious favor
that such radiant glory
and resounding praise
belongs forever to you. Amen.

JULY 11: SAINT BENEDICT
MORNING PRAYER
Legifer Prudens, Venerande Doctor / Lawgiver Most Wise

Legifer prudens, venerande
doctor,
qui nites celsis meritis per orbem,
denuo comple, Benedicte,
mundum
lumine Christi.

Lawgiver most wise,
teacher much revered,
throughout this wide world
you stand out for your merits sublime.
Fill up once more, O Benedict blessed,
this earth of ours
with Christ's holy, heavenly light.

It was through you that a religious order,
formed of God's holy people,
new to the Church, and united
in a wondrous bond, came to full flower.
Your voice,
through your magnificent rule,
knit all together in harmony most holy.

Floruit per te novus atque miro
gentium nexu sociatus ordo;
iuribus sacris tua vox subegit
dulciter omnes.

By your great rule, you made all
who live under it freedmen of Jesus,
and likewise slavemen of Jesus:
love, fostered by prayer,
abetted by a single work
undertaken for God,
retied their bonds in holy freedom.

Liberos Iesu pariterque servos
regula magna statuisti alumnos,
quos amor fotus precibus revinxit
et labor unus.

And now as brothers may they labor,
with you as their head;
may they strive might and main
with God's people's approval as well.
May they rejoice
in establishing once more,
and now forever,
the gifts of God's blessed peace.

Iamque fraterne, duce te,
laborent,
mutuo certent populi favore,
gaudeant pacis refovere semper
dona beatae.

Brilliance eternal be ever to the Father,
and to his begotten Son most high;
to the Spirit who is breathed forth
be glory and worship.
It is by their gracious favor
that such radiant glory and resounding
praise belongs forever to you. Amen.

Claritas Patri genitaeque Proli,
Flamini Sancto decus atque
cultus,
gratia quorum tibi tanta laudis
gloria lucet.
Amen.

JULY 22: SAINT MARY MAGDALENE
OFFICE OF READINGS AND EVENING PRAYER
Magdalae Sidus, Mulier Beata / Star-Brilliant Magdalene

Magdalae sidus, mulier beata,
te pio cultu veneramur omnes,
quam sibi Christus sociavit arcti
foedere amoris.

Star-brilliant Magdalene,
woman most blessed,
we honor you, one and all,
in devout homage true:
for Christ joined you to himself
in close-knit covenant of love
human and divine.

Cum tibi illius patefit potestas
daemonum vires abigens
tremenda,
tu fide gaudes potiore necti
grata medenti.

When his power became known to you,
that power, so awesome,
that put to flight
even the might of the demons,
in ever-deep'ning faith did you rejoice
to be gratefully united
to your heavenly healer most high.

Haeret hinc urgens tibi caritatis
vis ut insistas pedibus Magistri,
fervidis illum comitata semper
sedula curis.

From this sprang within you
that compelling power of love
that made you cling fast
to the feet of the Teacher,
following him always,
ever diligent in fervent concern.

And you lament your Lord as well:
full on fire,
stricken with fervent love,
you stand faithful by his cross.

Tuque comploras Dominum,
crucique
impetu flagrans pietatis astas;
membra tu terges studiosa et
ungis
danda sepulcro.

His limbs you carefully wipe clean
and anoint once more with oil
when they must be made ready
for the tomb.

And us, whom Christ's love
has brought forth:
make us, too,

Quos amor Christi peperit,
triumphis
nos fac adiungi socios per aevum,
atque Dilecto simul affluenter
pangere laudes.
Amen.

be joined to him in triumph
as his companions forever;
make us as well pour out to our Beloved
in full abundance all manner of praise.
Amen.

JULY 22: SAINT MARY MAGDALENE
MORNING PRAYER
Aurora Surgit Lucida / Up Springs the Dawn, Blazing and Bright

Aurora surgit lucida
Christi triumphos afferens,
cum corpus eius visere,
Maria, vis et ungere.

Up springs the dawn, blazing and bright,
bringing with itself the brilliant triumph
of Christ the Lord.
And this, O Magdalene, just when
you long to see his body,
and perchance to anoint it yet once
more with nard precious and rare.

Anhela curris; angelus
at ecce laetus praedocet
mortis refractis postibus
redisse quem desideras.

Breathless, you come in haste:
but lo, a joy-bearing angel is there
to tell you that the One
for whom you long
has burst the bondage gates of death
and returned, full radiant,
to life once more.

Sed te manet iucundius
intacti amoris praemium,
cum, voce pulsans vilicum,
tuum Magistrum conspicis.

Quae cum dolenti Virgine
haesisti acerbo stipiti,
tu prima vivi ab inferis
es testis atque nuntia.

Ah, but there awaits you
a yet more joyous reward
for your unfailing love
when, after your voice entreats the
garden keeper, your eyes behold
your Master Lord.

O flos venuste Magdalae,
o Christi amore saucia,
tu caritatis ignibus
fac corda nostra ferveant.

Da, Christe, tantae servulae
dilectionem persequi,
et nos ut in caelestibus
tibi canamus gloriam.
Amen.

With the sorrowing Virgin Mother
did you cling to that death-dealing tree.
And now you are to be the first witness,
the first herald to see and to tell
of the Living One, freed from the
netherworld's grim and dusky bonds.
[continued]

Aurora Surgit Lucida / Up Springs the Dawn, Blazing and Bright
[concluded]

O flower of Magdala,
comely and fair,
Magdalene, wounded by love for Christ,
make our hearts, like yours,
burn bright with the raging blazes of
love divine.

Christ Lord, grant
that we may strive to have a love
like that of this servant of yours,
so faithful, so true;
grant too that it may be our joy
to sing to you of your glory
in highest heaven above.
Amen.

JULY 25: SAINT JAMES THE APOSTLE
MORNING PRAYER
Te Nostra Laetis Laudibus / Our Hymns Extol You

Te nostra laetis laudibus
Iacobe, tollunt cantica,
quem Christus arte ex retium
ad tanta vexit culmina.

Ipso vocante, concitus
cum fratre linquis omnia,
ipsius et fis nominis
verbique praeco fervidus.

Testis potentis dexterae
praeclarus alta conspicis,
in monte celsam gloriam,
tristes in horto angustias.

Qui promptus exstas, poscitur
cum passionis poculum,
tu primus ex apostolis
pro Christi amore plecteris.

Iesu fidelis assecla
satorque lucis caelicae,
mentes fide clarescere,
da spe foveri pectora.

Christi sequi da sedulos
praecepta nos in saeculo,
hymnos ut olim gloriae
fundamus illi perpetim.
Amen.

Our hymns extol you,
O blessed St. James,
with the joyful praises they offer;
for you are one
whom Christ the Lord raised
from fisherman's state
to heights so profoundly glory-filled.

At Christ's divine call, you are moved,
in your brother's company,
to abandon everything:
and you become the ardent herald
of Christ's name, of Christ's word.

Renowned witness
of the power of his might,
yours it was to behold divine events:
on the mountain, his exalted glory;
in the garden, his sorrow and pain.

You are the one
who readily stands forth when
the cup with its suffering you seek.
You are the first of the Apostles
to suffer pangs for the love of Christ.

Fruitful follower of Jesus,
reason for heaven's holy light,
enlighten our minds
with the blaze of faith;
grant that our hearts may be consoled
with the holy virtue of hope.

Grant that, as Christ's fond followers,
we may obey those precepts of his
while we are in this life below,
and so may one day pour forth unto him
our hymns of glorious praise
for eras without end. Amen.

JULY 26: SAINTS JOACHIM AND ANNE
OFFICE OF READINGS AND EVENING PRAYER
Dum Tuas Festo, Pater O Colende / As This Assembled Throng

Dum tuas festo, pater o colende,
cantico laudes habet haec corona,
vocis ac mentis, Ioachim, benigne
accipe munus.

As this assembled throng,
O father most renowned,
brings you with festive song
the praises that are your due,
graciously receive, O Joachim,
the tribute
our minds and voices present.

Longa te regum series avorum
Abrahae prolem tulit atque David;
clarior mundi domina coruscas
prole Maria.

Long was the line of ancestor kings
that bore you, offspring of Abraham,
offspring of David.
But you shine forth e'en more brightly
than they because of your offspring,
Mary, the queen sovereign of the world.

Sic tuum germen benedicta ab
Anna
editum, patrum repetita vota
implet, et maesto properat referre
gaudia mundo.

And so it is your seed,
borne by blessed Anne,
who fulfills the oft-voiced desire
of the ancient ones,
and to a world
filled with sadness and sorrow
hastens to restore the joy of the Lord.

Laus tibi, Prolis Pater increatae;
laus tibi, summi Suboles Parentis;
summa laus, compar, tibi sit per
omne,
Spiritus, aevum.
Amen.

Praise to you,
Father of the Uncreated Son;
praise to you,
Child of the Parent most high.
Greatest praise, likewise, be to you,
O Holy Spirit,
for all ages to come.
Amen.

JULY 26: SAINTS JOACHIM AND ANNE
MORNING PRAYER
Nocti Succedit Lucifer / The Daystar Follows upon the Night

Nocti succedit lucifer
quem mox aurora sequitur,
solis ortum praenuntians
mundum lustrantis lumine.

The daystar follows upon the night,
and is itself soon followed by the dawn,
which proclaims the rising of the sun
that will bathe the world
in its resplendent light.

Christus sol est iustitiae,
aurora Mater gratiae,
quam, Anna, praeis rutilans
legis propellens tenebras.

The Sun of Justice is Christ the Lord;
the dawn is the Mother of all grace
whom you, Anna, precede in time;
e'er glowing like the time
before the dawn,
you put to total rout
the darkness of the law.

Anna, radix uberrima,
arbor tu salutifera,
virgam producens floridam
quae Christum nobis attulit.

Anna blest, O root most fecund,
you are a life-bearing tree,
bringing forth a flowering branch
which in turn brings its fruit,
the Christ, to us.

O matris Christi genetrix
tuque parens sanctissime,
natae favente merito,
nobis rogate veniam.

O mother of the mother of Christ,
and you, Joachim, father most holy,
by the favor and merits
of your holy daughter
beg for us
forgiveness's gladsome grace.

Iesu, tibi sit gloria,
qui natus es de Virgine,
cum Patre et almo Spiritu,
in sempiterna saecula.
Amen.

Jesus, to you be all glory,
born as you are of the Virgin,
with the Father and the kindly Spirit
for all ages to come.
Amen.

JULY 29: SAINT MARTHA
OFFICE OF READINGS AND EVENING PRAYER
Te Gratulantes Pangimus / Our Song We Sing to Show Our Joy

Te gratulantes pangimus
Martha, beata mulier,
quae meruisti saepius
Christum domi recipere.

Our song we sing to show our joy in you,
O Martha, blessed lady.
For you were the one who,
often, very often,
was given the gift of entertaining Christ
in your humble home.

Tantum libenter hospitem
curis ornabas sedulis,
in plurima sollicita
amoris dulci stimulo.

Most readily did you bestow
on such a Guest
the gift of your unremitting care;
you were concerned about many things
because of the happy goad
that love's demands imposed.

Pascis dum laeta Dominum,
soror ac frater avide
possunt ab illo gratiae
vitaeque cibum sumere.

While you with joy prepare
food for the Lord,
your sister and your brother
can eagerly receive
from Him the nourishment
of heavenly grace, heavenly life.

Capturo mortis tramitem
dante sorore aromata,
extremi tu servitii
vigil donasti munera.

He was to undertake death's grim path,
anointed with the precious nard
your sister provided of old.
You kept faithful watch for him,
and gave him the gift
of a final kindly deed.

Magistri felix hospita,
corda fac nostra ferveant,
ut illi gratae iugiter
sint sedes amicitiae.

Blessed hostess of the Master,
make our hearts be full on fire,
so that he might ever have a home
where pleasant friendship
might welcome him.

Sit Trinitati gloria,
quae nos in domum caelicam
admitti tandem tribuat
tecumque laudes canere.
Amen.

Let glory be given the Trinity:
may God grant us, at long last,
to be admitted to our heavenly home,
and, along with you, blessed Martha,
to sing his praises evermore. Amen.

JULY 29: SAINT MARTHA
MORNING PRAYER
Quas Tibi Laudes / May the Praise and the Votive Prayers

Quas tibi laudes ferimusque vota,
nos tuis possint meritis iuvare,
Martha, quam mire sibi corde
iungit
Christus amico.

May the praise and the votive prayers
we bring to you,
along with your holy merits,
O Martha, aid us now.
For it was you
whom Christ joined to himself
in wondrous fashion,
in loving embrace of heart.

Te frequens visit Dominus tuaque
in domo degit placida quiete
ac tuis verbis studiisque laetans
teque ministra.

Often was the Lord your guest,
and in your house
enjoyed peaceful rest:
he rejoiced in all that you said
and in all that you did
and in you yourself,
his hostess unsurpassed.

Tu prior fratrem quereris perisse,
cumque germina lacrimata
multum,
aspicis vitae subita Magistri
voce redire.

You were the first sadly to lament
that your brother had died;
along with your sister
you wept a great deal.
Then, at the sudden command
of the Master,
you saw your dead sibling return
unto fullness of life.

Quae fide prompta stabilem
fateris
spem resurgendi, Domino
probante,
impetra nobis cupide in perenne
pergere regnum.

You are the one who profess,
with ready faith,
a firm hope that the dead will rise
on that last day;
with the Lord's gracious approval,
obtain for us the grace
to enter eagerly
upon Christ's everlasting kingdom.

Laus Deo Patri, Genitoque virtus,
Flamini Sancto parilis potestas,
gloriam quorum petimus
per aevum
cernere tecum.
Amen.

Praise to God the Father;
power to God the Son;
equal might be to the holy Spirit,
whose glory every one of us
seeks to behold for eons to come,
while in your gracious company,
O blessed friend
of the Lord, blessed Martha. Amen.

JULY 31: SAINT IGNATIUS OF LOYOLA
MORNING PRAYER
Magnae Cohortis Principem / Our Praise Extols Ignatius

Magnae cohortis principem
Ignatium laus concinat,
clarum loquelis, actibus,
decem cientem milites.

Our praise extols Ignatius:
commander of an army great indeed,
a man in speech
and in action most renowned;
when he began he bestirred
a soon-to-grow group
of himself and nine fellow-soldiers.

Regi supremo caelitum
amore vinctus unico,
eius fovenda gloria
nil censuit iucundius.

Bound to the Eternal King
of the Heavens by a bond
that had no peer,
he judged nothing to be more pleasing
than to foster
that King's ever-greater glory.

Hinc se suosque devovet,
urgentis instar agminis,
ut iura Christi vindicet,
erroris umbras dissipet.

With this as beginning,
he dedicated himself and his men,
as if they were an aroused army,
to see to the safety of Christ's rights,
to scatter to the four winds
the shadows of error.

Sancto monente Spiritu,
certam salutis semitam
scrutator altus saeculis
doctorque prudens denotat.

Suis alumnis dissita
missis in orbis litora,
Ecclesiam quot expetit
frondere laetam gentibus!

Under the Holy Spirit's clear direction,
Ignatius, a prudent and careful teacher,
and one who had tasted
to its heights and to its depths
what he was to teach,
commited to writing for all the ages
a clear path
that leads to human salvation.

Sit Trinitati gloria,
quae nos det huius militis
exempla fortes persequi
in Christi honorem perpetim.
Amen.

[continued]

Magnae Cohortis Principem / Our Praise Extols Ignatius
[concluded]

By sending his sons into
scattered corners of the world,
how many souls did he seek
wherewith Mother Church might rejoice,
might full-flourish fair!

Glory be given the Trinity!
And may God grant
that we bravely follow
the example of this soldier-saint
in seeking unceasingly
the honor and glory of Christ
both now and for evermore.
Amen.

AUGUST 6: TRANSFIGURATION OF THE LORD
EVENING PRAYER I AND II
O Nata Lux de Lumine / Jesus, Redeemer of the World

O nata lux de lumine,
Iesu, redemptor saeculi,
dignare clemens supplicum
laudes precesque sumere.

Jesus, redeemer of the world,
light claiming birth from very light itself,
in your great mercy
accept the prayerful praises
of the people
who come to beg your favor.

Prae sole vultu flammeus,
ut nix amictu candidus,
in monte dignis testibus
apparuisti conditor.

Brilliant-blazing you appear,
beyond e'en the glare of Sun itself;
your garments become white,
like wintry snow.
On this mountain
you show yourself to be
the Creator almighty,
while lawgiver and prophet
alike look on in approving witness.

Vates alumnis abditos
novis vetustos conferens,
utrisque te divinitus
Deum dedisti credere.

Te vox paterna caelitus
suum vocavit Filium,
quem nos fideli pectore
regem fatemur caelitum.

With your new disciples,
you brought together ancient masters
from the earth long and far removed;
but to old and new alike,
with power divine
you granted belief
that you are God most high.

Qui carne quondam contegi
dignatus es pro perditis,
nos membra confer effici
tui beati corporis.

Laudes tibi nos pangimus,
dilectus es qui Filius,
quem Patris atque Spiritus
splendor revelat inclitus.
Amen.

The Father's thundering voice
from heaven
named you as his beloved Son.
With faithful heart we too
profess you as heavenly king on high.

[continued]

O Nata Lux de Lumine / Jesus, Redeemer of the World
[concluded]

You once deigned to be clothed
with mortal flesh
on behalf of fallen humankind;
grant too
that we may be made members
of that blessed body you then assumed.

We bring to you our praises,
for you are the beloved Son
whom the glorious splendor
of Father and Spirit
makes to stand revealed.
Amen.

AUGUST 6: TRANSFIGURATION OF THE LORD
OFFICE OF READINGS
Caelestis Formam Gloriae / The Vision of Heavenly Glory

Caelestis formam gloriae
quam spes quaerit Ecclesiae,
in monte Christus indicat,
qui supra solem emicat.

The vision of heavenly glory
in which the Church
places its fond hope,
Christ revealed on the mountain
when he showed himself
to be more brilliant
than e'en the Sun itself.

Res memoranda saeculis:
tribus coram discipulis,
cum Elia, cum Moyse
grata promit eloquia.

Something to be remembered
for all ages to come:
in the presence
of three of his companions,
and in the company of Elijah,
and in the company of Moses,
he spoke in winsome words.

Assistunt testes gratiae,
legis vatumque veterum;
de nube testimonium
sonat Patris ad Filium.

Witnesses of this graced event
were full ready at hand:
one testifying on behalf of the Law,
one testifying on behalf of the prophets
of old; and from the cloud,
the testimony and proclamation
of the Father to his Son
is thundered loud and clear.

Glorificata facie
Christus declarat hodie
quis honor sit credentium
Deo pie fruentium.

With heaven-suffused face,
Christ makes plain today
what honor awaits believers
when in loyal faith
they shall enjoy the Godhead blest.

Visionis mysterium
corda levat fidelium,
unde sollemni gaudio
clamat nostra devotio.

The mystery of this mountain-vision
raises up the hearts of the faithful;
from this, our loyal song
rings forth in solemn joy.

Pater, cum Unigenito
et Spiritu Paraclito
unus, nobis hanc gloriam
largire per praesentiam.
Amen.

Father, one with your Son
and with the Holy Spirit,
grant us this glorious grace
by your gracious protection. Amen.

AUGUST 6: TRANSFIGURATION OF THE LORD
MORNING PRAYER
Dulcis Iesu Memoria / How Winsome the Memory of Jesus!

Dulcis Iesu memoria, dans vera cordi gaudia, sed super mel et omnia eius dulcis praesentia.	How winsome the memory of Jesus! It grants true joys to the heart. But sweeter still, sweeter than honey and all else beside, is his true and blessed presence among us.
Nil canitur suavius, auditur nil iucundius, nil cogitatur dulcius quam Iesus Dei Filius.	In song, we find nothing more delightful, in the spoken word, nothing more pleasing, in thought, nothing more engaging, than Jesus, the sole-begotten Son of God.
Iesu, dulcedo cordium, fons veri, lumen mentium, excedit omne gaudium et omne desiderium.	Jesus, our souls' sweet surfeit, our fountain of truth, our inspiration of mind: he far surpasses every other joy, and anything else that we could e'er desire.
Quando cor nostrum visitas, tunc lucet ei veritas, mundi vilescit vanitas et intus fervet caritas.	When you come as guest within our hearts, then, truly, does truth shine forth in them; the world's empty show shows itself worthless indeed, and love's blazing flame is kindled brightly within us.
Da nobis largus veniam, amoris tui copiam; da nobis per praesentiam tuam videre gloriam.	In your generous kindness, grant us pardon for our sins; give us too an abundant share of your love. By your presence, grant that we will see your full glory.
Laudes tibi nos pangimus, dilectus es qui Filius, quem Patris atque Spiritus splendor revelat inclitus. Amen.	We bring to you our praises, for you are the beloved Son whom the glorious splendor of Father and Spirit makes to stand revealed. Amen.

AUGUST 8: SAINT DOMINIC
MORNING AND EVENING PRAYERS
Novus Athleta Domini / A New Champion of the Lord

Novus athleta Domini
collaudetur Dominicus,
qui rem confirmat nomini,
vir factus evangelicus.

A new champion of the Lord is Dominic;
let him be given due praise,
Dominic, one who matches
reality with his name,
for truly he has become
a "vir Dominicus," a man of the Lord,
a man who proclaims the Lord.

Conservans sine macula
virginitatis lilium,
ardebat quasi facula
pro zelo pereuntium.

Preserving unsullied purity's emblem
bright and true,
he was afire, like a torch ablaze,
with zeal for souls
that were being lost.

Mundum calcans sub pedibus
accinxit cor ad proelia,
nudus occurrens hostibus,
Christi suffultus gratia.

Trampling earthly concerns under foot,
he armed his heart to do battle;
devoid of this world's armor,
he yet met the enemy,
supported solely by the protection
of Christ's holy grace.

Pugnat verbo, miraculis,
missis per orbem fratribus,
crebros adiungens sedulis
fletus orationibus.

Battle he joined, by word,
by mighty signs,
by sending his brethren
throughout the world,
joining frequent tears
to unceasing prayers.

Sit trino Deo et simplici
laus, honor, decus, gloria,
qui nos prece Dominici
ducat ad caeli gloriam.
Amen.

To God Triune and One
be praise, honor, beauty, glory;
through the prayers of St. Dominic,
may he lead us to the glory of heaven.
Amen.

AUGUST 10: SAINT LAWRENCE
OFFICE OF READINGS AND EVENING PRAYER
Martyris Christi Colimus Triumphum / Now Celebrate We the Triumph

Martyris Christi colimus
triumphum,
dona qui mundi peritura spernit,
fert opem nudis, alimenta,
nummos
tradit egenis.

Now celebrate we the triumph
of this martyr of Christ.
Spurning the fleeting gifts
the world might have accorded him,
he brought clothing to the naked,
he provided food and funds
for the needy.

Igne torquetur, stabili tenore
cordis accensus superat minaces
ignium flammas in amore vitae
semper opimae.

Tortured he was, indeed, by fire.
But more inflamed was he
in that steadfast, steady heart
that was his; he overcame the flames
that menaced him
in his love of that ne'er-ending,
splendid life to come.

Spiritum sumpsit chorus
angelorum,
intulit caelo bene laureandum,
ut scelus laxet hominum,
precando
omnipotentem.

The angels' chorus received his spirit;
since he was full worthy
of all fitting praise,
they carried him into heaven,
so that he could relieve humankind
of its sin by his prayers
to the Almighty One.

Supplici voto rogitamus ergo
omnibus, martyr, veniam preceris,
cordis ardores, fidei tenacem
usque vigorem.

With humble but eager prayer
we now ask you,
O martyr, to beg of God
forgiveness for us all:
ask too for a loving, searing flame
for our hearts, to lead us to a faith
unshakeable and strong.

Gloriam Patri resonemus omnes,
eius et Nato modulemur apte,
cum quibus regnat simul et
creator
Spiritus almus.
Amen.

Now let us all
proclaim glory to the Father;
let us duly sing to his Son,
with whom reigns alike the faithful
Creator Spirit. Amen.

AUGUST 10: SAINT LAWRENCE
MORNING PRAYER
In Martyris Laurentii / In the Not-Unbloody Final Struggle

In martyris Laurentii
non incruento proelio,
armata pugnavit Fides
proprii cruoris prodiga.

In the not-unbloody final struggle
of Lawrence the Martyr,
it was an aroused faith
that poured out in fullest
measure its vital power
in battle severe.

Hic primus e septem viris
qui stant ad aram proximi,
levita sublimis gradu
et ceteris praestantior.

For Lawrence is the chief of the seven
who stand next to the altar:
a Levite high in rank,
a deacon who surpasses all others.

Hic dimicans fortissimus
non ense praecinxit latus,
hostile sed ferrum retro
torquens in auctorem tulit.

A brave man he:
as he engaged in battle,
he did not gird his side with a sword,
but rather turned
the enemy's own steel back upon him,
thrusting back the attack so cruel
upon the one whence it had come.

Sic, sancte Laurenti, tuam
nos passionem quaerimus;
quod quisque supplex postulat,
fert impetratum prospere,

And so, holy St. Lawrence,
it is thus that we seek
to invoke the passion you endured, so
each suppliant soul might carry off,
full-granted, whatever he has besought,

Dum caeli inerrabili
allectus urbi municeps,
aeternae in arce curiae
gestas coronam civicam.

For you have been chosen as a citizen
for the indescribable city
of heaven above:
you bear the highest of crowns
in the citadel of the eternal court.

Honor Patri cum Filio
et Spiritu Paraclito,
qui nos tuis suffragiis
ditent perenni laurea.
Amen.

Let honor then be given the Father,
with the Son and the Spirit Advocate:
may God, by your holy prayers,
enrich us too with an unending crown
of victory. Amen.

AUGUST 15: ASSUMPTION OF THE BLESSED VIRGIN MARY
EVENING PRAYER I AND II
Gaudium Mundi, Nova Stella Caeli / Joy of the World, Bright New Star

Gaudium mundi, nova stella caeli,
procreans solem, pariens
parentem,
da manum lapsis, fer opem
caducis,
virgo Maria.

Joy of the world,
bright new star of heaven,
you bring forth the very Sun himself,
you give birth to the very one
who made you:
O Mary, holy Virgin,
stretch out your hand
to those who have fallen,
bring aid to your children who are lost.

Te Deo factam liquet esse scalam
qua tenens summa petit Altus
ima;
nos ad excelsi remeare caeli
culmina dona.

Clear it is: you have become
a stairway for God,
whereby the Most Exalted One,
already possessing what is highest,
seeks yet what is lowest.
Clear too it is: by means of you
we make our way back
to the heights
of highest heaven above.

Te beatorum chorus angelorum,
te prophetarum et apostolorum
ordo praelatam sibi cernit unam
post Deitatem.

The chorus of blessed angels,
the ranked order
of prophets and apostles
gaze upon you, the only one
elevated above themselves,
in rank below only the Godhead itself.

Laus sit excelsae Triadi perennis,
quae tibi, Virgo, tribuit coronam,
atque reginam statuitque nostram
provida matrem.
Amen.

E'erlasting praise be given
to the Trinity on high,
who have delivered unto you,
holy Virgin,
a crown most sublime,
and have, in their provident care,
decreed that you are our queen,
that you are our mother.
Amen.

AUGUST 15: ASSUMPTION OF THE BLESSED VIRGIN MARY
OFFICE OF READINGS
Aurora velut Fulgida / Just as Bright-Shining Dawn

Aurora velut fulgida,
ad caeli meat culmina
ut sol Maria splendida,
tamquam luna pulcherrima.

Just as bright-shining dawn
makes its glowing way
to the very heights of heaven,
so is it with Mary:
she is like the sun, brilliant in splendor,
and like the moon, gleaming in beauty.

Regina mundi hodie
thronum conscendit gloriae,
illum enixa Filium
qui est ante luciferum.

The Queen of the world has today
ascended to a throne of glory,
having brought forth a Son,
her wondrous Son,
who was and is
before the daystar itself.

Assumpta super angelos
omnesque choros caelitum,
cuncta sanctorum merita
transcendit una femina.

Raised up on high above all angels,
above too all choirs
that populate heaven,
lo, this one human woman
surpasses all the merits
of all the saints as well.

Quem foverat in gremio,
locarat in praesepio,
nunc regem super omnia
Patris videt in gloria.

The one whom she had dandled
in her lap, the one whom she had
gently placed in the manger,
that very one does she now gaze upon:
the king who rules over all,
in the glory of the Father most high.

Pro nobis, Virgo Virginum,
tuum deposce Filium,
per quam nostra susceperat,
ut sua nobis praebeat.

O Virgin of Virgins, through you your Son
undertook our human condition.
Beg of him, on our behalf,
to accord us his own life divine.

Sit laus Patri cum Filio
et Spiritu Paraclito,
qui te prae cunctis caelica
exornaverunt gloria.
Amen.

Let high praise be given to the Father,
with the Son
and the Spirit Advocate as well;
they have enriched you
beyond all others
with glory full sublime. Amen.

AUGUST 15: ASSUMPTION OF THE BLESSED VIRGIN MARY
MORNING PRAYER
Solis, O Virgo, Radiis Amicta / O Virgin Blest, Clothed Are You

Solis, o Virgo, radiis amicta,
bis caput senis redimita stellis,
luna cui praebet pedibus
scabellum,
inclita fulges.

O Virgin blest, clothed are you
with the rays of the Sun itself;
with a crown of twice-six stars
are you adorned.
For your feet the moon itself
provides a footstool;
full resplendent are you in glory.

Mortis, inferi dominatrixque
culpae,
assides Christo studiosa nostri,
teque reginam celebrat
potentem
terra polusque.

You rule over death, over nether world,
over guilt itself;
mindful of us, you take your place
near Christ.
Earth and sky alike hail you
as their queen, peerless in power.

Protect those who remain faithful
to the faith divine;
bring back the scattered
to the sheepfold most holy.
Gather together those whom
for long ages the shadow of death
has kept in darkness drear.

Asseclas diae fidei tuere;
dissitos adduc ad ovile sacrum;
quas diu gentes tegit umbra
mortis
undique coge.

In your meekness, seek pardon
for the guilty;
aid those who weep,
those who are poor,
those who are sick.
For everyone, shine forth
as the sure hope of salvation
amidst the harsh lives that are theirs.

Sontibus mitis veniam precare,
adiuva flentes, inopes et aegros,
spes mica cunctis per acuta
vitae
certa salutis.

Laus sit excelsae Triadi
perennis,
quae tibi, Virgo, tribuit coronam,
atque reginam statuitque
nostram
provida matrem.
Amen.

E'erlasting praise be given
to the Trinity on high,
who have delivered unto you,
holy Virgin,
a crown most sublime,
and have, in their provident care,
decreed that you are our queen,
that you are our mother. Amen.

AUGUST 20: SAINT BERNARD
MORNING PRAYER AND EVENING PRAYER
Bernarde, Gemma Caelitum / Bernard, Jewel Descended

Bernarde, gemma caelitum,
laudes, tibi quas pangimus,
in nostra verte gaudia
salutis atque munera.

Bernard, jewel descended
from heaven above, receive the praises
that we pour forth unto you, and
transform them into the source
of our own joy, and into the gift
of salvation that we are given.

Te Christus ussit intimo
dilectionis vulnere
Sponsaeque fecit providus
scutum, columnam, lampada.

Christ set you on fire
with the internal wound of love,
and in his provident kindness
made you guarding shield,
defending pillar, and shining lamp
of his holy Bride most fair.

Almus dedit te Spiritus
os veritatis profluum
et angelorum pabuli
arcana mella proferens.

The faithful Spirit granted you
a mouth streaming forth with truth;
that Spirit brought forth from you
the hidden, honey-sweet food
of the angels themselves.

Amoris aestu candidi
te Virgo Mater imbuit,
quam nemo te facundius
vel praedicavit altius.

The Virgin Mother filled you
with the fires of white-hot love,
which none e'er proclaimed
more easily, more exaltedly than you.

Te quaesierunt arbitrum
reges, magistri, praesules,
cultorque solitudinis
fama replesti saeculum.

Kings, chieftains, prefects
sought you out
as counselor for themselves;
though you sought solitude,
you have filled the whole world
with the fame of your word.

Sit Trinitati gloria,
quae se videndam largiens,
tecum benigna gaudio
nos det perenni perfrui.
Amen.

Let glory be given to the Trinity,
who granted you a vision of Itself;
in its kindness sublime may it grant
that, in union with you,
we may enjoy delights unending. Amen.

AUGUST 22: BLESSED VIRGIN MARY, QUEEN
OFFICE OF READINGS

Rerum Supremo in Vertice / You Are Given Your Place, O Virgin

Rerum supremo in vertice
regina, Virgo, sisteris,
exuberanter omnium
ditata pulchritudine.

You are given your place,
O Virgin, O Queen,
at creation's highest point;
enriched abundantly are you
with beauty of every kind.

Princeps opus tu cetera
inter creata praenites,
praedestinata Filium
qui protulit te, gignere.

Amidst all the rest of created things
you shine forth
as the finest of God's works,
for it was your destiny to bear a Son:
a Son, but also
the very One who created you.

Ut Christus alta ab arbore
rex purpuratus sanguine,
sic passionis particeps
tu mater es viventium.

Just as Christ was king,
purpled, blood-stained
on that exalted tree,
so are you, sharer in his suffering,
the mother of all who live.

Tantis decora laudibus
ad nos ovantes respice,
tibique sume gratulans
quod fundimus praeconium.

Adorned with praises so high,
look upon us who rejoice in you;
in your joy, accept the proclaiming song
that we pour forth gladly unto you.

Patri sit et Paraclito
tuoque Nato gloria,
qui veste te mirabili
circumdederunt gratiae.
Amen.

To the Father, and to the Advocate blest,
and to the Son be great glory given;
they have enclothed you
with a garment of grace
most wondrous to behold.
Amen.

AUGUST 22: BLESSED VIRGIN MARY, QUEEN
MORNING PRAYER
O Quam Glorifica Luce Coruscas / How Glorious a Light

O quam glorifica luce coruscas,
stirpis Davidicae regia proles,
sublimis residens, virgo Maria,
supra caeligenas
aetheris omnes.

With how glorious a light
do you shine forth,
O queenly scion of David's royal line;
seated are you on high, O Virgin Mary,
above all the heavenborn
of Paradise sublime.

Tu, cum virgineo mater honore,
caelorum Domino
pectoris aulam
sacris visceribus casta parasti,
natus hinc Deus
est corpore Christus:

You are a mother,
but you boast a virgin's honored state;
chaste maiden, within your sacred body
you have prepared
the royal chamber of your heart
for the Lord of heaven;
and from there God has been born
in human form: Christ the Lord,

Quem cunctus venerans
orbis adorat,
cui nunc rite genu
flectitur omne,
a quo te petimus subveniente
abiectis tenebris gaudia lucis.

Whom the entire world
falls down and worships;
to whom every knee now rightly bends;
and from whom, through your aid,
O Virgin blest, we beg
that darkness may be put to flight
and that we may receive
the joys of light.

Hoc largire, Pater luminis omnis,
Natum per proprium,
Flamine Sancto,
qui tecum nitida vivit in aethra
regnans ac moderans
saecula cuncta.
Amen.

O Father of all brightness, grant us this,
through your own Son,
by means of the Sacred Spirit,
who lives and reigns with you
for e'ershining ages,
ruling and governing
the whole of creation.
Amen.

AUGUST 22: BLESSED VIRGIN MARY, QUEEN
EVENING PRAYER
Mole Gravati Criminum / Full-Burdened with the Weight of Our Sins

Mole gravati criminum
ad te, regina caelitum,
confugientes, poscimus
nostris ut adsis precibus.

Full-burdened with the weight
of our sins,
we flee to you, O queen of heaven
most high; and beg that you give
kindly ear to our prayers.

You are the gateway to eternal life;
give hearing to our plea,
for it is through you that our hope of life
has been restored, that hope which
ancient Eve stole full away
by her fall, by her sin.

Aeternae vitae ianua,
aurem nobis accommoda,
per quam spes vitae rediit,
quam Eva peccans abstulit.

You are the Queen,
the mother of the King.
Beg for your children the boon of life;
in your kind mercy obtain for us
the chance to perform
the penance we need.

Tu princeps, mater Principis,
vitam deposce famulis,
et paenitendi spatia
nobis indulgens impetra.

When you offer your prayer,
virgin of all virgins the holiest,
the whole saintly court
prays in union with you;
by your prayers, heavenly Queen,
the Lord God is made full appeased.

Orante te, sanctissima,
sanctorum orant agmina;
tuis, regina, precibus
concilietur Dominus.

Queenly mother of all that is,
bring to full fruition
the vows of your faithful children.
Once this brittle-frail life
is over and done,
lead us at last
to the realm of true rest eternal.

Regnatrix mater omnium,
vota comple fidelium,
ac vitam nos post fragilem
ad veram perduc requiem.

Sit laus Patri cum Filio
et Spiritu Paraclito,
qui te prae cunctis caelica
exornaverunt gloria.
Amen.

Let praise be given to the Father,
to the Son
and the Spirit Advocate as well;
they have adorned you
with heavenly glory in measure
far above all else there is. Amen.

AUGUST 24: SAINT BARTHOLOMEW
MORNING PRAYER
Relucens inter Principes / A Figure Shining Full Bright

Relucens inter principes
immensae Dei curiae,
Bartholomaee, laudibus
nostrisque intende precibus.

A figure shining full bright are you
amidst the chieftains
of the boundless court
of our God most high,
O Bartholomew: grant merciful ear,
we beg,
to the prayers, to the praise
that we pour out unto you.

In te convertit Dominus
dilectionis oculos,
quem pura insignem conspicit
sinceritate pectoris.

Christ the Lord cast his loving gaze
upon you, knowing as he did
that you were one who was
guileless and pure of heart.

Prophetae quem cecinerant,
quem longa clamant tempora,
Messias en mirifice
tibi laetanti proditur.

He of whom the prophets had sung,
whom long eons beseech e'en now
with fervent cry, the Messiah himself:
lo, in wondrous way,
he is made known to you,
and you receive him with joy.

Teque sibi conglutinat
sequelae talis foedere,
qua petat crucis aspera,
caeli sedes retribuat.

He bonds you to himself
in a sacred pact whereby
you would be that sort of disciple
who would seek
the harsh road of the cross,
and whom the heavens own realm
would seek to repay.

Christi, qui saeclis imperat,
amicus et apostolus,
Magistro vivis, homines
Magistri vita refoves.

Sit ipsi laus et gloria,
qui, te iuvante meritis,
aeternis nos in patria
frui concedat gaudiis. Amen.

[continued]

Relucens inter Principes / A Figure Shining Full Bright
[concluded]

Friend and apostle of Christ are you,
the Christ who rules
over ages uncounted.
As friend, you live for your Master;
as apostle, you restore men and women
far and wide with the life
and the love of that Master sublime.

Let praise and glory be given to Him;
and may He, aided by your holy merits,
grant that we too
may enjoy e'erlasting joys
in our home and fatherland
in high heaven above.
Amen.

AUGUST 28: SAINT AUGUSTINE
MORNING AND EVENING PRAYERS
Fulget in Caelis Celebris Sacerdos / Great Renown Has This Priest

Fulget in caelis celebris sacerdos,
stella doctorum rutilat corusca,
lumen intactum fidei per orbis
climata spargens.

Great renown has this priest,
who now shines forth
in the heavens above;
as a blazing star he gleams
brilliant and bright among learned men,
and spreads the light of faith
undiminished through all the regions
of the world.

Cive tam claro, Sion o superna,
laeta dic laudes Domino salutis,
qui modis miris sibi vinxit ipsum
lumine complens.

Enjoying such a citizen within you,
O Sion most high, joyfully chant
your praises to the Lord of salvation,
who in ways many and wondrous
has clasped this saint unto himself,
and has filled him
with bright-shining light.

Hic fidem sacram vigil usque
firmat,
arma et errorum subigit potenter,
sordidos mores lavat
et repellit
dogmate claro.

This vigilant man still fosters a faith
that is sacred and strong;
powerfully does he overcome
the weapons error has.
He purges evil habits,
and puts them to flight
with his teaching clear and power-filled.

Qui, gregis Christi speculator
almus,
enites clero monachisque forma,
tu Dei nobis faciem benignam
fac prece semper.

Faithful watchman
o'er the flock of Christ,
you are prominent as model for priest,
as model for monk:
by your prayers,
render the face of God ever kindly to us.

Laus, honor, virtus Triadi beatae,
cuius in terris studuisti amanter
alta scrutari nitidaque in astris
luce potiris.
Amen.

Praise, honor, power be
to the blessed Trinity,
whose profound mysteries
you lovingly studied
while you were on earth,
and whose brilliant light on high
you have received to ponder carefully
in the heavens above. Amen.

AUGUST 29: SUFFERING OF SAINT JOHN THE BAPTIST
MORNING PRAYER
O Nimis Felix, p. 224

OFFICE OF READINGS AND EVENING PRAYER
Praecessor Almus Gratiae / The Kindly Precursor of Grace Was He

Praecessor almus gratiae
et veritatis angelus,
lucerna Christi et perpetis
evangelista luminis,

The kindly precursor of grace was he,
the messenger of truth;
a lamp showing forth Christ the Lord,
he announced the good news
of unending light to come,

Prophetiae praeconia,
quae voce, vita et actibus
cantaverat, haec astruit
mortis sacrae signaculo.

And proclaimed prophecies from of old.
But whatever he had made known
by voice, life, or action,
he has added to e'en more greatly
by the seal of his own sacred death.

Nam nasciturum saeculis,
nascendo quem praevenerat,
sed et datorem proprii
monstraverat baptismatis,

For the One who was to be born
for the ages—
Whom in birth he had preceded,
and Whom he had pointed out
as the one who ought to be baptizing
rather than baptized—

Huiusce mortem innoxiam,
qua vita mundo est reddita,
signat sui praesagio
baptista martyr sanguinis.

This same One's innocent death,
by which life has been restored
to the world, has the martyr-baptist
marked out in advance
by the shedding of his own holy blood.

Praesta, Pater piissime,
sequi Ioannis semitas,
metamus ut plenissime
aeterna Christi munera.
Amen.

O Father most faithful, grant
that we may follow the path
that John laid out,
so that we may reap in full abundance
the e'erlasting rewards
of Christ our Lord.
Amen.

SEPTEMBER 3: SAINT GREGORY THE GREAT
MORNING PRAYER
Anglorum Iam Apostolus / Once an Apostle to Anglian Shores

Anglorum iam apostolus,
nunc angelorum socius,
ut tunc, Gregori, gentibus,
succurre iam credentibus.

Once an apostle to Anglian shores,
now a companion to Angel hosts above,
come now,
O Gregory well termed the Great,
to the aid of loyal believers,
just as you succored
pagan peoples of old.

Tu largas opum copias
omnemque mundi gloriam
spernis, ut inops inopem
Iesum sequaris principem.

A great mass of wealth,
and all the glory the earth can offer
you treat with scorn,
so that as a poor man
you might follow Jesus the poor man,
Jesus the leader supreme.

Te celsus Christus pontifex
suae praefert Ecclesiae;
sic Petri gradum percipis,
cuius et normam sequeris.

And Christ, the exalted high priest,
places you in charge of his Church;
and thus you accept
the position of Peter, whom you take as
pattern and as norm.

Scripturae sacrae mystica
mire solvis aenigmata,
excelsaque mysteria
te docet ipsa Veritas.

You wondrously make plain
the mystic puzzles
that Holy Writ contains,
and Truth Himself is your teacher
in matters of mystery sublime.

O pontifex egregie,
lux et decus Ecclesiae,
non sinas in periculis
quos tot mandatis instruis.

Bridge-builder most eminent,
light and glory of holy Church,
do not allow those
to suffer danger's perils
whom you have trained by counsel
so well, so oft given.

Sit Patri laus ingenito,
sit decus Unigenito,
sit utriusque parili
maiestas summa Flamini.
Amen.

Let praise be given
to the Father unbegotten,
let honor be given
to the sole-begotten Son,
let supreme dominion belong
to the Spirit alike of Father and Son.
Amen.

SEPTEMBER 8: NATIVITY OF THE BLESSED VIRGIN MARY
OFFICE OF READINGS AND EVENING PRAYER
Beata Dei Genetrix / Blessed Mother of God

Beata Dei genetrix,
nitor humani generis,
per quam de servis liberi
lucisque sumus filii;

Blessed mother of God,
shining splendor of the human race,
through you
we are freed from slavish state;
through you
we have become children of the light.

Maria, virgo regia,
David stirpe progenita,
non tam paterna nobilis
quam dignitate subolis,

Mary, queenly virgin,
offspring of David's royal line,
not so much ennobled are you
by the ancestry you so rightly claim,
as by the high estate of the royal child
that you yourself have regally borne.

Tu nos, avulso veteri,
complanta novo germini;
per te sit genus hominum
regale sacerdotium.

Take away far from us
the old lineage that was ours;
graft us into a brand-new shoot:
by you may the race of humankind
become a royal priesthood
in truth and deed.

Tu nos culparum nexibus
sacris absolve precibus;
tua promentes merita
ad caeli transfer praemia.

By your holy prayers,
loose us from the bonds of guilt;
betake unto the rewards of heaven
those of us who proclaim aloud
the measure
of your own glorious worth.

Sit Trinitati gloria,
o Virgo nobilissima,
quae te suorum munerum
thesaurum dat magnificum.
Amen.

To the Trinity be glorious praise,
O Virgin Mother most high;
to us has God given you
as treasury overflowing
with his own magnificence and wealth.
Amen.

SEPTEMBER 8: NATIVITY OF THE BLESSED VIRGIN MARY
MORNING PRAYER
O Sancta Mundi Domina / O Lady Ruling o'er the World

O sancta mundi domina,
regina caeli inclita,
O stella maris fulgida,
virgo mater mirifica,

O lady ruling o'er the world,
most holy one,
Queen of heaven, most renowned one,
O star of the sea, bright-shining one,
Virgin and mother, most marvelous one,

Show yourself to us,
O daughter most pleasing;
shine forth among us now,
youthful maiden,
as the one who is about to bring forth
offspring most exalted:
the Christ-God, the Christ-man.

Appare, dulcis filia,
nitesce iam, virguncula,
florem latura nobilem,
Christum Deum et hominem.

Lo, we celebrate each year the holy rites
that mark the day of your birth.
On that day, though newly born indeed,
yet set full apart
by the progeny to be yours,
you became glorious
in the sight of the world far and wide.

Natalis tui annua
en colimus sollemnia,
quo stirpe delectissima
mundo fulsisti genita.

Through you are we,
citizens of lowly earth,
now also made
denizens of high heaven above,
granted calm and rest
by a peace full well renowned,
in a manner far beyond
all reckon and measure.

Per te sumus, terrigenae
simulque iam caligenae,
pacati pace nobili,
more non aestimabili.

Let glory be given the Trinity
throughout the ages' long roll;
by the Triune's own bounteous gift
are you termed
the blessed mother of our holy Church.
Amen.

Sit Trinitati gloria
per saeculorum saecula,
cuius vocaris munere
mater beata Ecclesiae.
Amen.

SEPTEMBER 13: SAINT JOHN CHRYSOSTOM
MORNING AND EVENING PRAYERS
Laude Te Cives Superni Coronant / Heaven's Denizens Heap Full
Praise upon You

Laude te cives superni coronant,
magne Ioannes, sociusque noster
iungitur cantus, generose praesul,
celse magister.

Heaven's denizens heap full praise
upon you, O John, great saint;
and our song joins
in companionship with theirs,
O eminent patron,
O teacher most sublime.

Aureo profers vehementer ore
verba quae dives facilisque amoris
vena progignit, feriunt vel acri
vulnere noxas.

With lips of gold do you boldly proclaim
those words which your genius,
rich, filled with ready love,
brings forth: but words which smite
evil, and deal it
a mighty blow.

Ipse virtutum speculum nitescis
ac tuae plebi meritis coruscas,
omnibus, Pauli velut aemulator,
omnia factus.

Like a mirror, imaging all virtues,
you shine forth;
to your admiring throng
you surpass all in merit,
and like one who mirrors great St. Paul
to all men and women
you have become all things.

Nemo te frangit, nihil imperantum
te domant irae, rutilaeque
honorem
obtines palmae venerandus exsul,
pectore martyr.

No one wears down your resolve;
the anger of princes cows you not at all.
You garner the glory
of a bloody victory-palm
as an exile much revered,
and a martyr in your heart.

Nunc tuis valde precibus iuvemur,
ut Dei sedem celeres petamus,
dulcibus tecum sonituri amoris
vocibus hymnos.
Amen.

Now may we be greatly aided
by your prayers,
that thus we may seek in haste
the homeland of God;
with lucent voices are we prepared,
in company with you,
to sing hymns
about God's love so great. Amen.

SEPTEMBER 14: EXALTATION OF THE HOLY CROSS

EVENING PRAYER I (if celebrated) AND II
Vexilla Regis Prodeunt: see pages 52-53

OFFICE OF READINGS
Salve, Crux Sancta / Hail, O Sacred Cross

Salve, crux sancta,
salve mundi gloria,
vera spes nostra,
vera ferens gaudia,
signum salutis,
salus in periculis,
vitale lignum
vitam portans omnium.

Hail, O sacred cross,
Hail, glory of the entire world;
you are our true hope,
you are the bearer of true joy.
You are the mark of salvation,
the rescue granted us
midst dangers most dire,
the life-giving wood
that bears upon itself
the Life of us all.

Te adorandam,
te crucem vivificam,
in te redempti,
dulce decus saeculi,
semper laudamus,
semper tibi canimus,
per lignum servi,
per te, lignum, liberi.

Without ceasing, we praise you,
cross meriting reverence,
cross meriting awe.
We praise you, yoke that restores life,
we: who have been redeemed
through you,
most kindly glory of the ages.
Forever our song rises unto you,
for by a tree were we enslaved,
and by you yourself a tree
were we freed.

Laus Deo Patri
sit in cruce Filii,
laus coaequali
sit Sancto Spiritui;
civibus summis
gaudium et angelis,
honor sit mundo
crucis exaltatio.
Amen.

Let praise be given God the Father
through the cross of his glorious Son,
and let praise likewise be given
to the Holy Spirit,
equal in majesty to Father and Son.
Let joy attend the citizens of heaven,
joy attend the angels above;
and let the exaltation
of the holy Cross
be glorious honor for the world below.
Amen.

SEPTEMBER 14: EXALTATION OF THE HOLY CROSS
MORNING PRAYER
Signum Crucis Mirabile / The Standard of the Cross

Signum crucis mirabile
totum per orbem praenitet,
in qua pependit innocens
Christus, redemptor omnium.

The standard of the Cross,
most wondrous to behold,
shines forth throughout the length
and the breadth of all the world.
On that holy Cross
hung the Christic One:
shamed by no sin,
but of all sinners the Savior.

Haec arbor est sublimior
cedris, habet quas Libanus,
quae poma nescit noxia,
sed ferre vitae praemia.

Taller stands this tree
than do the cedars
that live in lofty Lebanon;
no ill-bringing fruit
does it know itself to bear,
but rather the boon of everlasting life.

Te, Christe, rex piissime,
huius crucis signaculo
horis, momentis omnibus
munire nos non abnuas,

O Christ, most faithful King,
by the sign of this Cross
refuse not to protect us
at every hour, every moment of the day,

So that at each hour,
each moment of each day,
with worthy lips
and with hearts dedicated to you,
we may be able to offer you
the praises that we owe.

Ut ore tibi consono
et corde devotissimo
possimus omni tempore
laudes referre debitas.

To the Father almighty,
to you, Jesus Lord,
to the Spirit most high
may fitting glory be ever given,
for you allow us to enjoy ceaselessly
the victory of the Cross.
Amen.

Patri, tibi, Paraclito
sit aequa, Iesu, gloria,
qui nos crucis victoria
concedis usque perfrui.
Amen.

SEPTEMBER 15: OUR LADY OF SORROWS
Stabat Mater Dolorosa / She Stayed Standing There, the Mother in Sorrow Rent

OFFICE OF READINGS: Stanzas 1-9
MORNING PRAYER: Stanzas 10-16
EVENING PRAYER: Stanzas 17-22

[1] Stabat mater dolorosa
iuxta crucem lacrimosa,
dum pendebat Filius.

[2] Cuius animam gementem,
contristatam et dolentem,
pertransivit gladius.

[3] O quam tristis et afflicta
fuit illa benedicta
mater Unigeniti!

[4] Quae maerebat et dolebat
pia mater, cum videbat
Nati poenas incliti.

[5] Quis est homo
qui non fleret,
Matrem Christi si videret
in tanto supplicio?

[6] Quis non posset contristari,
piam matrem contemplari
dolentem cum Filio?

[7] Pro peccatis suae gentis
vidit Iesum in tormentis
et flagellis subditum.

[8] Vidit suum dulcem natum
morientem, desolatum,
cum emisit spiritum.

[9] Christe, cum sit hinc exire,
da per matrem me venire
ad palmam victoriae.

[1] She stayed standing there,
the Mother, in sorrow rent,
next to the cross,
lo, with bitter tears overcome,
sadness bent,
while on that rood there hung her Son.

[2] In her grieving spirit,
sore afflicted and vast empained,
has a shining, sadding, sword of sorrow
been soul-blood stained.

[3] O how grieved, how sore beset
that most holy Mother of the One
whom alone saw fit the Father to beget
as beloved, sole-born Son.

[4] O how sad, how heavy of heart
that dutiful Mother,
who painful gaze must needs impart
on the torments of her glorious Son.

[5] Who be the man, the woman so cold
as not to weep,
Christ's mother to behold
in straits so awful,
in suffering untold?

[6] Who could fail to sorrow in turn,
on pondering the mother
of the Christic One,
as grieves she for her only Son?

Stabat Mater Dolorosa [continued]

[10] Eia, mater, fons amoris
me sentire vim doloris
fac, ut tecum lugeam.

[11] Fac ut ardeat cor meum
in amando Christum Deum,
ut sibi complaceam.

[12] Sancta mater, istud agas,
Crucifixi fige plagas
cordi meo valide.

[13] Tui Nati vulnerati
tam dignati pro me pati
poenas mecum divide.

[14] Fac me tecum flere,
Crucifixo condolere,
donec ego vixero.

[15] Iuxta crucem tecum stare
ac me tibi sociare
in planctu desidero.

[16] Quando corpus morietur,
fac ut animi donetur
paradisi gloria.

[17] Virgo virginum praeclara,
mihi iam non sis amara;
fac me tecum plangere.

[18] Fac ut portem
Christi mortem,
passionis fac me sortem
et plagas recolere.

[19] Fac me plagis vulnerari,
cruce hac inebriari
et cruore Filii.

[7] For the sins of her own kind
and her own race did she her Jesus
in torment find, fated fell tortures
bravely to embrace.

[8] She gazed on him: beloved Son,
in dying undone,
as sent he forth his spirit soul.

[9] Christ God, when time shall come
for me to leave this life
and come to thee,
grant that through mother of thine
I may come to great reward divine.

[10] Lo, O Mother,
font of love for us on earth,
make me feel sharp sorrow's dearth,
that with you I too might grieve.

[11] Make it be that soul of mine
might blaze in love for Christ divine:
so might I, too,
be pleasing unto Him.

[12] Mother most holy,
grant this to me,
your daughter, your son:
the wounds of the Crucified One—
stamp them in my heart ineradicably.

[13] Grant to me a share
of the sufferings of your Child,
wounded, deemed so suited
to be so meek, so mild
as to suffer for a sinner like me.

Stabat Mater Dolorosa [continued]

[20] Flammis urar ne succensus,
per te, Virgo, sim defensus
in die iudicii.

[21] Fac me cruce custodiri,
morte Christi praemuniri,
confoveri gratia.

[22] Quando corpus morietur,
fac ut animae donetur
paradisi gloria. Amen.

[14] Grant me truly to weep,
with you bitterly to sigh, to cry:
make me sorrow
with your Crucified One,
till at last I come to die.

[15] Placed next to the cross
with you to stand,
in grief with you to be yoked:
your hand, my hand: for this I long.

[16] When this mortal body of mine
shall come to sentence of death,
grant that to soul of mine
may be given the breath
of glory eternal in Paradise.

[17] Virgin, of all virgins
greatest in renown,
turn thou now not to me
fierce-wrathed in frown;
make me, rather, a sharer in your grief.

[18] To carry that death of Christ,
that death accepted so free:
to share in his cruel passion
grant thou me,
and to bear anew his wounds.

[19] By wounds of his proud marked,
may I drink to its dregs
that cup of the cross so stark,
the blood shed by him
who was and is your Son.

Stabat Mater Dolorosa [concluded]

[20] In flames eternal
 let me not be enfired;
through you, O Virgin, may I find
the safe harbor I have desired
for the dreaded day of judgment divine.

[21] Make me:
by Christ's cross safeguarded,
by Christ's death true warded,
by his grace be cherished lovingly.

[22] When this mortal body of mine
shall come to sentence of death,
grant that to soul of mine may be given
the breath of glory eternal in Paradise.
Amen.

SEPTEMBER 21: SAINT MATTHEW
MORNING PRAYER
Praeclara Qua Tu Gloria / O Levi Most Blessed

Praeclara qua tu gloria,
Levi beate, cingeris,
laus est Dei clementiae,
spes nostra ad indulgentiam.

O Levi most blessed,
the splendid glory that surrounds you
is full-deserved praise
of the mercy of God,
is why we can hope
for forgiveness divine.

Teloneo quando assidens
nummis inhaeres anxius,
Matthaee, Christus advocans
opes tibi quas praeparat!

While you sat at your taxer's table,
how concerned were you,
as you clutched close your coins;
but, O Levi turned Matthew,
what riches sublime
has the Christ who has called you
prepared for you to enjoy!

Iam cordis ardens impetu
curris, Magistrum suscipis,
sermone factus inclito
princeps in urbe caelica.

Already ablaze with desire,
felt deep in your heart,
you run after Him, you choose Him
as your Master, your Teacher supreme.
Now you have become,
by the renowned words of the Lord,
a chieftain exalted
in the heavenly city on high.

Tu verba vitae colligens
Davidque facta Filii,
per scripta linquis aurea
caeleste mundo pabulum.

Christum per orbem nuntians
confessus atque sanguine,
dilectionis vividae
supremo honoras pignore.

You gathered together
the words of eternal life,
gathered too the deeds
of the Son of David;
now through the writings,
precious as gold,
that you have left us
you provide a heavenly food
for the world here below.

O martyr atque apostole,
evangelista nobilis,
tecum fac omne in saeculum
Christo canamus gloriam.
Amen.

[continued]

Praeclara Qua Tu Gloria / O Levi Most Blessed
[concluded]

Christ you made known
throughout the world far and wide;
him you proclaimed as well
by your own blood
in harsh martyrdom shed:
No higher pledge
of shining love possible,
than what you lay down
in ultimate honor of Him.

O martyr and apostle,
evangelist so renowned,
make it be that, for all ages to come,
we may join with you and sing
glorious paeans of praise
to Christ Jesus our Lord.
Amen.

SEPTEMBER 29: SAINTS MICHAEL, GABRIEL, AND RAPHAEL
OFFICE OF READINGS
Festiva Vos, Archangeli / Anchangels Blest, Our Gladsome Songs

Festiva vos, archangeli,
haec nostra tollunt cantica,
quos in superna curia
insignit ingens gloria.

Tu nos, cohortis caelicae
invicte princeps, Michael,
dextra corusca robora
Deique serva gratiae.

Qui nuntius delectus es
mysteriorum maximus,
nos lucis usque, Gabriel,
fac diligamus semitas.

Nobis adesto, Raphael,
ad patriam petentibus
morbos repelle corporum,
affer salutem mentium.

Vosque angelorum candida
nos adiuvetis agmina,
possimus ut consortio
vestro beati perfrui.

Summo Parent*i* et Filio
honor sit ac Paraclito,
quos vester uno praedicat
concentus hymno perpetim.
Amen.

Archangels blest,
these, our gladsome songs,
lift up on high your glorious praises
on this, your festal day;
great indeed is the honor
that marks you
in heaven's grand, exalted court.

To you, O Michael,
unconquerable leader
of the heavenly host,
we pray:
by your sword-flashing right hand
strengthen us,
and preserve us
for God's most gracious grace.

And you, O Gabriel:
chosen were you to be
the greatest revealer
of mysteries sublime.
Make us, we pray,
e'er love the paths
that light marks out for us.

Be present to us, O Raphael,
as we seek our homeward path.
Ward off sickness
from our mortal frames;
bring us health of mind and soul.

[continued]

Festiva Vos, Archangeli / Archangels Blest, Our Gladsome Songs
[concluded]

And all of you,
white-robed hosts of angels above,
come to our aid, we pray,
so that in happiness we may enjoy
your blessed company
for ages without end.

To the Father most high, and to his Son,
to the Spirit blest too
be glory e'er given;
to the Triune God
does angelic song, in harmony blest,
offer praise in hymn, all voices united,
for eons without end. Amen.

SEPTEMBER 29: SAINTS MICHAEL, GABRIEL, AND RAPHAEL
MORNING PRAYER
Tibi, Christe, Splendor Patris / O Christ God, Brilliant Splendor

Tibi, Christe, splendor Patris,
vita, virtus cordium,
in conspectu angelorum
votis, voce psallimus;
alternantes concrepando
melos damus vocibus.

Collaudamus venerantes
inclitos archangelos,
sed praecipue primatem
caelestis exercitus,
Michaelem in virtute
conterentem Satanam.

Quo custode procul pelle,
rex Christe piissime,
omne nefas inimici;
mundos corde et corpore
paradiso redde tuo
nos sola clementia.

Gloriam Patri melodis
personemus vocibus,
gloriam Christo canamus,
gloriam Paraclito,
qui Deus trinus et unus
exstat ante saecula. Amen.

[1] *Prior to the reformation of the liturgical calendar that followed Vatican II, September 29 was the feast of St. Michael the Archangel only, and the present hymn reflects that fact. In the calendar now in use, today's celebration combines the feasts of the Archangels: Michael (today), Gabriel (formerly March 24), and Raphael (formerly October 24).*

It might be of passing interest to note that, traditionally, there are seven archangels: Michael, Gabriel, Raphael, Uriel, Sealtiel, Jehudiel, and Barachiel.

O Christ God, brilliant splendor
of the Father most high,
our life, our hearts' whole strength,
in the sight of the angels
we bring our praise to you
with vows and song.
One after another
we make joyful sound to you,
pouring forth melodious strain.

All the archangels most high
we greatly praise, greatly revere;[1]
but particularly do we sing
of the chieftain of the heavenly host,
Michael, as by his invincible might
he brings down to crushing defeat
Satan, adversary of ours,
enemy of ours.

As Michael stands guard,
drive far from us,
O Christ our King most faithful,
all the awful snares
of the enemy dreadful;
by your mercy's sole power
cleanse us in spirit and body,
restore us
to your land of Paradise on high.

With tuneful voices, let us make
glorious praise resound to the Father,
let us sing equal praise to Christ,
and the same praise
to the Advocate most high:
as Godhead three yet one
have they existed before ages began.
Amen.

SEPTEMBER 29: SAINTS MICHAEL, GABRIEL, AND RAPHAEL
EVENING PRAYER
Angelum Pacis Michael ad Istam / Earnestly We Ask, Christ Jesus

Angelum pacis Michael ad istam,
Christe, demitti rogitamus aulam,
cuncta quo crebro veniente
crescant
prospera nobis.

Earnestly we ask, Christ Jesus our Lord,
that your angel of peace, Michael,
might be sent down
to this hall of ours;
because of his oft-granted presence
among us
may all things be well for us.

Angelus fortis Gabriel, ut hostem
pellat antiquum, volitet superne,
saepius templum cupiens favendo
visere nostrum.

And may your angel Gabriel,
on wings of strength,
descend here from heaven
to put the ancient enemy to flight and,
through a desire sprung
from his gracious favor,
to be present
in our temples and churches
full often.

Angelum nobis medicum salutis
mitte de caelis Raphael, ut omnes
sanet aegrotos pariterque nostros
dirigat actus.

Send to us from heaven on high
your physician angel Raphael,
to cure all who are sick,
and also
to guide our every action.

Christe, sanctorum decus
angelorum,
adsit illorum chorus usque nobis,
ut simul tandem Triadi per aevum
carmina demus.
Amen.

Christ, glory of the holy angels,
let their choirs e'er be present to us,
so that at long last we may,
in company with them,
sing our praises to our Triune God
for ages without end.
Amen.

SEPTEMBER 30: SAINT JEROME
MORNING AND EVENING PRAYER
Festiva Canimus Laude Hieronymum / With Festive Praise We Sing

Festiva canimus laude
Hieronymum,
qui nobis radiat sidus ut eminens
doctrinae meritis ac simul actibus
vitae fortis et asperae.

With festive praise we sing of Jerome,
who, as a blazing star,
stands out in our sight
by what his teaching full deserves
and by the life he led, so brave, so stern.

He strove to peer deeply
into the word of faith,
into doctrine sublime,
and to make it clear and open to all.
But he also, when aroused,
was stern as a lion, and strove
to confound faith's enemies
with o'erpowering voice
and flaming word.

Hic verbum fidei sanctaque
dogmata
scrutando studuit pandere lucide,
aut hostes, vehemens ut leo,
concitus
acri voce refellere.

With labor great, with labor eager
did he cultivate the verdant fields
of Holy Writ,
received from heaven above;
richly provisioned by its words,
he brought forth
the pleasing food of grace
for peoples one and all.

Insudans alacer prata virentia
Scripturae coluit caelitus editae;
ex his et locuples dulcia protulit
cunctis pabula gratiae.

Though he much preferred the
peaceful silence of the desert serene,
he none the less stood guard
o'er Bethlehem town,
the Lord's own cradle site,
so that he too might submit his flesh
to the cross,
and give himself closely to the Father
as gift and offering, as victim free.

Deserti cupiens grata silentia,
ad cunas Domini pervigil astitit,
ut carnem crucians se daret
intime
Patri munus et hostiam.

We beg of you, Lord God most blest:
by the prayers of this magnificent
teacher of ours, guide us, cherish us,
so that we might be allowed to pour
forth our joyous praises to you
for all ages to come. Amen.

Tanti nos, petimus te, Deus
optime,
doctoris precibus dirige, confove,
ut laetas liceat nos tibi in omnia
laudes pangere saecula.
Amen.

OCTOBER 2: HOLY GUARDIAN ANGELS
OFFICE OF READINGS
Aeterne Rerum Conditor / Timeless Creator of All That Is

Aeterne rerum conditor,
qui mare, solum, aethera
gubernas, iustus redditor
cunctis secundum opera,

Timeless Creator of all that is,
you gently rule
ocean, land, and sky above;
and in equity most fair do you reward
your children, one and all,
according to their deeds.

Superbum qui iam spiritum
eiusque cunctos complices
condemnas in interitum
veros firmasti supplices,

The proud one, spirit though he was,
and all his cohorts,
you have now condemned
to perdition, to hell;
but those who call upon you in truth
you have established
firmly in your favor.

Precamur te fidentius,
hos defensores dirige,
nobis per quos propitius
salutis dona porrige.

We cry to you, with confidence great:
guide these defenders
you have given us.
Through them, in your mercy,
grant us the gifts of salvation.

Nos consolando visitent,
purgent, inflamment, doceant,
ad bona semper incitent,
vim daemonum coerceant.

May they come to be with us
and encourage us;
may they cleanse us,
inspire us, instruct us.
May they e'er urge us on to do good,
and may they keep locked in chains
the power of Satan
and his legion of minions.

O angelorum gloria,
securo gressu pergere
fac horum nos custodia,
ut te possimus cernere.

You are the angels' proud boast;
make us go forward
with untroubled step,
with these angels as our guardians,
so that we may eventually arrive
at the vision of your Godhead divine.

Sint, angelorum Domine,
honoris tibi cantica,
qui miro praebes ordine
illis nobisque caelica.
Amen.

Lord, let the angels' songs of praise
ring out to you;
for it is in marvelous manner
that you lavish heavenly gifts
on them and on us. Amen.

OCTOBER 2: HOLY GUARDIAN ANGELS
MORNING PRAYER
Orbis Patrator Optime / O Most Excellent Creator

Orbis patrator optime,
quaecumque sunt qui dextera
magna creasti, nec regis
minore providentia,

O most excellent Creator
of this world of ours,
whatever in any way exists,
you, by the power
of your strong right hand,
have brought into being
and with no less fatherly care
do you rule it, do you guide it.

Adesto supplicantium
tibi reorum coetui,
lucisque sub crepusculum
lucem novam da mentibus.

Be present, we pray,
to the throng of us guilty souls
who cry out unto you,
and at the darkling shadows
of early morn
grant to our spirits
a bright and renewed light.

Tuusque nobis angelus,
signatus ad custodiam,
hic adsit, a contagio
qui criminum nos protegat.

May your angel,
whom you have charged with our care,
be present unto us here,
to protect us from shameful stain of sin.

Nobis draconis aemuli
calumnias exterminet,
ne rete fraudulentiae
incauta nectat pectora.

May that angel bring to naught
the cunning trickery of the dragon,
evil and envious of us,
so that he does not
snare souls unsuspecting
with his net of fraud and deceit.

Metum repellat hostium
nostris procul de finibus;
pacem secundet civium
fugetque pestilentiam.

And may he drive far away from where
we dwell all fear of enemies;
may he foster peace among our people,
and put to full flight all disease,
all pestilence most foul.

Deo Patri sit gloria,
qui, quos redemit Filius
et Sanctus unxit Spiritus,
per angelos custodiat.
Amen.

To God the Father be glory,
so that through his angels on high,
he may guard and protect all those
whom the Son has redeemed,
whom the Holy Spirit has anointed.
Amen.

OCTOBER 2: HOLY GUARDIAN ANGELS
EVENING PRAYER

Custodes Hominum Psallimus Angelos / We Sing the Praises of the Angels

Custodes hominum psallimus
angelos,
naturae fragili quos Pater addidit
caelestis comites, insidiantibus
ne succumberet hostibus.

We sing the praises of the angels,
guardians bestowed
upon the human race,
assigned by Heavenly Father's love
as companion friends of our frail frame,
lest we fall into the treacherous snares
of our dread enemy most foul.

Nam quod corruerit proditor
angelus,
concessis merito pulsus
honoribus,
ardens invidia pellere nititur
quos caelo Deus advocat.

For since the betrayer angel
fell from grace,
rightly bereft of the place
that had been his,
he has been ablaze with envy,
and with hate
has striven to put to frightened flight
those whom God invites
to heaven above.

And so, O guardian ever watchful,
fly quickly to us here below.
Bar from the land entrusted to you
all sickness of soul,
and whatever would hinder
those who dwell herein
from enjoying the calm and peace
that God would give unto them.

Huc, custos, igitur pervigil advola,
avertens patria de tibi credita
tam morbos animi quam
requiescere
quidquid non sinit incolas.

Sanctae sit Triadi laus pia iugiter,
cuius perpetuo numine machina
triplex haec regitur, cuius in omnia
regnat gloria saecula.
Amen.

To the Holy Trinity be given
due praise without end,
for by their godhead unceasing
is our threefold world
of earth, sea, and sky well ruled,
and their glory reigns supreme
for all ages to come.
Amen.

OCTOBER 4: SAINT FRANCIS OF ASSISI
MORNING AND EVENING PRAYERS
In Caelesti Collegio / Amidst His Companions in Heaven

In caelesti collegio
Franciscus fulget gloria,
insigni privilegio
Christi portans insignia.

Amidst his companions in heaven
Francis stands out,
shining, resplendent in glory,
for by priceless privilege does he bear
the wound marks of Christ his Lord.

Hic coetus apostolici
est factus consors pauperis,
crucem in se dominici
signum reportans foederis.

He it was, too, who sought out
a twelvefold band of companions true:
apostolic men, poor men,
as he carried about within himself
the cross of the Lord,
the mark of the Lord's own covenant.

His martyr desiderio
crucem post Christum baiulat,
quem martyrum consortio
Christus in caelis copulat.

A martyr he was, at least in desire,
carrying the cross
behind Christ his Lord; and so now
in heaven has that self-same Lord
admitted him to the fellowship
of that glorious, red-robed band.

Crucem per abstinentiam
Franciscus ferens iugiter,
iam confessorum gloriam
adeptus est feliciter.

By fasts frequent, by fasts untold
did Francis e'er carry
the cross of his Lord.
And so now, in joy beyond measure,
has he taken his glorious place
among confessors young,
confessors old.

Candens decore niveo,
passum hic sequens Dominum,
nunc castitatis praemio
gaudet in choro virginum.

Resplendent in snow-white, beauteous
robe he followed the Lord
who had suffered
where'er he chose to go;
now does he rejoice in chastity's reward
amidst the choir
of sacred virgins on high.

Pater, Natus cum Flamine
nos per Francisci vulnera
lustrent divino lumine,
aeterna dantes munera.
Amen.

May Father, Son, and Spirit blest,
through Francis's holy wounds,
purify us with light divine,
and so grant us heaven's full joy
for ages without end. Amen.

OCTOBER 7: OUR LADY OF THE ROSARY
MORNING AND EVENING PRAYERS
Te Gestientem Gaudiis / In Transport with Ecstatic Joys

Te gestientem gaudiis,
te sauciam doloribus,
te iugi amictam gloria,
o Virgo Mater, pangimus.

In transport with ecstatic joys,
yet gashed by sorrows
sharp and profound,
but still, robed in glory without end:
as all of these, O Virgin Mother,
we portray you here today.

Ave, redundans gaudio
dum concipis, dum visitas,
et edis, offers, invenis,
mater beata, Filium.

Hail, O joyful Mary!
you are filled to o'erbrimming
with gladness as you conceive
your child, as you visit your cousin,
as, O Blessed Mother,
you bring him forth,
you bring him to the temple,
you find him in the temple,
him: your sacred Son divine.

Ave, dolens et intimo
in corde agonem, verbera,
spinas crucemque Filii
perpessa, princeps martyrum.

Ave, in triumphis Filii,
in ignibus Paracliti,
in regni honore et lumine
regina fulgens gloria.

Hail, O sorrowful Mary!
Sore aggrieved, you endured bravely
within the depths of your heart
the agony, the blows, the thorns,
the cross of your Son: and in his death
you became the sovereign
of all martyrs fair.

Venite, gentes, carpite
ex his rosas mysteriis,
et pulchri amoris inclitae
matri coronas nectite.

Hail, O glorious Mary!
You shine forth in queenly glory amidst
the rising and ascending triumphs
of your Son,
the fiery tongues of the Spirit,
the resplendent beauty
to which you rose up in assuming
your regal rule of the kingdom on high.

Iesu, tibi sit gloria,
qui natus es de Virgine,
cum Patre et almo Spiritu,
in sempiterna saecula.
Amen.

[continued]

Te Gestientem Gaudiis / In Transport with Ecstatic Joys
[concluded]

Come then, O nations!
From these thorned mysteries
reap roses full and fair;
for the regal mother
weave together crowns
of beauty and of love.

Jesus, may glory be given to you,
for you were born of the Virgin holy;
glory too be given to the Father
and the Spirit blest
for ages without pause or end. Amen.

OCTOBER 15: SAINT TERESA OF AVILA
MORNING PRAYER
Regis Superni Nuntia / From Your Father's House You Steal Away

Regis superni nuntia
domum paternam deseris,
terris, Teresa, barbaris
Christum datura aut sanguinem.

From your father's house
you steal away, O Teresa;
a herald of heaven's king would you be;
to pagan lands would you bring
either the good news of Christ,
or else your own blood,
martyr-shed instead.

Sed te manet suavior
mors, poena poscit dulcior:
divini amoris cuspide
in vulnus icta concides.

But a gentler death is to be yours;
sufferings of a kindlier sort
summon you.
You will be struck
by the dart-point of divine love,
and you will fall headlong
into the wound
that will all-engulf you.

O caritatis victima,
tu corda nostra concrema,
tibique gentes creditas
inferni ab igne libera.

You are love's fair victim,
its sacrifice most fair.
Our hearts then, too, set full aflame.
Rescue from the fires of hell most foul
the peoples far and near
that are entrusted to your patronal care.

Te, sponse, Iesu, virginum,
beati adorent ordines,
et nuptiali cantico
laudent per omne saeculum.
Amen.

To you, O Jesus, spouse of virgins blest,
may the massed array of holy choirs
bring their full adoring worship,
and with bridal song bright and clear
sing your praises for ages without end.
Amen.

OCTOBER 15: SAINT THERESA OF AVILA
EVENING PRAYER
Haec Est Dies, Qua Candidae / This Is the Day

Haec est dies, qua candidae
instar columbae, caelitum
ad sacra templa spiritus
se transtulit Teresiae,

This is the day,
when like a bright-shining dove,
Teresa's soul took heavenward flight
to the sacred lands on high.

Sponsique voces audiit:
"Veni, soror, de vertice
Carmeli ad Agni nuptias;
veni ad coronam gloriae."

She heard the words of her Beloved
ringing out clear:
"Come, my sister, from Mt. Carmel's top
to the wedding feast of the Lamb;
come, receive your crown of glory!"

Te, sponse, Iesu, virginum,
beati adorent ordines,
et nuptiali cantico
laudent per omne saeculum.
Amen.

To you, O Jesus, spouse of virgins blest,
may the massed array of holy choirs
bring their full adoring worship,
and with bridal songs bright and clear
sing your praises for ages without end.
Amen.

OCTOBER 18: SAINT LUKE
OFFICE OF READINGS
O Vir Beate, Apostolis / O Blessed Man, Companion of the Apostles
[see page 206]

MORNING AND EVENING PRAYERS
Plausibus, Luca, Canimus Triumphum / With Much Applause

Plausibus, Luca, canimus triumphum quo nites fuso rutilo cruore, atque praecelsis meritis adeptam rite coronam.	With much applause, O great St. Luke, do we sing of the triumph you have achieved; renowned full well are you therein by your life-blood: stark, and red, and shed. We sing as well of the heavenly crown that your matchless merits have now achieved.
Spiritus ductu, studiosus orbi mira quae pastor docuit supernus Christus ac fecit miserans amore, tradis amanter.	Led on by the Spirit, in your zeal for this world you gave to it, in loving script, the marvelous teachings which Christ, supreme Shepherd of all, handed down, and the marvelous deeds he did for us all, in his love so great, in his mercy so fair.
Providus chartis perhibes venustis gesta quae Iesu celebrant alumnos, eius et gentis nova quae patescunt in nova saecla.	Wisely, indeed, do you recount, from pages already written, the events that honor the disciples of Jesus: and new events as well, events of his people that would become known for ages to come.
O comes Pauli, speculator alti cordis illius sed et aemulator, caritas Christi fac ut usque nostrum pectus adurat.	O companion of Paul, you closely observed the depths of his great soul, and you imitated it as well: make it be that the love of Christ may e'er set on fire our spirits as well.
Tu malis nostris medicus fer artem, confer et laetum fidei levamen, ut Deo tandem potiamur, ipsi semper ovantes. Amen.	Physician most kind, bring your healing art to cure the ills that we suffer; bring us the blessed balm that the true faith provides, so that we ourselves may one day possess God our Father, and rejoice in Him without measure or end. Amen.

OCTOBER 28: SAINTS SIMON AND JUDE
MORNING PRAYER
Commune Vos, Apostoli / Let It Be a Shared Song of Praise

Commune vos, apostoli,
extollat hymni iubilum,
quos advocat par gratia,
coronat una gloria.

Let it be a shared song of praise
that lifts up your names on high,
O apostolic pair:
equal were the graces
given to summon you,
equal the glorious crown
appointed to reward you.

Ardore pulsus caelico,
Christi premis vestigia,
Simon, et illum nuntias
zelo peractus impigro.

Driven on, O Simon,
by a fervor sent from heaven,
you follow closely
in the footsteps of Christ;
inspired by unwearied zeal,
you proclaim to all
the good news of the Lord.

Tu carne frater, assecla
fraterque Christi spiritu,
Iuda, Magistrum praedicas
scriptisque fratres erudis.

Nec pertimescit sanguinem
uterque purum fundere,
ut veritatis enitens
sit testis atque victima.

A brother are you, O Jude,
by natural birth;
a brother in spirit of Christ are you,
and his faithful follower as well.
You proclaim
your Master's words and deeds,
and by what you wrote
you instruct all your brethren as well.

O summa caeli sidera,
nos detis ut per aspera,
fide valentes integra,
tendamus ad caelestia.

Patri per aevum gloria
Natoque cum Paraclito,
quorum supernis gaudiis
simul fruemur perpetim.
Amen.

Nor does either of you fear
to pour out your most holy blood;
and thus do you strive
to be truth's witnesses,
and the sacrificial victims
it claims as well.

[continued]

Commune Vos, Apostoli / Let It Be a Shared Song of Praise
[concluded]

You are the great glories
of high heaven above;
grant to us that,
through hardships dire,
we may be able, with faith unsullied fair,
to wend our way safely
to our eternal home.

Through ages endless let glory be given
to the Father, and to the Son as well,
in company with the Advocate blessed;
in their company may we share
their eternal happiness for ages without
end. Amen.

NOVEMBER 1: ALL SAINTS
EVENING PRAYER I AND II
Christe, Redemptor Omnium / Christ Lord, Redeemer of All

Christe, Redemptor omnium,
conserva tuos famulos,
beatae semper Virginis
placatus sanctis precibus.

Christ Lord, Redeemer of all,
each and every one,
be pleased with the holy prayers
of Mary, ever the Virgin pure,
and keep each of us, your servants,
safe from every harm.

Beata quoque agmina
caelestium spirituum,
praeterita, praesentia,
futura mala pellite.

And you as well,
O serried and blessed ranks
of spirits celestial,
keep far from us all evil:
past, present, and yet to be.

Vates aeterni iudicis
apostolique Domini,
suppliciter exposcimus
salvari vestris precibus.

You prophets of the eternal Judge,
and you apostles of the Lord,
humbly do we make our plea to you
to be kept sound, safe,
by your holy prayers.

Martyres Dei incliti
confessoresque lucidi,
vestris orationibus
nos ferte in caelestibus.

You glorious martyrs
of our glorious Lord,
you confessors shining bright,
by your holy prayers,
be our guides into our heavenly home.

Chori sanctarum virginum
monachorumque omnium,
simul cum sanctis omnibus
consortes Christi facite.

You choirs of virgins most holy,
choirs too of religious one and all,
make us too be companions of Christ,
in company with all your fellow saints.

Sit Trinitati gloria,
vestrasque voces iungite
ut illi laudes debitas
persolvamus alacriter.
Amen.

Let all glory be given to the Holy Trinity!
O all you saints,
join your voices together with ours,
so that we may joyfully sing
the praises we owe
to our Triune God.
Amen.

NOVEMBER 1: ALL SAINTS
OFFICE OF READINGS
Christe, Caelorum Habitator Alme / Christ, Most Kindly Dweller

Christe, caelorum habitator alme,
vita sanctorum, via, spes
salusque,
hostiam clemens, tibi quam
litamus,
suscipe laudis.

Christ, most kindly dweller
in the heavens above,
life of your saints, way to the Father,
hope that is ours, salvation of all:
in your great mercy,
accept the offering of praise
which we humbly bring
in full sacrifice to you.

Omnium semper chorus
angelorum
in polo temet benedicit alto,
atque te sancti simul universi
laudibus ornant.

The choir of all the angels
blesses you endlessly
in high heaven above;
in harmony with them,
all of your saints together
heap high praise upon you.

Virginis sanctae meritis Mariae
atque cunctorum pariter piorum,
contine poenam, pie, quam
meremur
daque medelam.

Through the merits of Mary, Virgin blest
and of all the holy ones as well,
revoke the punishment,
O Faithful One,
which we have earned;
grant us your gracious healing instead.

Hic tuam praesta celebrare
laudem,
ut tibi fidi valeamus illam
prosequi in caelis Triadi canentes
iugiter hymnos.
Amen.

Grant that we may proclaim
your praise here below,
so that, in full faithfulness to you,
we may continue it in the heavens,
endlessly singing songs of glory
to the Trinity on high.
Amen.

NOVEMBER 1: ALL SAINTS
MORNING PRAYER
Iesu, Salvator Saeculi / Jesus, Gracious Savior of All That Is

Iesu, salvator saeculi,
redemptis ope subveni,
et, pia Dei genetrix,
salutem posce miseris.

Jesus, gracious savior of all that is,
with all your mighty power
come to the aid
of those you have redeemed.
And you, too, O loving Mother of God,
beg that we wretched humans
may enjoy safe-haven's boon.

Coetus omnes angelici
patriarchum cunei
ac prophetarum merita
nobis precentur veniam.

All the serried ranks of angels,
all the patriarchs,
formed up in battle array,
all the prophets,
showing their merits so fair:
may they, one and all,
beg forgiveness for us.

Baptista tui praevius
et claviger aethereus
cum ceteris apostolis
nos solvant nexu criminis.

Chorus sacratus martyrum,
sacerdotum confessio
et virginalis castitas
nos a peccatis abluant.

The Baptist who foretold you,
the heavenly guardian
of the keys of the kingdom,
and all the other apostles as well:
may they win for us freedom full
from transgression's tangled toils.

Monachorum suffragia
omnesque cives caelici
annuant votis supplicum
et vitae poscant praemium.

The sacred choir of martyrs,
the ranks of holy priests
who proclaim God in voices so clear,
the throng of virgins most chaste:
may they, one and all, wash us clean
from the stain of sin.

Sit, Christe, tibi gloria
cum Patre et Sancto Spiritu,
quorum luce mirifica
sancti congaudent perpetim.
Amen.

[continued]

Iesu, Salvator Saeculi / Jesus, Gracious Savior of All That Is
[concluded]

May the prayers of those vowed souls,
vowed men, vowed women,
may, indeed, each and every denizen
of high heaven above
grant ear to our plea
as we call upon them;
may they beg for us
the reward of everlasting life.

O Christ, to you be lasting praise,
with the Father and the Spirit blest,
in whose radiant light
the saints rejoice for time unending.
Amen.

NOVEMBER 11: SAINT MARTIN OF TOURS
OFFICE OF READINGS AND EVENING PRAYER
Iste Confessor Domini Sacratus / This Man Is a Confessor

Iste confessor Domini sacratus,
festa plebs cuius celebrat per
orbem,
hodie laetus meruit secreta
scandere caeli.

Qui pius, prudens, humilis,
pudicus,
sobrius, castus fuit et quietus,
vita dum praesens vegetavit
eius
corporis artus.

Ad sacrum cuius tumulum
frequenter
membra languentum modo
sanitati,
quolibet morbo fuerint gravati,
restituuntur.

Unde nunc noster chorus in
honorem
ipsius, hymnum canit hunc
libenter,
ut piis eius meritis iuvemur
omne per aevum.

Sit salus illi, decus atque virtus,
qui supra caeli residens
cacumen,
totius mundi machinam
gubernat
trinus et unus.
Amen.

This man is a confessor
who is sacred to the Lord;
throughout the whole world
do faithful throngs
celebrate his festal day,
for today has he deserved, in fullest joy,
to ascend on high
to heaven's secluded groves.

Dutiful was he, wise, humble, undefiled;
temperate too,
chaste and peaceable as well,
while mortal life here on earth
quickened his bodily limbs.

At his holy tomb,
the bodies of those who suffer
are oft now restored
to full, perfect health,
whatever the disease
that held them in thrall.

And so now our chorus
willingly sings a hymn in his honor,
chanting joyful hymn to him gladly,
so that we may be aided
by his merits so many
for every age that is yet to come.

Let saving power, let glory and strength
as well be given to Him
who is enthroned
above the heights of high heaven
and governs the workings
of the entire world:
to Him, who is Three and yet One.
Amen.

NOVEMBER 11: SAINT MARTIN OF TOURS
MORNING PRAYER
Martine, Par Apostolis / Martin, Counterpart Are You

Martine, par apostolis,
festum colentes tu fove;
qui vivere discipulis
aut mori vis, nos respice.

Martin, counterpart are you,
in stature so high,
with the very apostles of the Lord;
look now with love and care
on those who celebrate your festal day.
In your sight, the choice was equal:
to live on, in behalf of your brothers,
or to die and be with Christ:
look now upon us, we pray.

Fac nunc quod olim gesseras,
nunc praesules clarifica,
auge decus Ecclesiae,
fraudes relide Satanae.

Do now what you did of old:
exalt Holy Church's leaders,
build up the honor of the Church,
beat back the snares that Satan sets.

Qui ter chaos evisceras,
mersos reatu suscita;
diviseras ut chlamydem,
nos indue iustitiam.

A three-time foiler are you of death
spawned by
the darkling kingdom below;
restore now those
whom damning guilt buries deep.
You divided your cloak with the beggar,
to clothe him from the cold;
clothe us now
with justice's garment fair.

Ut specialis gloriae
quondam tuae memineris,
pontificum nunc ordini
pio favore subveni.

As once you bore in mind
the special glory granted unto you,
now, with faithful succor,
come to the aid of those
who like you bear the shepherd's staff.

Sit Trinitati gloria,
Martinus ut confessus est,
eius fidem qui iugiter
in nos per actus inserat.
Amen.

To the Trinity be endless glory,
as great St. Martin did proclaim,
Martin: may he constantly implant in us
by what he was and did,
firmest faith in God one and three.
Amen.

NOVEMBER 18: DEDICATION OF THE BASILICAS OF SAINTS PETER AND PAUL
MORNING PRAYER
Iam, Bone Pasto, Petre / Goodly Shepherd, Peter Most Blest

Iam, bone pastor, Petre,
clemens accipe vota precantum,
et peccati vincula resolve,
tibi potestate tradita,
qua cunctis caelum
verbo claudis, aperis.

Goodly shepherd, Peter most blest,
in your mercy receive now the prayers
of those who call upon you,
and loose the bonds of their sins
by the power you have been given,
that power which you use,
at your sole command,
to close or open
the gates of heaven for all.

Doctor egregie, Paule,
mores instrue et mente polum
nos transferre satage,
donec perfectum
largiatur plenius,
evacuato quod
ex parte gerimus.

And you, teacher most renowned,
Paul the great,
show us how we should live on earth;
strive to transport us to heaven
in our thoughts at least,
until that which is perfect
be accorded us in full measure,
and that which we have
but imperfectly achieved
be banished far away.

Sit Trinitati sempiterna gloria,
honor, potestas, atque iubilatio,
in unitate,
cui manet imperium
ex tunc et modo
per aeterna saecula.
Amen.

Let glory everlasting,
honor, might, and all joy as well
be given the Trinity on high,
in its triune oneness;
kingly power be to our God
now and for all ages to come.
Amen.

NOVEMBER 21: PRESENTATION OF THE BLESSED VIRGIN MARY
OFFICE OF READINGS
Salve, Mater Misericordiae / O Mother, Whence Mercy Springs

Salve, mater misericordiae,
mater spei et mater veniae,
mater Dei et mater gratiae,
mater plena sanctae laetitiae.
(O Maria.)

O mother, whence mercy springs,
O mother, source of hope,
source of forgiveness blest,
O mother, from whom God took flesh,
in whom grace found
its surging channel,
O mother, flowing over with holiest joy:
O Mary!

Vallis vernans virtutum liliis,
tota fluens summis deliciis,
mater sancta, tuis suffragiis
condescende nostris miseriis.
(O Maria.)

A valley are you, spring-blooming
with fairest lilies
that are your many virtues;
you are all o'erbrimming
with sublimest delights.
O mother most holy,
with your powerful help,
come down and heal all the ailments
that so sorely beset us.
O Mary!

Te creavit Pater ingenitus,
obumbravit te Unigenitus,
fecundavit te Sanctus Spiritus;
ipsis honor ex corde penitus.
(O Maria.)

The unbegotten Father created you,
The sole-begotten One
overshadowed you,
The Holy Spirit made you fruitful:
to them be lasting honor
from deepest place within our hearts.
O Mary!

NOVEMBER 21: PRESENTATION OF THE BLESSED VIRGIN MARY
MORNING PRAYER
Maria, Virgo Regia / Mary, Regal Virgin

Maria, virgo regia,
sponsa regis et filia,
te Dei sapientia
elegit ante saecula.

Mary, regal virgin, betrothed to a King,
and yet his child as well,
the wisdom of God most high
selected you
before e'er the ages began.

Puella carens macula,
Dei domus eburnea,
te dedicavit caelitus
missus ab eo Spiritus.

A girl-child were you,
with no hint of stain,
God's own abode, made of ivory fair;
God's Holy Spirit, sent down
from Trinity's realm in heaven above,
set you apart
for your glorious role to come.

Caritatis signaculum,
totius boni speculum,
aurora veri luminis,
arca divini seminis,

Symbol of charity itself are you,
a mirror imaging forth
every possible good;
you are true light's bright dawn,
the chosen treasure chest,
guarding well
the child, human and divine.

In domo summi principis
tu affluis deliciis;
virga Jesse florigera,
repleris Dei gratia.

In the palace of the King of Kings
you now abound in delights full fair.
Jesse's own rod you are,
full flower forging;
you are filled with the grace of God.

O margarita candida
et stella mundi splendida,
fac puris esse moribus
nos vera templa Spiritus.

O gleaming pearl of price untold,
most glorious star
shining bright on our world below,
make us be pure in thought and deed
and so be true temples
of the Spirit blest.

Sit Trinitati gloria,
o Virgo nobilissima,
quae te suorum munerum
thesaurum dat magnificum.
Amen.

To the holy Trinity be all glory given,
O Virgin most renowned,
for God has given us you yourself
as treasure-house resplendent
of all his glorious gifts.
Amen.

NOVEMBER 30: SAINT ANDREW
MORNING PRAYER
Captator Olim Piscium / Once You Were a Fisherman

Captator olim piscium,
iam nunc piscator hominum,
tuis, Andrea, retibus
mundi nos rape fluctibus.

Once were you a fisherman, and now,
a fisher of men: in your net, O Andrew,
catch us up safe
from the world's surging waves.

Peter's brother you were, when still
in living flesh, nor unlike to him
in the way that you died:

Germanus Petri corpore
nec mortis dispar ordine;
quos una caro genuit,
crux caelo fratres edidit.

those whom the same womb bore,
the cross raises up, as brothers still,
to high heaven above.

O brother-born, offshoot
most renowned, full equal to his

O germen venerabile,
o par corona gloriae!
Ecclesiae patres pii
crucis sunt aeque filii.

is the crown of glory given to you.
Fathers most faithful of Christ's
holy Church, sons just as faithful
of Christ's holy cross.

Ad Iesum fratri praevius
indexque vitae strenuus,
et nobis esto miseris
beati dux itineris.

For your brother you led
the way to Jesus; insistent,
you pointed out the road to life.
Be for us poor souls as well
faithful guide of happy journey.

Companion outstanding
to your brother beloved,

Fratris comes egregius,
Ecclesias impensius
da caritate exercitas
pastori Petro subditas.

grant that the churches
may strive even harder
to be ever more fervently
submissive to Peter,
their shepherd true.

Vir Christo dilectissime,
amore fac nos currere,
ut laeti adepti patriam
Deo canamus gloriam.
Amen.

Man beloved of Christ, make us too
run along our path with love,
so that we may joyfully come
to our homeland and then sing
hymns of glory to God on high. Amen.

DECEMBER 7: SAINT AMBROSE
MORNING PRAYER
Fortem Piumque Praesulem / Let a Brave and Faithful Bishop

Fortem piumque praesulem
canamus omnes, turbidas
qui fluctuantis saeculi
terris procellas expulit.

Let a brave and faithful bishop
be the theme of the song
we all sing today;
he it was who set at rest
the raging storms
that marked the roiling age
in the days when he lived on earth.

Non sceptra concussus timet,
non imperantem feminam,
temploque, clausis postibus,
arcet cruentum caesarem.

Though by royal scepter beaten,
he showed no fear;
nor did he yield
to an empress's demands.
He kept a blood-stained emperor
away from the church,
closing firm the doors
with full righteous force.

Arcana sacrae paginae
altus magister explicat;
divina pandens dogmata,
mira nitet facundia.

Fide ciente spiritum,
praeclara fundit carmina;
fide coaequans martyres,
deprendit artus martyrum.

Of teachers the finest,
he makes clear the hidden secrets
of scripture's sacred pages;
Holy Church's sacred teachings
he makes plain,
and outstrips all with his eloquent word.

Iam nunc furentem tartari
lupum flagello submove;
scientiae nos lumine
fove, tuere iugiter.

Sit Trinitati gloria,
quam, te rogante prospere,
hymnis in aula caelica
laudemus usque in saeculum.
Amen.

Faith sets his heart on fire,
and so he pours out beauty
in everything he writes;
In faith too he is the equal
of the martyrs, and discovers
the strengths that are theirs.
[continued]

Fortem Piumque Praesulem / Let a Brave and Faithful Bishop
[concluded]

Now, holy Ambrose,
with flashing whip put to flight
the wolf-hound of hell
as he rages about.
But guard us, protect us forever,
with your mind's e'er brilliant lore.

To the Sacred Trinity be great glory!
And, O saint most renowned,
with our hymns may we,
by dint of your powerful prayer,
praise God one-in-three forever
in the holy halls of heaven on high.
Amen.

DECEMBER 8: IMMACULATE CONCEPTION
EVENING PRAYER I AND II
Praeclara Custos Virginum / Most Splendid Patron of Virgins Blest

Praeclara custos virginum
Deique mater innuba,
caelestis aulae ianua,
spes nostra, caeli gaudium;

Most splendid patron of virgins blest,
Mother of God, wife of man
yet knowing not man,
doorway to the celestial courts on high,
our great hope,
joy of the heavens above;

Inter rubeta lilium,
columba formosissima,
e stirpe virga germinans
nostro medelam vulneri;

Midst the thorn-thickets, a lily most fair;
a dove, most beautiful to behold;
a rod from Jesse's line, blooming forth,
providing powerful potion
for the wound that is ours;

Turris draco*ni* impervia,
amica stella naufragis,
defende nos a fraudibus
tuaque luce dirige.

Tower of strength,
unthreatenable by the dragon himself,
shining star, in friendship guiding
sailor by shipwreck bereft:
defend us, too,
from the evil one's deceits;
guide us, too,
with your most blessed light.

Erroris umbras discute,
syrtes dolosas amove,
fluctus tot inter, deviis
tutam reclude semitam.

Quae labe nostrae originis
intacta splendes unica,
serpentis artes aemuli
elude vindex inclita.

Scatter the shadows where error lurks;
take away the rocks
of sandy ocean bank
that cause such groaning grief.
In the midst of waves so many, so high,
show forth safe passage to us
who wander about
in places we know not.

Patri sit et Paraclito
tuoque Nato gloria,
qui sanctitatis unicae
te munerarunt gratia.
Amen.

[continued]

Praeclara Custos Virginum / Most Splendid Patron of Virgins Blest
[concluded]

Only you shine forth untouched
by the fall we suffered
when yet our race was still new.
Most beauteous defender,
make mocking sport
of the envious serpent's sinister snares.

To the Father, and to the Advocate blest,
to your Son as well: be glory given,
for they have gifted you
with the grace of a holiness
that none can match.
Amen.

DECEMBER 8: IMMACULATE CONCEPTION
OFFICE OF READINGS
Te Dicimus Praeconio / We Call Upon You with Hymns of Praise

Te dicimus praeconio,
mater Dei purissima;
nostris benigna laudibus
tuam repende gratiam.

We call upon you with hymns of praise,
O Mother of God, pure and undefiled;
in your kindness, grant your powerful
favor in return for the songs we sing
unto you.

Sontes Adami posteri,
infecta proles gignimur;
labis paternae nescia
tu sola, Virgo, crederis.

Children of Adam are we, guilt-born;
as offspring bereft do we enter the
world. We know by faith, O Virgin blest,
that you are the only one
untouched by our ancestral stain.

Caput draconis invidi
tu conteris vestigio,
gerisque sola gloriam
intaminatae originis.

The head of the envious dragon
you crush with your heel:
you alone rightly bear
the glory of a birth unsullied and fair.

You are the glory of our race;
you take away the shame-shadow
that mother Eve so sorrowingly bore.
Keep us safe as we call upon you;
raise us up when we slip and fall.

Nostrae decus propaginis,
quae tollis *Evae* opprobrium,
tu nos tuere supplices,
tu nos labantes erige.

Serpentis antiqui potens
astus retunde et impetus,
ut caelitum perennibus
per te fruamur gaudiis.

In your great power, turn aside
the cunning of the ancient serpent;
ward off from us his attacks so dire,
so that at length, by your petition,
we may know the everlasting joys
that heaven accords.

To the Father, and to the Advocate blest,
to your Son as well be glory given,
for they have gifted you with the grace
of a holiness that none can match.
Amen.

Patri sit et Paraclito
tuoque Nato gloria,
qui sanctitatis unicae
te munuerarunt gratia.
Amen.

DECEMBER 8: IMMACULATE CONCEPTION
MORNING PRAYER
In Plausu Grati Carminis / In Grateful Song Let Us Sound Our Applause

In plausu grati carminis
adsit nova laetitia,
dum Dei matris Virginis
sumit vita principia.

In grateful song
let us sound our applause
at now a new source of joy,
as the life of God's Virgin Mother
takes its beginning.

Maria, mundi gloria,
lucis aeternae filia,
te praeservavit Filius
ab omni labe penitus.

Mary, the great glory of our world,
daughter of light unending:
your Son has sheltered you completely
from every speck of stain.

Humankind's primal blot
has besmeared each and every age;
you alone do we vaunt to be
untouched by sin
from e'er first you came forth
from your mother's womb.

Originalis macula
cuncta respersit saecula;
sola post natum vitiis
numquam contacta diceris.

Caput serpentis callidi
tuo pede conteritur;
fastus gigantis perfidi
David funda devincitur.

The head of the canny serpent
you crush underfoot
with the step of your heel;
the arrogance of a treacherous giant
is cut down by the sling-stone
of David's royal line.

Columba mitis, humilis,
fers, carens felle criminis,
signum Dei clementiae,
ramum virentis gratiae.

Dove most meek, dove most humble,
spared the poison of sin's grim guilt,
you bear the symbol of God's mercy,
you bear the branch of vibrant grace.

To the Father, and to the Advocate blest,
to your Son as well: be glory given,
for they have gifted you with the grace
of a holiness that none can match.
Amen.

Patri sit et Paraclito
tuoque Nato gloria,
qui sanctitatis unicae
te munerarunt gratia.
Amen.

DECEMBER 26: SAINT STEPHEN
OFFICE OF READINGS
Festum Celebre Martyris / Let Us Celebrate in Fitting Fashion

Festum celebre martyris
digne colamus Stephani,
qui primus in certamine
palma nitet victoriae.

Let us celebrate in fitting fashion
the glorious feast
of St. Stephen the Martyr.
He was the first
to conquer in the struggle,
the first to emerge radiant,
holding fast to the victor's crown.

Martyr fidelis, comminus
falsis renitens testibus,
Iesu videbat gloriam,
stantis Patris ad dexteram.

Faithful martyr, in verbal combat,
hand to hand, did he battle
against witnesses many and untrue;
his it was to see
the glory of Jesus himself,
standing by the right hand
of his Father on high.

Nunc te precamur, inclite,
succurre, martyr, concite;
nobis rogatus impetra
caeli ut patescat regia.

Now do we call upon you,
holy saint so blest:
aid us, O martyr;
bestir our spirits full well.
In answer to our prayers,
obtain for us the grace
that the heavens
may open for us as well.

Lotus cruoris flumine,
splendescis alto lumine;
nostri memor nunc supplica
tecum fruamur gloria.

Washed in the flow of your own blood,
you shine forth with a heavenly light.
Be mindful of us now
and beg that, with you,
we too may enjoy glory that never ends.

May the Child, born of the Virgin,
in his favoring mercy,
grant us these boons:
that Child who,

Praestet favens haec munera
natus Puer de Virgine,
cum Patre et almo Spiritu
regnans per omne saeculum.
Amen.

with the Father and the benign Spirit,
rules for ages everlasting. Amen.

DECEMBER 26: SAINT STEPHEN
MORNING PRAYER
Christus Est Vita Veniens / Christ Is the True Life That Comes

Christus est vita veniens in
orbem,
qui ferens vulnus removensque
mortem,
ad Patris dextram repetendo,
regnat
sede superna.

Christ is the true life that comes
into this world; He bears our wounds,
and takes away the death
that we have earned.
Now has he reclaimed once more
his seat at the Father's right hand;
he reigns from his throne
in great heaven above.

Hunc sequens primus Stephanus
minister
sortis illatae titulo est decorus,
quam dedit spirans Domini
benignus
Spiritus illi.

The first to follow him heavenward
is Stephen, his deacon. Truly worthy
is he of the protomartyr's name,
a name which the death that was his
imposed on him, but also a death
which, with kindly breath,
the Spirit of the Lord assigned unto him.

Saxeo nimbo lapidatus instat,
sustinet mortis rabiem profanam,
hostibus quaerit veniam misertus
pectore grato.

Under a shower of stones does he
stand firm, murdered by men;
an unholy madness does he witness
at the time of his death.
But he has pity and, with a heart
well pleasing to the Lord, begs
full forgiveness for his frenzied foes.

Quaesumus flentes, benedicte
prime
martyr et civis sociate iustis:
caelitus, clarae regionis heres,
mitte favores.

O first of the martyrs, blessed soul
sublime, fellow-citizen of heaven's
denizens, you have inherited
the realms of happiness:
we come with tearful petition: grant us
your favors from high heaven above.

Gloriae laudes Triadi beatae
martyrum laeti comites canamus,
quae dedit primas Stephano ex
agone
ferre coronas.
Amen.

May we, as joyous companions
of the martyrs above, sing glorious
praises to our triune God blest;
For God it was, three-in-one, who
granted the first palm of the martyrs'
struggles to Stephen:
Saint and Protomartyr,
Amen.

DECEMBER 27: SAINT JOHN THE EVANGELIST
OFFICE OF READINGS
Virginis Virgo Venerande Custos / A Chaste Young Man

Virginis virgo venerande custos,
praeco qui Verbi coleris fidelis,
terge servorum facinus tuorum,
sancte Ioannes.

A chaste young man,
much to be admired,
guardian of the chaste Virgin blest:
we honor you,
O faithful herald of the Word,
and we beg you, John the blessed:
wipe away the sin-guilt
that stains your faithful followers.

Fonte prorumpens fluvius perenni
curris, arentis satiator orbis;
hausit ex pleno, modo qui
propinat,
pectore pectus.

As a river, bursting forth from an
endless spring, you hasten to refresh
a world that has become sere,
a world become dry.
What is itself now a font has drunk
from the Christ-font's full bounty;
and now provides that others
may abundantly drink.

Tu, decus mundi iubar atque caeli
impetra nostris veniam ruinis;
da sacramentum penetrare
summum,
quod docuisti.

Ornament of the world,
splendor of high heaven as well,
beg forgiveness for our failures:
grant that we may begin to enter upon
the supreme mystery,
which you have taught.

Patris arcanum speculando
Verbum
gratiam fundis fidei per orbem;
nos ad aeternam speciem
fruendam,
dux bone, transfer.

By probing the depths
of the hidden Word of the Father,
you pour out the grace of faith
throughout the whole world;
most excellent leader, bring us, too,
to the enjoyment
of everlasting splendor.

Sit decus summo sine fine
Christo,
sancta quem virgo genuit Maria,
qui Patri compar Flaminique
Sancto
regnat in aevum.
Amen.

Let glory be given without ceasing
to Christ our Lord on high,
whom the holy Virgin Mary brought to
birth, and who, alike with the Father
and the Holy Spirit, lives and reigns
for ages without end. Amen.

DECEMBER 27: SAINT JOHN THE EVANGELIST
MORNING PRAYER

Cohors Beata Seraphim / Let the Blessed Choir of Seraphim Chant

Cohors beata Seraphim,
quem Christus arcte diligit
laudet, chorusque canticis
noster resultet aemulis.

Let the blessed choir of Seraphim
chant aloud the praise of the one
whom Christ so dearly loved;
and let us, in chorus responding,
sing loudly forth
in rivaling strains of laud.

Hic discit, almus edocet
hic unde Verbum prodeat,
sinumque matris impleat,
sinum Patris non deserens.

He first comes to learn;
then it is also he who nourishes and
teaches us whence the Word has come,
how he filled his mother's womb,
but did not leave the embrace
of his heavenly Father.

Felix Ioannes, deligit
et te Magister, providus,
ut clara Thabor lumina
hortique cernas taedia.

Blessed St. John, in his foreknowing
care the Lord chose you to witness
the blazing light on Thabor's
bright mount, and the heart-strickening
grief in the garden so grim.

Tu, raptus in sublimia,
arcana caeli conspicis,
Agni sed et mysteria
Ecclesiaeque percipis.

Taken up into highest heights above,
you view the apocalyptic mysteries
in bright heaven concealed;
but yours to see as well
are the mysteries of the Lamb
and of the Church on earth below.

O digne fili Virgine,
successor alti nominis,
nos adde Matri filios,
nos conde Christi in pectore.

O son, full worthy to be entrusted
with the Virgin's care,
bearer not the first of a noble name,
unite us as sons with your Mother blest;
place us next to Christ's own breast.

Verbo sit ingens gloria,
caro quod est et creditur,
cum Patre et almo Spiritu
in sempiterna saecula.
Amen.

To the Word be great glory, the Word
which is flesh, in whom is our faith,
with the Father and the blessed Spirit
for ages without end. Amen.

DECEMBER 28: HOLY INNOCENTS
OFFICE OF READINGS
Hymnum Canentes Martyrum / Let Us Proclaim in Song

Hymnum canentes martyrum
dicamus Innocentium,
quos terra deflens perdidit,
gaudens sed aethra suscipit;

Let us proclaim in song the brief lives
and the deaths of these martyrs;
innocent and holy are they, without fault
or blame. Rachel's earth wept
as they went forth and left it;
but heaven delighted
in receiving them with joy.

Quos rex peremit impius,
pius sed Auctor colligit,
secum beatos collocans
in luce regni perpetis.

Wicked the king who killed them, but
faithful the Creator who received them,
placing them with himself in fullest bliss
amidst the brilliant splendor
of that kingdom which has no end.

Praeclara Christo splenduit
mors innocens fidelium;
caelis ferebant angeli
bimos et infra parvulos.

Innocent the death, innocent
the faithful ones who died.
Their deaths, a brilliant oblation
to Christ the sovereign Lord.
Into the heavens above
did angels carry two-year-olds, and
those of fewer days still.

O quam beata civitas,
in qua Redemptor nascitur,
natoque primae martyrum
in qua dicantur hostiae!

How very blessed the city
where Christ the Redeemer was born!
and where the first
of martyrdom's thralls
are consecrated to the newborn Child.

Astant nitentes fulgidis
eius throno nunc vestibus,
stolas suas qui laverant
Agni rubentes sanguine.

Now, with gleaming vesture, they stand
shining bright around his throne:
in brilliant red are they clothed,
for they have washed their garments
in the blood of the Lamb.

Iesu, tibi sit gloria,
qui natus es de Virgine,
cum Patre et almo Spiritu
in sempiterna saecula.
Amen.

Jesus, to you be great glory,
for you have been born of the Virgin;
to the Father as well, and to
the kindly Spirit be praises
now and for evermore. Amen.

DECEMBER 28: HOLY INNOCENTS
MORNING PRAYER
Audit Tyrannus Anxius / How Troubled the Tyrant Cruel

Audit tyrannus anxius
adesse regem principem,
qui nomen Israel regat
*ten*eatque David regiam.

How troubled the tyrant cruel,
as he hears that a leader, a king,
has come to rule over Israel's name
and to take sway
over the royal palace of David.

Exclamat amens nuntio,
"Successor instat, pellimur,
satelles, i, ferrum rape,
perfunde cunas sanguine!"

In madness dire, he shouts,
after he hears the news,
"So! Our successor is at hand,
and we are driven away.
Go, my retinue! Take sword to hand,
fill the cradles with blood!"

Quo proficit tantum nefas?
Quid crimen Herodem iuvat?
Unus tot inter funera
impune Christus tollitur.

What does such an awful crime
achieve? How is Herod helped
by a deed so all-appalling?
For one child, the Christ,
is yet preserved from harm
in the midst of murder so foul.

Salvete, flores martyrum,
quos lucis ipso in limine,
Christ*i* insecutor sustulit
ceu turbo nascentes rosas.

Hail, you flower-crowns of martyrdom!
He who would kill the Christ
had you put to death
on the very threshold of life,
like new-budding roses
carried off in a whirlwind dire.

Vos prima Christi victima,
grex immolatorum tener,
aram sub ipsam simplices
palm*a* et coronis luditis.

You are the first sacrifices of Christ,
a tender flock of victims,
in offering made.
Beneath the very altar of sacrifice
you enjoy your play, albeit play
with palm and crown of martyrdom true.

Iesu, tibi sit gloria,
qui natus es de Virgine,
cum Patre et almo Spiritu
in sempiterna saecula.
Amen.

Jesus, to you be great glory,
for you have been born of the Virgin;
to the Father as well,
and to the kindly Spirit be praises
now and for evermore. Amen.

COMMONS

COMMON OF THE DEDICATION OF A CHURCH

COMMON OF THE BLESSED VIRGIN MARY
Feasts of the Blessed Virgin
B.V.M. on Saturdays

COMMON OF THE APOSTLES

COMMON OF MARTYRS
for Several or Many Martyrs
for One Martyr

COMMON OF PASTORS
for Several or Many Pastors
for One Pastor

COMMON OF DOCTORS OF THE CHURCH

COMMON OF VIRGINS
for Several or Many Virgins
for One Virgin

COMMON OF HOLY MEN
for Several or Many Holy Men
for One Holy Man

COMMON OF HOLY WOMEN
for Several or Many Holy Women
for One Holy Woman

COMMON OF RELIGIOUS

OFFICE OF THE DEAD

COMMON OF THE DEDICATION OF A CHURCH
OFFICE OF READINGS
Christe, Cunctorum Dominator Alme / Christ Lord, Kindly Ruler

Christe, cunctorum dominator
alme,
plebs tibi supplex resonat in
aula,
annuo cuius redeunt colenda
tempore festa.

Hic locus nempe vocitatur aula
regis immensi nitidique caeli
porta, quae vitae patriam
petentes
accipit omnes.

Haec tuam plebem sacra cogit
aedes,
haec sacramentis pia ditat
usque,
caelicis escis alit in perennis
munera vitae.

Quaesumus ergo, Deus,
ut sereno
adnuas vultu famulos
gubernans,
qui tui summo celebrant amore
gaudia templi.

Aequa laus summum celebret
Parentem
teque, Salvator, pie rex, per
aevum;
Spiritus Sancti resonet per
omnem
gloria mundum.
Amen.

Christ Lord, kindly ruler of all that is,
your people re-echo their prayers to you
in this church, this royal court,
whose festal days
have come once more
for celebration in yearly cycle due.

For this place is wont to be called
the courtyard of the all-powerful king,
and the gateway to brilliant heaven;
it embraces all who seek
their homeland, their land of life.

This sacred dwelling place
gathers together your holy people;
with its sacraments
it enriches them beyond measure,
and with its heavenly food
it nourishes them, helps them onward
towards the rewards of eternal life.

We ask of you, then,
God of power and might,
that with kindly mien
you grant your favor
to those servants
whom you govern, and who
with love unbounded celebrate the joys
of this, your temple.

Let equal praise be given
to the Father most high,
and to you, O Savior,
kindly King, for all ages to come;
and let the glory given to the Holy Spirit
sound forth throughout the entire world.
Amen.

COMMON OF THE DEDICATION OF A CHURCH
MORNING PRAYER
Angularis Fundamentum / Cornerstone and Foundation Both

Angularis fundamentum
lapis Christus missus est,
qui parietum compage
in utroque nectitur,
quem Sion sancta suscepit,
in quo credens permanet.

Cornerstone and foundation both
was Christ sent to be,
Christ, who in the very junction of two
walls
is joined to each, and joins both
equally:
Christ, whom holy Sion takes unto
itself,
Christ, in whom it stands firm in its
belief.

Omnis illa Deo sacra
et dilecta civitas,
plena modulis in laude
et canore iubilo,
trinum Deum unicumque
cum fervore praedicat.

That entire city,
sacred to God, beloved of God,
filled with measures of praise
and joyful song,
pays gladsome laud
to God who is Triune, to God who is
One.

Hoc in templo, summe Deus,
exoratus adveni,
et clementi bonitate
precum vota suscipe;
largam benedictionem
hic infunde iugiter.

In this temple, God sublime,
come to us in answer to earnest plea;
and with merciful goodness
hear our vows and prayers,
pour forth your abundant blessing
here
ceaselessly.

Hic promereantur omnes
petita acquirere
et adepta possidere
cum sanctis perenniter,
paradisum introire
translati in requiem.

May all deserve to receive here
what they have sought in prayer,
and to enjoy those blessings received
with the saints forever;
may they deserve, when transported
into rest,
to enter into Paradise itself.

Gloria et honor Deo
usquequaque altissimo,
una Patri Filioque
atque Sancto Flamini
quibus laudes et potestas
per aeterna saecula.
Amen.

Ceaseless glory and honor to God
almighty,
alike to Father and Son and Sacred
Spirit;
to them be praise and might
for ages e'er to come.
Amen.

COMMON OF THE DEDICATION OF A CHURCH
EVENING PRAYER I AND II
Urbs Ierusalem Beata / Jerusalem, Blessed City

Urbs Ierusalem beata,
dicta pacis visio,
quae construitur in caelis
vivis ex lapidibus,
angelisque coronata
sicut sponsa comite,

Nova veniens e caelo,
nuptiali thalamo
praeparata, ut intacta
copuletur Domino.
Plateae et muri eius
ex auro purissimo;

Portae nitent margaritis
adytis patentibus,
et virtute meritorum
illuc introducitur
omnis qui ob Christi nomen
hic in mundo premitur.

Tunsionibus, pressuris
expoliti lapides
suis coaptantur locis
per manum artificis;
disponuntur permansuri
sacris aedificiis.

Gloria et honor Deo
usquequaque altissimo,
una Patri Filioque
atque Sancto Flamini,
quibus laudes et potestas
per aeterna saecula.
Amen.

Jerusalem, blessed city,
named "Vision of Peace,"
e'en now is being built in heaven
out of living stones;
encircled by angels bright, it stands
forth, spouse-like,
surrounded by bridal retinue.

It comes from the heavens above,
newly made and
readied for nuptial couch,
so that in total purity
it might be joined to its Lord.
Its streets, its walls
are made of purest gold;

Its gates sparkle with pearls and,
as its temples open wide,
by the power of his or her merits is each
one led therein,
whoso here in this world
suffered because of the name
of Christ the Lord.

By bruising blows, by affliction's force
are its stones polished fine
and prepared for their fated places
by the hand of the Artist Divine:
readied are they to remain forevermore
in the holy shrine.

Glory and honor be evermore
to God most high,
alike to Father and to Son
and to Sacred Spirit as well;
to them be praise and power
for all ages to come. Amen.

COMMON OF THE BLESSED VIRGIN MARY
EVENING PRAYER I
Maria, Quae Mortalium / Mary Mother, with Greatest Love

Maria, quae mortalium
preces amanter excipis,
rogamus ergo supplices,
nobis adesto perpetim.

Mary Mother, with greatest love
you receive the prayers
of your mortal children.
We come to you in petition, then:
be present to us for all time to come.

Adesto, si nos criminum
catena stringit horrida;
cito resolve compedes
quae corda culpis illigant.

Be present to us,
should sin's savage chains
bind us fast;
hasten to loose the bonds
which enfetter our hearts
in wicked guilt.

Succurre, si nos saeculi
fallax imago pellicit,
ne mens salutis tramitem,
oblita caeli, deserat.

Come to our aid,
should the world's deceptive guise
entice us,
lest our hearts forget heaven
and stray from the path of salvation.

Succurre, si vel corpori
adversa sors impendeat;
fac sint quieta tempora,
aeternitas dum luceat.

Come to our aid,
should fateful adversity threaten
even our bodily frame;
make our days be peaceful,
until the brightness of eternity
shines forth.

Tuis et esto filiis
tutela mortis tempore,
ut, te iuvante, consequi
perenne detur praemium.

For us your children,
be thou safeguard firm
when death shall draw near,
that with your gracious help
we may be gifted with achieving
the eternal reward.

Patri sit ac Paraclito
tuoque Nato gloria,
qui veste te mirabili
circumdederunt gratiae.
Amen.

To the Father, and to the Advocate,
and to your Son be glory,
to the God who has surrounded you
with glorious garment of grace. Amen.

COMMON OF THE BLESSED VIRGIN MARY
OFFICE OF READINGS
Quem Terra, Pontus, Aethera / The One Whom Earth, Whom Sea

Quem terra, pontus, aethera
colunt, adorant, praedicant
trinam regentem machinam,
claustrum Mariae baiulat.

The One whom earth,
whom sea, whom sky above
worship, adore, proclaim
as rules he o'er their threefold domain:
This is the One
whom the safe harbor of Mary's
womb does truly contain.

Cui luna, sol, et omnia
deserviunt per tempora,
perfusa caeli gratia
gestant puellae viscera.

The One to whom moon,
to whom sun, to whom all else beside
pledge e'erlasting fealty:
He it is
whom the young maiden's womb,
filled with heaven's surpassing grace,
carries true.

Beata mater munere
cuius, supernus artifex,
mundum pugillo continens,
ventris sub arca clausus est.

Blessed the mother,
by reason of heavenly gift:
in the treasure-box of her womb
the architect of heaven,
bearing in the palm of his hand the
world entire, is safe enclosed.

Beata caeli nuntio,
fecunda Sancto Spiritu,
desideratus gentibus
cuius per alvum fusus est.

Blessed is she by word from heaven,
made fertile by the Holy Spirit's
o'ershadowing power;
by means of her womb is brought forth
the One for whom
the nations have longed.

Iesu, tibi sit gloria,
qui natus es de Virgine,
cum Patre et almo Spiritu
in sempiterna saecula.
Amen.

Jesus Lord, to you be glory,
born of the Virgin sublime,
in union with the Father
and the kindly Spirit
for eons surpassing all measure of time.
Amen.

COMMON OF THE BLESSED VIRGIN MARY
MORNING PRAYER
O Gloriosa Domina / O Regal, Glorious Lady

O gloriosa Domina,
excelsa super sidera,
qui te creavit provide,
lactas sacrato ubere.

O regal, glorious Lady,
exalted beyond heaven above,
at your sacred breast you nourish
the very One who created you,
with foresight keen and true.

What doleful Eve took away,
you restore
by the blessed fruit of your womb;
so that those who weep in sorrow
may enter the starry realms,
you in your kindness fashion the path
for them to follow.

Quod Eva tristis abstulit
tu reddis almo germine;
intrent ut astra flebiles,
sternis benigna semitam.

Tu regis alti ianua
et porta lucis fulgida;
vitam datam per Virginem,
gentes redemptae, plaudite.

You are the gateway
of the King himself,
the King most high;
you are the doorway of light,
bright, glorious light.
O ye peoples, now ransomed,
now redeemed,
praise the life you are given
through the Virgin most pure.

Patri sit et Paraclito
tuoque Nato gloria,
qui veste te mirabili
circumdederunt gratiae.
Amen.

To the Father, to the Advocate,
and to your Son as well
let praise be sung,
to the God, one yet three,
who has surrounded you
with the brilliant garment
of most wondrous grace.
Amen.

COMMON OF THE BLESSED VIRGIN MARY
EVENING PRAYER II
Ave, Maris Stella / Hail, O Star of Ocean Blest

Ave, maris stella,
Dei mater alma,
atque semper virgo,
felix caeli porta.

Hail, O Star of Ocean blest,
faithful mother of God most high,
yet ever a virgin: the blessed
Gate of Heaven are you.

Sumens illud "Ave"
Gabrielis ore,
funda nos in pace,
mutans Evae nomen.

Since you did receive that "Hail!,"
that greeting from Gabriel's lips,
and since you have changed
what "Eve" had come to mean,
make firm our peace,
our life-basing peace.

Solve vincla reis,
profer lumen caecis,
mala nostra pelle,
bona cuncta posce.

Shatter the iron fetters of the guilty;
bring forth bright light for the blind.
Put to flight the evils we face;
petition for us all that is good.

Monstra te esse matrem,
sumat per te preces
qui pro nobis natus
tulit esse tuus.

Show us all that you are a mother true;
may He receive our prayer through you,
He who was born for us,
and allowed himself to be your son.

Virgo singularis,
inter omnes mitis,
nos culpis solutos
mites fac et castos.

Virgin holy, unique among all peoples
Virgin completely mild,
free us from our faults;
make us meek and pure.

Vitam praesta puram,
iter para tutum,
ut videntes Iesum
semper collaetemur.

Make our lives be lives that are pure;
make our path a path that is safe,
so that we may truly see Jesus,
and in Him have real and lasting joy.

Sit laus Deo Patri,
summo Christo decus,
Spiritui Sancto
honor, tribus unus.
Amen.

To God the Father be praise,
to Christ most exalted be glory,
to the Holy Spirit be honor:
To the three persons in one
be gladsome song forever. Amen.

COMMON OF THE BLESSED VIRGIN MARY
B.V.M. ON SATURDAY
OFFICE OF READINGS
O Virgo Mater, Filia / You Are Both Virgin and Mother

O virgo mater, filia
tui beata Filii,
sublimis et humillima
prae creaturis omnibus.

You are both virgin and mother,
most blessed daughter
of your own most blessed Son.
Exalted are you
above all other creatures,
yet most lowly as well.

Divini tu consilii
fixus ab aevo terminus
tu decus et fastigium
naturae nostrae maximum.

From all ages were you chosen
to be where the divine plan
would come to fulfillment;
you are the glory
of our human nature,
and its highest expression as well.

Quam sic prompsisti nobilem
ut summus eius conditor
in ipsa per te fieret
arte miseranda conditus.

So noble did you render
that nature we share
that its divine Creator
came to partake of it
by means of you,
through mercy's artful device.

In utero virgineo
amor revixit igneus,
cuius calore germinant
flores in terra caelici.

In virgineal womb did fiery love
take life once more;
by that love's ardent glow
do heavenly flowers blossom forth
on this earth of ours.

Patri sit et Paraclito
tuoque Nato gloria,
qui veste te mirabili
circumdederunt gratiae.
Amen.

To the Father, to the Advocate,
to your Son be glory given,
to the triune God
who has surrounded you
with vesture most grace-filled,
most marvelous to behold. Amen.

COMMON OF THE BLESSED VIRGIN MARY
B.V.M. ON SATURDAY
MORNING PRAYER
O Gloriosa Domina [p. 320], or:
Quae Caritatis Fulgidum / For Those in Heaven Above

Quae caritatis fulgidum
es astrum, Virgo, superis,
spei nobis mortalibus
fons vivax es et profluus.

For those in heaven above, O Virgin,
you are the gleaming star of love itself;
and for those of us mortals
still on earth, a flowing and abundant
fountain of hope.

Sic vales, celsa Domina,
in Nati cor piissimi,
ut qui fidenter postulat,
per te securus impetret.

So powerful you are,
Maiden Mother most high,
over the heart of your dutiful Son,
that whoe'er, with trusting prayer,
seeks some boon, most assuredly,
through your powerful aid,
receives it full-fold.

Opem tua benignitas
non solum fert poscentibus,
sed et libenter saepius
precantum vota praevenit.

To earnest suppliants not only does
your gracious kindness bring
the aid they seek;
oft enough, it tarries not,
but readily anticipates the prayers
those suppliants will bring.

In te misericordia,
in te magnificentia;
tu bonitatis cumulas
quicquid creata possident.

In you we find mercy;
in you we find grandeur.
Whate'er degree of goodness
created things possess,
finds in you its abundant crown.

Patri sit et Paraclito
tuoque Nato gloria,
qui veste te mirabili
circumdederunt gratiae.
Amen.

To the Father,
and to the Advocate as well,
and to your own Son be glory paid:
the God-in-Three
who have surrounded you
with the magnificent raiment of grace.
Amen.

COMMON OF APOSTLES
EVENING PRAYER I AND II OUTSIDE OF PASCHAL TIME
Exsultet Caelum Laudibus / Let Heaven Break Forth in Joyful Praise

Exsultet caelum laudibus,
resultet terra gaudiis:
Apostolorum gloriam
sacra canunt sollemnia.

Let heaven break forth
in joyful praise; let earth resound
in turn with cries of gladness:
for these holy festivals
proclaim the glory
of Christ's Apostles most renowned.

Vos, saecli iusti iudices
et vera mundi lumina,
votis precamur cordium,
audite preces supplicum.

And you, just judges of this, our age,
true lights brightening this, our world:
with the prayerful vows of our hearts
we call upon you.
Listen to the trusting cries of those
who plead with you.

Qui caelum verbo clauditis
serasque eius solvitis,
nos a peccatis omnibus
solvite iussu, quaesumus.

You are those who,
with but a single word
bind the gate of heaven shut, or
loose whatever would keep it closed.
By your powerful command, then,
we beg: free us from all bond of sin.

Quorum praecepto subditur
salus et languor omnium,
sanate aegros moribus,
nos reddentes virtutibus,

In your mandate's scope
lies the sickness and lies the health
of peoples one and all.
Cure those whose evil habits
render them akin to the ill,
we beg; restore us, as well,
to virtue's sound state,

Ut, cum iudex advenerit
Christus in fine saeculi,
nos sempiterni gaudii
faciat esse compotes.

So that, when Christ the Judge
shall come at the end
of the world's long age,
He may make us sharers
in that joy which has no end.

Deo sint laudes gloriae,
qui dat nos evangelicis
per vos doctrinis instrui
et prosequi caelestia.
Amen.

To the God of glory be praise,
the God who allows us to be formed
by gospel doctrines taught us by you,
blessed Apostles,
the God who grants too that we come
thereby to achieving
heaven's unending bliss. Amen.

COMMON OF APOSTLES
EVENING PRAYER I AND II DURING PASCHAL TIME
Tristes Erant Apostoli / Heavy-Hearted, the Apostles Mourned

Tristes erant Apostoli
de nece sui Domini,
quem morte crudelissima
saevi damnarant impii.

Heavy-hearted, the Apostles mourned
the murder of their Master and Lord,
whom wicked men, cruel men,
had condemned
to a shameful, painful death.

Sermone blando Angelus
praedixit mulieribus:
"In Galilea Dominus
videndus est quantocius."

With consoling words, the Angel
foretold to the women:
"In Galilee is the Lord to be seen,
as quickly as you can."

Illae dum pergunt concitae
Apostolis hoc dicere,
videntes eum vivere,
osculant pedes Domini.

As they went off in haste
to tell the Apostles,
they saw him alive,
and they kissed the feet of the Lord.

Quo agnito, discipuli
in Galilea propere
pergunt videre faciem
desideratam Domini.

Once this was known, the disciples
go in haste to Galilee,
to see the face, the longed-for face,
of their beloved Lord.

Esto perenne mentibus
paschale, Iesu, gaudium,
et nos renatos gratiae
tuis triumphis aggrega.

Be thou, O Jesus, lasting Easter joy
for our spirits; unite us, renewed now,
with the triumphs of grace
that you have won.

Sit, Christe, tibi gloria,
qui regno mortis obruto,
pandisti per Apostolos
vitae lucisque semitas.
Amen.

O Christ, may glory be given to you:
you have overturned the realm of death,
and, through the Apostles,
opened up the paths of life and light.
Amen.

COMMON OF APOSTLES
OFFICE OF READINGS OUTSIDE OF PASCHAL TIME
MORNING PRAYER DURING PASCHAL TIME
O Sempiternae Curiae / O Princely Rulers

O sempiternae curiae
regis supremi principes,
quos ipse Iesus edocens
donavit orb*i* Apostolos,

O princely rulers of the supernal
King's e'erlasting court,
The Lord Jesus himself trained you,
and gave you to the world
as his heralds, authentic and true.

Superna vos Ierusalem,
lucerna cuius Agnus est,
gemmas micantes possidet,
praeclara vos fundamina.

The heavenly Jerusalem,
whose light is sourced
in the Lamb himself,
embraces you as its own,
as its ornaments bejeweled,
as its foundation without peer.

Vos et celebrat gratulans
nunc sponsa Christ*i* Ecclesia,
quam sermo vester exciit,
quam consecrastis sanguine.

So too does Christ's own Spouse,
the Church, now gratefully praise you
in song: that same Spouse
that your preaching nourished
when first it began to grow,
that same Church
which you consecrated
by the shedding of your blood.

Cadentibus cum saeculis
iudex Redemptor sederit,
qua laude vos sedebitis
senatus altae gloriae!

When the eons
shall have finished passing, and
when the Redeemer Judge
shall at last have mounted
his dread throne,
with what unspeakable praise
will you likewise take your seats,
you, the Church's high senate,
that senate of supreme renown!

Nos ergo vestra iugiter
prex adiuvando roboret,
fudistis ut quae semina
in grana caeli floreant.

Aeterna Christo gloria,
qui fecit esse nuntios
vos Patris, atque Spiritus
replevit almo numine.
Amen.

[continued]

O Sempiternae Curiae / O Princely Rulers
[concluded]

May therefore your prayers now always
be our help and strength:
those same prayers
that you poured out as seeds
that would blossom forth
into the flora of heaven itself.

To Christ be glory without end;
He has named you messengers
of his own Father,
and He has filled you
with the gracious godhead
of the Spirit as well. Amen.

COMMON OF APOSTLES
MORNING PRAYER WITHIN PASCHAL TIME
Claro Paschali Gaudio / With Gleaming Paschal Joy

Claro paschali gaudio
sol mundo nitet radio.
cum Christum iam Apostoli
visu cernunt corporeo.

With gleaming paschal joy the sun,
with its gentle beam,
smiles down upon the world,
as the Apostles now gaze upon Christ
with sight body-bounded.

Ostensa sibi vulnera
in Christi carne fulgida,
resurrexisse Dominum
voce patentur publica.

The wounds displayed to them,
those wounds that shine forth
in Christ's risen flesh,
make clear and plain proclamation:
the Lord has risen indeed!

Rex, Christe, clementissime,
tu corda nostra posside,
ut tibi laudes debitas
reddamus omni tempore.

Christ, O King most merciful,
take full possession
of these hearts of ours,
so that in every time and place
we may render you the praises
that are your unquestioned due.

Esto perenne mentibus
paschale, Iesu, gaudium,
et nos renatos gratiae
tuis triumphis aggrega.

Be thou, O Jesus,
everlasting Easter joy
for these spirits of ours;
place us,
now reborn to grace as we are,
with the other victories you have won.

Sit, Christe, tibi gloria,
qui regno mortis obruto,
pandisti per Apostolos
vitae lucisque semitas.
Amen.

O Christ, to you be glory:
for you have overturned
the kingdom of death;
through your Apostles,
you have opened to us
the ways that lead to life and light.
Amen.

COMMON OF SEVERAL OR MANY MARTYRS
EVENING PRAYER I AND II
Sanctorum Meritis Inclita Gaudia / Let Us Loudly Proclaim

Sanctorum meritis inclita gaudia
pangamus, socii, gestaque fortia;
nam gliscit animus promere
cantibus
victorum genus optimum.

Hi [hae] sunt quos [quas]
retinens mundus inhorruit,
ipsum nam sterili flore
peraridum
sprevere penitus teque secuti
[secutae] sunt,
rex, Christe, bone caelitum.

Hi [Hae] pro te furias saevaque
sustinent;
non murmur resonat, non
querimonia,
sed corde tacito mens bene
conscia
conservat patientiam.

Quae vox, quae poterit lingua
retexere
quae tu martyribus munera
praeparas?
Rubri nam fluido sanguine laureis
ditantur bene fulgidis.

Te, trina Deitas unaque, poscimus,
ut culpas abluas, noxia subtrahas,
des pacem famulis, nos quoque
gloriam
per cuncta tibi saecula.
Amen.

Let us loudly proclaim
how incomparable are the joys
that flow from the merits of the saints;
as their companions, let us affirm
how wondrously brave
their deeds have truly been.
For our hearts swell in glad desire
to tell in song of this wondrous breed
of warriors victorious.

These are they whom the world, while
yet they tarried in it, shuddered at,
and would not claim as its own;
for completely did they spurn it,
see it as dusty-dry, bearing only
unfruitful seed. No, it was you, O Christ,
whom they followed: you, O Christ,
good king of the heavens above.

For love of you they endure
men's violent passions,
suffer their ferocious deeds.
No grumbling do they voice,
no complaint; nay, with silent heart,
but with mind well aware, their souls
they possess in patient peace.

What the word, what the voice
that could make plain the rewards
you prepare for your martyrs?
For ruddy with the blood
they have shed, they are enriched
with bright and shimmering crowns.

You, Godhead three yet Godhead one,
we beg: wash away our guilt,
keep from us all that would harm us;
grant peace to our families,
and grant that we may give you glory
for ages without end. Amen.

COMMON OF SEVERAL OR MANY MARTYRS
OFFICE OF READINGS
Rex Gloriose Martyrum / King Most Glorious of Witness-Martyrs

Rex gloriose martyrum,
corona confitentium,
qui respuentes terrea
perducis ad caelestia,

King most glorious
of witness-martyrs so brave,
Crown and reward of Confessors:
those who profess your name,
to the rewards of heaven itself do you
guide those who spurn
the alluring charms of earth.

Aurem benignam protinus
appone nostris vocibus;
tropea sacra pangimus,
ignosce quod deliquimus.

Lend unfailing and kindly ear
to our voices as we cry;
as we sing sacred hymns
to laud the martyrs' triumphs high,
forgive us for the mistakes,
the failures,
in what we ourselves have done.

Tu vincis in martyribus
parcendo confessoribus;
tu vince nostra crimina
donando indulgentiam.

You glean glory in granting
your martyrs' victories, while sparing
from martyr's path confessors
as they proclaim your holy name.
Conquer the evil deeds
we ourselves have done
by granting us their forgiveness full.

Praesta, Pater piissime,
Patrique compar Unice,
cum Spiritu Paraclito
regnans per omne saeculum.
Amen.

Grant this, Father most faithful,
grant it, only-begotten One,
to the Father full equal,
with the Spirit Advocate
reigning for ages e'er yet to come.
Amen.

COMMON: SEVERAL OR MANY MARTYRS
MORNING PRAYER
Aeterna Christi Munera / The Ne'er-Ending Rewards of Christ the Lord

Aeterna Christi munera
et martyrum victorias,
laudes ferentes debitas,
laetis canamus mentibus.

The ne'er-ending rewards
of Christ the Lord, and the victories
that the martyrs have won:
of all these let us sing
with spirits raised on high,
let us bring them the laud
that is their just due.

Ecclesiarum principes,
belli triumphales duces
caelestis aulae milites
et vera mundi lumina.

The martyrs: princely leaders
of the churches,
victorious chieftains in the sacred war,
soldiers of the heavenly realm,
true luminaries of this world here below.

Terrore victo saeculi
poenisque spretis corporis,
mortis sacrae compendio
lucem beatam possident.

Earth's fierce fears are overcome;
the penalties that flesh can suffer
are deemed as nil.
After brief struggle, after holy death,
now do Christ's holy martyrs possess
the blessed light of life itself.

Tortoris insani manu
sanguis sacratus funditur,
sed permanent immobiles
vitae perennis gratia.

Their holy blood is poured out at the
hand of their frenzied executioner;
but they remain unmoved, rock-firm
for the sake of a life they hope for, a life
that has no end.

Devota sanctorum fides
invicta spes credentium,
perfecta Christi caritas
mundi triumphat principem.

The unwavering faith of the saints,
the unconquerable hope
of those who believe,
the supreme and perfect love
of Christ the Lord:
all triumph over the prince
who would rule this world.

In his paterna gloria
in his voluntas Spiritus,
exsultat in his Filius,
caelum repletur gaudio.

Te nunc, Redemptor,
quaesumus,
ut martyrum consortio
iungas precantes servulos
in sempiterna saecula. Amen.

[continued]

Aeterna Christi Munera / The Ne'er-Ending Rewards of Christ the Lord
[concluded]

In these lies the glory
of God the Father;
in them, the will of the Holy Spirit.
The Son rejoices in them,
and the whole of heaven
is filled with joy.

And now, Redeemer blest,
we ask of you:
join, for ages without end,
to the fellowship of the martyrs
these poor servants of yours
who now bring their
prayerful pleas to you. Amen.

COMMON OF ONE MARTYR
EVENING PRAYER I AND II
Deus, Tuorum Militum / God Our Father, Destiny, and Crown

Deus, tuorum militum
sors et corona, praemium,
laudes canentes martyris
absolve nexu criminis.

God our Father, Destiny, and Crown,
and Reward supreme
of your soldiers' courageous deeds,
free us from the snares of sin,
free us who chant
your martyr's gladsome praises.

Hic [Haec] testis ore protulit
quod cordis arca credidit,
Christum sequendo repperit
effusione sanguinis.

This is a martyr, a witness who with lips
proclaimed what hidden places of heart
held fast in faith: by following Christ,
he (she) discovered Him
in the very shedding
of his (her) own blood.

His [Haec] nempe mundi gaudia
et blandimenta noxia
caduca rite deputans,
pervenit ad caelestia.

Poenas cucurrit fortiter
et sustulit viriliter;
pro te refundens sanguinem,
aeterna dona possidet.

For he (she), rightly seeing
that the world's joys
and its harmful allures
were but fleeting, passing,
ended the course rather in claiming, in
possessing eternal bliss, eternal life.

Ob hoc precatu supplici
te poscimus, piissime;
in hoc triumpho martyris
dimitte noxam servulis,

Ut consequamur muneris
ipsius et consortia,
laetemur ac perenniter
iuncti polorum sedibus.

He (she) endured
stern torments bravely,
survived them with a courage
that did not break;
he (she) poured out his (her) blood
for you, and so now holds fast
to rewards that do not fade.

[continued]

Laus et perennis gloria
tibi, Pater, cum Filio,
Sancto simul Paraclito
in saeculorum saecula.
Amen.

Deus, Tuorum Militum / God Our Father, Destiny and Crown
[concluded]

And therefore we ask of you
in humble prayer,
O Lord most faithful:
on this day that marks
your martyr's triumph on high,
forgive the faults of your servants
here below,

So that we too may be given a share
in his (her) rewards, the rewards
of his (her) high station,
and may be admitted
to the abode of heaven itself
and thus rejoice for ages without end.

Praise, and endless glory,
be given to you, O Father,
in company with your Son,
and the Holy Spirit as well,
for ages without end.
Amen.

COMMON OF ONE VIRGIN MARTYR
EVENING PRAYER I AND II
Virginis Proles Opifexque Matris / Offspring of a Virgin

Virginis Proles opifexque Matris,
Virgo quem gessit peperitque
Virgo, virginis festum canimus
    tropaeum:
    accipe votum.

Offspring of a Virgin,
    yet yourself creator
    of your own mother,
it was a Virgin who bore you,
a Virgin who brought you forth.
Today we sing
the triumphant praise of a virgin;
hear thou our prayer.

Haec tua virgo, duplici beata sorte,
dum gestit fragilem domare
corporis sexum, domuit cruentum
    corpore saeclum.

This virgin of yours is blessed
    by twofold title:
while she strove to overcome
the weakness her bodily sex entailed,
    at the same time
and with that same frail body,
    she also vanquished
    the bloodstained cruelty
    the world imposed.

Inde nec mortem nec amica
    mortis
saeva poenarum genera
    pavescens,
sanguine fuso meruit sacratum
    scandere caelum.

And thus she stood in terror
    neither of death,
    nor of death's friend,
    savage punishment dire.
By pouring out her blood
she was privileged to ascend on high
    to heaven's bliss.

Because of her prayers,
    O Godhead most kindly,
    forgive now our sins;
because of those prayers,
free us from our wicked deeds,
and let there now break forth,
    from purified hearts
and for ages upon ages to come,
    our joyful song. Amen.

Huius obtentu, Deus alme, nostris
parce iam culpis, vitiis revulsis,
quo tibi puri resonet per aevum
    pectoris hymnus.
    Amen.

COMMON OF ONE MARTYR
OFFICE OF READINGS
Beate[a] Martyr, Prospera / Holy Martyr, Make This Day

Beate[a] martyr, prospera
diem triumphalem tuum,
quo sanguinis merces tibi
corona vincenti datur.

Holy martyr, make this day
a favorable time,
this the day of your triumph bright;
today the heavenly crown, the reward
of the blood you have shed,
is bestowed upon you,
O conquering champion.

Hic te ex tenebris saeculi,
tortore victo et iudice,
evexit ad caelum dies
Christoque ovantem reddidit.

This is the day that exalted you
up to heaven itself:
it took you out of the darkness
of this world; it put to shame
your executioner and your judge,
it placed you in joy with Christ.

Nunc angelorum particeps
colluces insigni stola,
quam testis indomabilis
rivis cruoris laveras.

Now you are in the company
of the angels, and you stand,
shimmering in the brilliant robe
that, as witness indomitable,
you have full washed in the sacred,
bloody stream.

Adesto nunc et obsecra,
placatus ut Christus suis
inclinet aurem prosperam,
noxas nec omnes imputet.

Be with us now: beg Christ
to be appeased, to grant us
a favorable hearing,
and not to hold us blameful
for all the evil we have done.

Paulisper huc illabere
Christi favorem deferens,
sensus gravati ut sentiant
levamen indulgentiae.

No; let it be but a short time
till you bring down to us and fill us
with the favor of Christ himself,
so that our minds, overwhelmed
as now they are with guilt,
may know the soothing balm
of forgiveness blest.

Honor Patri cum Filio
et Spiritu Paraclito,
qui te corona perpeti
cingunt in aula gloriae.
Amen.

Honor be given to the Father, as to
the Son and the Advocate Spirit, who
in the palace of heaven encircle you
now with unending crown. Amen.

COMMON OF ONE VIRGIN MARTYR
OFFICE OF READINGS
O Christe, Flos Convallium / Christ Lord, Splendid Crown

O Christe, flos convallium,
te laudibus extollimus,
quod hanc ornasti virginem
palmis quoque martyrii.

Christ Lord, splendid flower
of valleys so far,
we lift up your holy name in praise,
for you have honored this virgin blest
with e'en the great and high palm
of martyrdom.

Prudent was she, brave,
and wise as well;

Haec prudens, fortis, sapiens,
fidem professa libere,
pro te dira supplicia
excepit imperterrita.

freely she professed her faith,
and for your sake
went forth undaunted, unafraid
to undertake sufferings most awful,
sufferings most cruel.

She spurned the allurements
the prince of the world held out,
and so was enriched

Sic spreto mundi principe,
tuo ditata munere,
cruento parta proelio
aeterna tulit praemia.

with your gift instead:
from bloody battle came she forth
a victor, and bore off rewards eternal,
rewards ne'er knowing end.

Because of her holy merits,
O Redeemer most kind,

Huius, Redemptor, meritis
nos pius adde socios,
ut, mente pura, fructibus
tui fruamur sanguinis.

join us to her as her companions,
so that, in purity of heart,
we may enjoy the rewards
you have won by your precious blood.

Jesus, born of the Virgin most holy,
to you be due glory given,
with the Father and the kindly Spirit

Iesu, tibi sit gloria,
qui natus es de Virgine,
cum Patre et almo Spiritu
in sempiterna saecula.
Amen.

for ages without end.
Amen.

COMMON OF ONE MARTYR
MORNING PRAYER
Martyr Dei, Qui [Quae] Unicum / Holy Martyr of God

Martyr Dei, qui [quae] unicum
Patris sequendo Filium,
victis triumphas hostibus,
victor [victrix] fruens
caelestibus,

Holy martyr of God,
because you were a follower
of the sole-begotten
Son of God the Father,
your enemies now lie vanquished,
and you glory in your victory,
enjoying the rewards of heaven above.

By the gift of your holy prayer,
wash away the guilt
that stains us deep,
keep at bay the loathsome touch
of the evil one,
and put to flight the irksome burdens
our lives now know.

Tui precatus munere
nostrum reatum dilue,
arcens mali contagium,
vitae repellens taedium.

The chains that bound
your sacred body
are now shattered, all undone;
through your love
for the Son of God most high,
free us from the chains
this world of ours now employs
to hold us in thrall.

Soluta sunt iam vincula
tui sacrati corporis;
nos solve vinclis saeculi
amore Filii Dei.

Let glory be given to the Father,
in company with the Son
and the Spirit Advocate:
to the Godhead, one in three,
who in heaven's bright halls
surrounds you with a crown
whose luster never dims.
Amen.

Honor Patri cum Filio
et Spiritu Paraclito,
qui te corona perpeti
cingunt in aula gloriae.
Amen.

COMMON OF ONE VIRGIN MARTYR
MORNING PRAYER
O Castitatis Signifer / Lord God, You Are the Standard-Bearer

O castitatis signifer
et fortitudo martyrum,
utrisque reddens praemia,
audi benignus supplices.

Haec virgo magni pectoris,
beata sorte duplici
binaque palma nobilis,
hic tollitur praeconiis.

Haec te fateri pertinax,
tortoris acre bracchium
armavit in se strenue
tibique fudit spiritum.

Sic saevientis vulnera
et blandientis vincere
mundi docens illecebram,
fidem docet nos integram.

Huius favore debita
nobis remittas omnia,
tormenta tollens criminum
tuamque subdens gratiam.

Iesu, tibi sit gloria,
qui natus es de Virgine,
cum Patre et almo Spiritu,
in sempiterna saecula.
Amen.

Lord God, you are the standard-bearer
of great purity bright, the martyrs'
strength, strength that none
can overcome: as today you bestow
the rewards of chaste holiness,
and the rewards as well
of martyrdom brave,
in your kindness lend ear to those
who cry out trustingly to you.

This is a virgin great-hearted, brave,
blessed in her double role,
renowned full high in two-fold crown,
and now raised up high
on full-swelling praise.

Constant in professing your name,
she vigorously provoked
her tormentor's harsh arm
to strike against her;
and she poured out her spirit unto you.

And so, as she teaches us to overcome
the blows of the raging executioner,
and to conquer full the blandishments
an alluring world has to offer,
she instructs us well as to what
an unbroken faith truly can be, truly is.

Through the prayerful favor of this,
your virgin, forgive us all the debts
we have incurred. Take from us
the sufferings our ill deeds deserve,
and grant us your own grace instead.

Jesus, to you be glory given,
you who are Virgin-born,
and the Father as well
and the kindly Spirit too,
for ages without number,
ages without end. Amen.

COMMON OF SEVERAL OR MANY PASTORS
EVENING PRAYER I AND II
Sacrata Nobis Gaudia / Each Year This Day Brings Us Back

Sacrata nobis gaudia
dies reduxit annua,
laudantur in qua debito
cultu duces ovilium.

Each year this day brings us back
to the holy joys we feel: this day,
on which the chieftains of the flock
are acclaimed with proper pomp,
due celebration.

For lo: so as to guard their flock,
they spurn no efforts;
the sheep they keep safe, and
pasture them with food
that is very good for them.

En pro gregis custodia
nullos labores neglegunt,
tutantur illum, sanius
impertientes pabulum.

They keep the wolves
away from the gates;
thieves they drive off
to distances great and far.
They fill the sheep
with rich and abundant food;
never do they abandon their flock.

Arcent lupos e finibus,
procul latrones exigunt,
replent oves pinguitudine,
ovile numquam deserunt.

And now,
O holy shepherds of the flock,
you have achieved so many,
such great joys:
beg for us in turn a kindly sentence
at the tribunal
of the great Judge on high.

Tot nunc potiti gaudiis,
gregum duces sanctissimi,
nobis rogate gratiam
apud tribunal iudicis.

O Christ, High Priest Eternal,
may glory be given to you,
as equally to the Father
and the kindly Spirit,
for ages without limits or end. Amen.

Aeterne, Christe, pontifex,
tibi sit aequa gloria
cum Patre et almo Spiritu
in sempiterna saecula.
Amen.

COMMON OF SEVERAL OR MANY PASTORS
OFFICE OF READINGS
Dum Sacerdotum Celebrant Fideles / As Your Faithful People Celebrate

Dum sacerdotum celebrant fideles
festa sollemni veneranda cultu,
in tuas laudes honor hic redundat,
summe Sacerdos.

As your faithful people celebrate
your priests' festal day with solemn rite,
as is right, as they should,
the honor they pay to them
reflects back unto
the sincere and heartfelt praise
given you, O High Priest Supernal.

Cuius ex dono potuere patres
semitas lucis populos docere,
moribus sanctis regere atque verbo
pascere vitae.

By your generous gift,
these your holy priests were able
to teach your people the pathways
that lead to eternal light,
to rule over them
by the holy way of life they imparted,
and to feed them
with word of life ne'er-ending.

Sed ne adversis poterant moveri
a tuae certo fidei tenore,
quos futuorum rata praemiorum
spes animabat.

But lest, by adversity's grim touch,
they might be moved away
from the clear pathway
that faith in you provides,
the firm-founded hope of future reward
encouraged them onward.

Unde post vitae fragilis labores
rite decursos, patrias adepti
caelitus sedes, solida beati
pace fruuntur.

And so, after duly passing through
the labors of this fragile life,
they took possession of fatherland,
homeland, in heaven above;
and now are they blessed,
now do they enjoy
unshakeable peace.

Gloriae summum decus atque laudis,
rex, tibi, regum, Deitas perennis,
quicquid est rerum celebret
per omne tempus et aevum.
Amen.

Let the supreme meed
of glorious praise be accorded you,
O King of Kings, O Godhead Ceaseless;
let all that exists sing forth your praise
through each age and time. Amen.

COMMON OF SEVERAL PASTORS
MORNING PRAYER
Hi Sacerdotes Domini Sacrati / These Are Priests of the Lord

Hi sacerdotes Domini sacrati,
consecratores Domini fideles
atque pastores populi fuere
imprigo amore.

These are priests of the Lord,
set apart to sanctify faithfully,
to shepherd with indefatigable love,
the Lord's own holy people.

Namque susceptae
benedictionis
dona servantes, studuere,
lumbos
fortiter cincti, manibus coruscas
ferre lucernas.

For they have safeguarded
the gifts of the blessing
they have received.
They have striven,
with loins bravely girt,
to bear in their hands torches
that flame brightly aglow.

Sicque suspensi vigilesque,
quando
ianuam pulsans Dominus
veniret,
obviaverunt properant*i* alacres
pandere limen.

And thus, wakeful, watchful,
when the Lord came
and knocked at the door,
they went to meet him,
and flung open the gate full wide
as he came in hurried haste.

Gloriae summum decus atque
laudis,
rex, tibi, regum, Deitas perennis,
quicquid est rerum celebret
per omne
tempus et aevum.
Amen.

Let the supreme meed
of glory and praise
be yours, O King of Kings,
O Godhead supernal;
let whatever exists exalt you
through time and through eternity.
Amen.

COMMON OF ONE PASTOR
EVENING PRAYER I AND II
Vir Celse, Forma Fulgida / O Man Exalted, Shining Pattern

Vir celse, forma fulgida virtutis, hymnum suscipe, qui iure dum te praedicat, Dei canit magnalia.	O man exalted, shining pattern of what virtue ought to be, receive our song of prayer. For whoever justly proclaims your praise, thereby sings of the great deeds of God.
Qui sempiternus Pontifex stirpem Deo mortalium revinxit, atque reddidit paci novo nos foedere,	The same High Priest who freed and won back to God the race of mortal men, and who restored us to peace in the gift of the new covenant,
Te fecit ipse providus sui ministrum muneris, Patri daturum gloriam eiusque vitam plebibus.	Did himself, in his provident care, establish you as his servant, so as to give glory to the Father and life to his people.
[Pro Papa] Tu Petri ovile caelitus sumptis regebas clavibus, gregemque verbo gratiae, puris fovebas actibus.	*(For a Pope)* You received the keys from on high, and ruled over Peter's own flock; you nurtured your sheep with grace-filled words, with actions most pure.
[Pro Episcopo] Virtute factus ditior te consecrantis Spiritus, praesul, salutis pinguia tu tradidisti pabula.	*(For a Bishop)* Enriched by the power of the Spirit who set you apart, you were the leader: you distributed salvation's rich nurture to your people.
[Pro Presbytero] Regalis huius culminis adeptus altitudinem, verbo fuisti et moribus doctor, sacerdos, hostia.	*(For a Priest)* Having reached the summit of this regal height, in word and in way of life were you teacher, priest, and victim pure. [continued]
Locatus in caelestibus, sanctae memento Ecclesiae, oves ut omnes pascua Christi petant felicia.	
Sit Trinitati gloria, qui sancti honoris munia tibi ministro sedulo dignis coronat gaudiis. Amen.	

Vir Celse, Forma Fulgida / O Man Exalted, Shining Pattern
[concluded]

Now safe at home
in high heaven above,
be mindful of Holy Church,
so that all of Christ's sheep
might seek
the pastures of blessedness.

Let glory be given
to the Trinity on high:
for you, their faithful servant,
have they crowned with
the reward of saintly honor,
with joys that know no end. Amen.

COMMON OF ONE PASTOR
OFFICE OF READINGS
Christe, Pastorum Caput / Christ Lord, Shepherd Supreme

Christe, pastorum caput
atque princeps,
gestiens huius celebrare festum,
debitas sacro pia turba psallit
carmine laudes.

Christ Lord, shepherd supreme,
of all shepherds the chief,
your holy people strive to celebrate
this shepherd's festal day;
they pour forth due praises
in sacred song.

(For a Pope)

[Pro Papa]
Quas oves Petro dederas,
ovile
orbis ut totus fieret sacratum,
hic tuo nutu positus supremo
culmine rexit.

The sheep you had entrusted to Peter
so that the entire world
might become a sacred sheepfold,
this holy man, placed over them
by your will,
duly ruled from his throne sublime.

(For a Bishop)

[Pro Episcopo]
Strenuum bello pugilem
superni
chrismatis pleno tuus unxit
intus
Spiritus dono, posuitque
sanctam
pascere gentem.

This vigorous champion
has your very Spirit
anointed for holy warfare,
full-gifting him from within
with heavenly anointing;
and that Spirit has set him to the task
of shepherding your holy flock.

(For a Priest)
This holy man you chose,
and united him to youself
as minister and as priest.
You granted him the task
of coming to the aid of your people
as captain of the host,
as good and faithful foster father.

[Pro Presbytero]
Hunc tibi electum faciens
ministrum
ac sacerdotem socians,
dedisti
dux ut astaret populo fidelis
ac bonus altor.

[continued]

Christe, Pastorum Caput atque Princeps / Christ Lord, Shepherd Supreme
[concluded]

Hic gregis doctor fuit atque forma lux erat caeco, misero levamen, providus cunctis pater omnibusque omnia factus.	Teacher of your flock was he, its model as well; a light for the blind, a solace for those in woe, a provident father for all: for all people, all things become.
Christe, qui sanctis meritam coronam reddis in caelis, docili magistrum fac sequi vita, similique tandem fine potiri.	Christ Lord, you bestow upon the saints their due reward in heaven above. Make us follow this our teacher with lives open to his teaching, and so obtain the same final glory-crown as he.
Aequa laus summum celebret Parentem teque, Salvator, pie rex, per aevum; Spiritus Sancti resonet per omnem gloria mundum. Amen.	Let equal praise extol the supreme Father, and you as well, Savior God, King most faithful, for all ages to come; and may the glory given the Holy Spirit echo far and wide throughout the entire world. Amen.

COMMON OF ONE PASTOR
MORNING PRAYER
Inclitus Rector / A Ruler So Renowned

Inclitus rector pater atque
prudens,
cuius insignem colimus
triumphum,
iste confessor sine fine laetus
regnat in astris.

[Pro Papa]
Qui Petri summa cathedra
residens,
praesul immensi gregis et
magister,
regna per claves Domini potenter
caelica pandit.

[Pro Episcopo]
Qui sacerdotis, ducis, ac magistri
munus insumpsit populis
sacratum,
praesul et vitae sapiens paravit
dona beatae.

[Pro Sacerdote]
Ipse dux clarus fuit et magister,
exhibens sacrae documenta vitae
ac Deo semper satagens placere
pectore mundo.

Nunc eum nisu rogitemus omnes,
abluat nostrum pius ut reatum,
et sua ducat prece nos ad alta
culmina caeli.

Sit Deo soli decus et potestas,
laus in excelsis, honor et perennis,
qui suis totum moderans
gubernat
legibus orbem.
Amen.

A ruler so renowned, a father so wise,
whose shining triumph
we celebrate now, a confessor he,
whose joy knows no end,
as he reigns in high heaven above.

(For a Pope)
Seated upon Peter's own exalted chair,
he presided over his uncountable flock;
as teacher did he use
the keys of the Lord to unlock
and with power fling open the very gates
of the kingdom of heaven itself.

(For a Bishop)
He accepted the task,
sacred to his people:
he was priest, leader, and teacher alike.
A wise provider was he,
preparing his flock
for the gifts of e'er-blessed life.

(For a Priest)
Renowned was he
as leader and as teacher, showing forth
shining evidence of a holy life
and ever striving to please his God
with blazing purity of mind and heart.

Earnestly now let us all entreat him,
by his faithful love all of our guilt
to wash away, and with his holy prayers
to lead us to the regal heights
of heaven above.

To God alone be glory, be power, be
praise on high, be honor without end:
to God, who with a father's own care
rules the entire universe
with provident, loving laws. Amen.

COMMON OF DOCTORS OF THE CHURCH
EVENING PRAYER I AND II and OFFICE OF READINGS
Aeterne Sol, Qui Lumine / O Sun Ne'er Setting

Aeterne sol, qui lumine
creata comples omnia,
suprema lux et mentium,
te corda nostra concinunt.

O Sun ne'er setting, eternal, most
high, you brim-fill all you have made
with your splendor bright.
You are the supreme light
of our minds;
our hearts justly sing your praises.

Tuo fovente Spiritu,
hic viva luminaria
fulsere, per quae saeculis
patent salutis semitae.

By your Spirit's nurturing breath
have living torches, glowing, gleaming,
shone here brilliant,
shone here bright.
Through them, the paths of salvation
lie clear for eons to come.

Quod verba missa caelitus,
nativa mens quod exhibet,
per hos ministros gratiae
novo nitore claruit.

What your words, sent down from
heaven above, have meant,
what of those words created mind
has labored to make clear:
all has become more and more
known through these,
your ministers of grace.

Horum coronae particeps,
doctrina honestus lucida,
hic vir beatus splenduit
quem praedicamus laudibus.

This holy man shares
in the glory-crown of these
wise ministers: unwavering
has he been in clearest teaching.
Exemplary has he been:
this, the very one whom we extol
today with our praises.

Ipso favente, quaesumus,
nobis, Deus, percurrere
da veritatis tramitem,
possimus ut te consequi.

By his favoring intercession,
we ask you, O Lord,
to grant us to run faithfully along
the pathway of truth, and so be able
to possess you at long last.

Praesta, Pater piissime,
Patrique compar Unice,
cum Spiritu Paraclito
regnans per omne saeculum.
Amen.

Grant this, Father most faithful:
grant it, only-begotten one,
Co-equal of the Father,
with the Spirit advocate
ruling for all ages to come. Amen.

COMMON OF DOCTORS OF THE CHURCH
MORNING PRAYER
Doctor Aeternus Coleris Piusque / We Worship You as Teacher

Doctor aeternus coleris piusque
Christe, qui leges aperis salutis,
verba qui vitae merito putaris
solus habere.

We worship you as teacher
from time limit free,
as Anointed One most faithful.
You make known the laws
that lead to salvation;
you alone are rightly thought to possess
the words of eternal life.

Teque clamamus, bone Pastor
orbis,
caelitus semper solidasse
Sponsae
verba, constanter quibus illa
mundo
lumen adesset.

Goodly Shepherd of the Universe,
we proclaim that from on high
you have always confirmed
and made certain the words
of your Spouse, the Church:
the words that make her
ceaselessly present
as faithful light to the world.

Ipse quin praebes famulos
coruscos,
aureas stellas velut emicantes,
certa qui nobis reserent beatae
dogmata vitae.

Of a truth: you yourself show forth
your holy ones, shining clear, golden
stars in the heavens flashing bright:
they are those who unlock for us
the sure, certain secrets
of life without end.

Unde te laudes recinant, Magister,
Spiritus fundis bona qui stupenda
ore doctorum, tua quo potenter
lux patet alma.

And so do our praises resound unto you,
O Master most renowned:
for you pour forth
the marvelous riches of the Spirit
through the mouths of your teachers,
so that your kindly light
may e'er powerfully shine forth.

Quique nunc iustus celebratur,
instet
ut tuam plebem per amoena lucis
des gradi, donec tibi dicat hymnos
lumine pleno.
Amen.

May then whoever is now
acclaimed as being just
enteat you eagerly,
that you grant your people
progress through light's pleasant glow,
until at last they sing hymns of joy
to you in the blessed, brilliant light
of heaven above. Amen.

COMMON OF SEVERAL OR MANY VIRGINS
EVENING PRAYER I AND II and MORNING PRAYER
Iesu, Corona Virginum / Jesus, Crowning Reward of Virgins Blest

Iesu, corona virginum,
quem Mater illa concipit
quae sola virgo parturit,
haec vota clemens accipe,

Jesus, crowning reward
of virgins blest, you it was
whom that Mother conceives—
that Mother who alone
was also a virgin—
conceived and indeed bore.
In your mercy, receive
these votive prayers of ours.

Qui pascis inter lilia
saeptus choreis virginum,
sponsus decorus gloria
sponsisque reddens praemia.

Surrounded are you
by the choirs of the virgins;
you grant fit pasture amidst the lilies
to those who virgins truly are:
a spouse brilliant in glory,
a spouse bestowing due rewards
on the bridal spouses
you have made your own.

Quocumque pergis, virgines
sequuntur, atque laudibus
post te canentes cursitant
hymnosque dulces personant.

Where'er you go, your virgin spouses
follow closely upon you;
with chants of praise they run
eager and oft after you,
and break forth
in songs and harmony most fine.

Te deprecamur, largius
nostris adauge mentibus
nescire prorsus omnia
corruptionis vulnera.

We bring our plea to you:
increase greatly our minds' powers,
so that no experience we may have
of any wound
the seducer might bestow.

Iesu, tibi sit gloria,
qui natus es de Virgine,
cum Patre et almo Spiritu
in sempiterna saecula. Amen.

Jesus, to you be glory,
born as you were of a Virgin pure.
Glory too to Father and kindly Spirit,
for all ages to come. Amen.

COMMON OF SEVERAL OR MANY VIRGINS
OFFICE OF READINGS
Gaudentes Festum Colimus / With Joy Unbounded Do We Come

Gaudentes festum colimus sanctarum Christi virginum, quae puro corde Dominum secutae sunt in laudibus.	With joy unbounded do we come to celebrate the festal day of Christ's holy virgins, who with unsullied hearts followed their Lord and sang forth his praises.
O castitatis lilium, rex virginum sanctissime, tu, custos pudicitiae, fraudes repelle daemonum.	O lily-flower of chastity bright, Most Holy King of virgins pure, you are guardian of modesty's shining shrine: ward off far from us demon-snares, demon-hordes.
Qui castis in visceribus placaris clementissime, nostros reatus dilue, dimittens quae peccavimus.	Most merciful King, in chastity of mortal frames you take full delight. Wash away our faults; drive far from us the sins we have committed.
Grates precantes agimus; erramus, viam dirige; tu, pater indulgentiae, nobis succurre, quaesumus.	In humble prayer we offer heartfelt thanks. Yes, we do stray, do fall: but still we pray that you would correct our way. Father of forgiveness itself, come to our aid: this in hope we beg.
Iesu, tibi sit gloria, qui natus es de Virgine, cum Patre et almo Spiritu in sempiterna saecula. Amen.	Jesus, to you be glory; you were born of a Virgin. Glory too be given to the Father, and to the kindly Spirit as well, for ages that no mortal can tell. Amen.

COMMON OF ONE VIRGIN
OFFICE OF READINGS
Dulci Depromat Carmine / In Resounding, Wondrous Harmony

Dulci depromat carmine
devota plebs sollemnia,
dum in caelorum culmine
haec virgo micat gloria.

Virgo, quae Christi laudibus
vacavit iam viriliter,
sanctorum nunc agminibus
coniungitur feliciter.

Vicit per pudicitiam
infirmae carnis vitium;
sprevit mundi blanditiam
Christi sequens vestigium.

Per hanc nos, Christe, dirige
servans a cunctis hostibus;
culparum lapsus corrige
nos imbuens virtutibus.

Iesu, tibi sit gloria,
qui natus es de Virgine,
cum Patre et almo Spiritu
in sempiterna saecula.
Amen.

In resounding, wondrous harmony
do God's people break forth
in songs of praise,
fitting unto this solemn day
of festal dedication bright,
while in the heights
of high heaven above
this virgin shines forth
in glory and splendor.

A virgin blest, she devoted her days
to Christ's praises
in manner stouthearted and true;
now she has been joined
to the company of the
saints in happiness sublime.

Through a maiden's holy virtue
did she overcome
the sickening sinfulness
of fallible flesh;
Christ's own footsteps did she pursue,
and spurned the foul allurements
the world held forth.

Through this virgin's prayer, O Christ,
guide us; keep us safe from all
that would harm us.
Save us from the falls
our faults would bring;
fill us with the virtues that you are
wont to grant.

Jesus, to you be glory:
you, who were born of a Virgin blest.
Glory, too, to the Father
and kindly Spirit,
for ages without halt or rest. Amen.

COMMON OF ONE VIRGIN
MORNING PRAYER
Aptata, Virgo, Lampade / With Lamp Well Trimmed, O Virgin

Aptata, virgo, lampade
ad nuptias ingressa es
aeterni regis gloriae,
quem laudant turbae caelicae.

With lamp well trimmed, O virgin,
have you entered into the wedding feast
of the eternal king of glory,
to whom the host of heaven
sings full praise.

Grata conviva superis,
caelesti sponso iungeris
amplexu casti foederis,
pudoris dives meritis.

Table-guest most pleasing
to the heavenly court,
you are now united to your
heavenly spouse in the gentle embrace
of a chaste marriage pact;
rich are you in what
purest virtue deserves.

Normam vivendi instrue,
nos prece tua confove,
possimus ut resistere
hostis nostri versutiae.

Draw up for us a rule for holy living;
cherish us with your faithful prayer,
so that we might be well able
to resist the cunning wiles
of our wicked foe.

Exemplar vitae virginum,
Maria roget Filium,
ut eius adiutorium
nos iuvet per exsilium.

And may Mary, model of what a virgin
should be and do,
ask her Son to grant us his help
to keep us safe
in our time of exile drear.

Sit Deitati gloria
per infinita saecula
pro virginis victoria,
qua gaudet caeli curia.
Amen.

May glory be given
to the Godhead on high,
through ages uncountable yet to come,
because of the victory
which this virgin won
and which brings joy to all in heaven
above. Amen.

COMMON OF SEVERAL OR MANY HOLY MEN
EVENING PRAYER I AND II and OFFICE OF READINGS
Inclitos Christi Famulos / Sing We Now of the Glorious Companions

Inclitos Christi famulos canamus,
quos, fide claros nitidisque gestis,
hac die tellus sociata caelo
laudibus ornat.

Sing we now of the glorious
companions of Christ;
renowned are they for their faith,
their shining deeds,
and today earth joins heaven
in heaping praise upon them.

Quippe qui mites, humiles, pudici,
nesciam culpae coluere vitam,
donec e terris animus volavit
liber ad astra.

For they were, indeed,
meek, humble, chaste;
theirs was a life
unacquainted with fault,
all the way until the time came
for their souls to take flight,
in full freedom, from earth below
to the heavens above.

Inde iam gaudent miseris adesse,
flentium tergunt lacrimas, medentur
mentium plagis, vitiata reddunt
membra saluti.

From there they now rejoice in being
present to us wretched souls;
they wipe away our tears,
they cure our spirits' wounds,
they restore to full health
our sin-tainted bodies.

Nostra laus ergo resonet benignis
his Dei servis referatque grates,
qui pia pergant ope nos iuvare
rebus in arctis.

Let then our praise resound
to these kindly servants of God;
let it bring them our thanks,
for they continue, with steadfast aid,
to assist us in
the hardship of our lives and deeds.

Sit Deo soli decus et potestas,
laus in excelsis honor ac perennis,
qui suis totum moderans gubernat
legibus orbem.
Amen.

To God alone be glory and power,
praise on high, and everlasting honor,
for gently does he govern,
with kindly, loving law
the whole of the world.
Amen.

COMMON OF SEVERAL OR MANY HOLY MEN
MORNING PRAYER
Beata Caeli Gaudia / The Blessed Joys of Heaven

Beata caeli gaudia,
confessionis praemium,
Christi o fideles asseclae,
iam possidetis affatim.

The blessed joys of heaven, the reward
that comes from professing the name
of the Lord: all these do you,
O faithful followers of Christ,
hold now fast in abundance full and fair.

Laudes benignis auribus
audite, quas effundimus
nos exules de patria
vobis sacrato cantico.

With kindly ear, attend to the praises
which we offer: which we, doleful exiles
from our fatherland above,
pour forth to you
in sacred songs and hymns.

Amore Christi perciti
crucem tulistis asperam,
oboedientes, impigri
et caritate fervidi.

On fire with the love of Christ,
you bore the cross most drear:
faithful to the Lord, unwearied,
heated full through with charity's flame.

Sprevistis artes daemonum
fallaciasque saeculi;
Christum fatendo moribus
migrastis inter sidera.

You spurned the wiles of the
Satan-horde and the deceiving
pretensions of the world;
by professing Christ
in what you were and did
you have come to take your place
amidst heaven's stars above.

Iam nunc potiti gloria,
adeste votis omnium
ardenter exoptantium
exempla vestra prosequi.

Now you have attained
full glory on high. Be attentive then
to the prayers of all those
who with burning hearts desire
to tread your homeward-leading,
heavenward-leading path.

Sit Trinitati gloria,
quae pro sua clementia
vobisque suffragantibus
nos ducat ad caelestia.
Amen.

May glory be Trinity bound;
may our Triune God, in his merciful ways
lead us, with the help of your prayers,
to the rewards of heaven above.
Amen.

COMMON OF ONE HOLY MAN
EVENING PRAYER I AND II and OFFICE OF READINGS
Iesu, Redemptor Omnium / Jesus, Redeemer of All

Iesu, redemptor omnium,
perpes corona caelitum,
in hac die clementius
nostris faveto vocibus,

Jesus, Redeemer of all,
crowning reward without end
of heaven's throng above;
on this day we ask: grant e'en more
merciful ear to our abject pleas.

Sacri tui qua nominis
confessor almus claruit,
cuius celebrat annua
devota plebs sollemnia.

On this day, your faithful confessor,
who professed aloud your holy name,
has become renowned: the very one
whose anniversary festival
your faithful people celebrate in joy.

Per illa quae sunt saeculi
gressu sereno transiit,
tibi fidelis iugiter
iter salutis persequens.

Through the infamous snares
and concerns that belong
to this world of ours
did he pass with tranquil step,
pursuing rather the path to salvation,
in steadfast, full fidelity to you.

At rite mundi gaudiis
non cor caducis applicans,
cum angelis caelestibus
laetus potitur praemiis.

He lent his heart, rightly,
to none of the alluring pleasures
of the world; and now, in company
with the angels on high, he happily
enjoys your heavenly rewards.

Huius benignus annue
nobis sequi vestigia;
huius precatu servulis
dimitte noxam criminis.

In your kindness grant that we
may follow the footsteps
of this holy man;
because of his prayers,
grant your servants forgiveness
for the guilt their sins have earned.

Sit, Christe, rex piissime,
tibi Patrique gloria
cum Spiritu Paraclito,
in sempiterna saecula.
Amen.

O Christ, King most faithful, may glory
be given to you, be given
to the Father too, with the Spirit
Advocate as well for all ages to come.
Amen.

COMMON OF ONE HOLY MAN
MORNING PRAYER
Iesu, Corona Celsior / Jesus, You Are Reward More Exalted

Iesu, corona celsior
et veritas sublimior,
qui confitenti servulo
reddis perenne praemium,

Da supplicanti coetui
huius rogatu caelitis,
remissionem criminum
rumpendo nexum vinculi.

Nil vanitatis diligens,
terrena sic exercuit,
ut mente tota fervidus
tibi placeret unice.

Te, Christe, Rex piissime,
hic confitendo iugiter,
calcavit hostem fortiter
superbum ac satellitem.

Virtute clarus et fide,
orationi sedulus,
ac membra servans sobria,
dapes supernas obtinet.

Deo Patri sit gloria,
tibique soli Filio,
cum Spiritu Paraclito
in sempiterna saecula.
Amen.

Jesus, you are reward more exalted
than reward itself,
truth truer than truth itself:
you grant joy without end
to this humble servant of yours,
who boldly professes your name.

So too, by the intercession of this
your saint, your heaven-dweller on high,
grant to your people
what they beg of you:
forgive the sins they have committed,
shattering thereby the bond-chain
that holds them thrall-fast.

Your holy saint strove
for nothing offered by vain allure,
and dealt with earthly matters
so as solely to serve you alone,
with singleminded heart,
with ardent-hearted zeal.

O Christ most faithful, this holy man,
by professing your name
with constancy most faithful,
trod firmly underfoot the ancient enemy,
and that enemy's proud satanic band.

Renowned was he in faith, in virtue;
unwavering was he in prayer.
He kept himself sober and pure,
and now finds honored place
at your eternal banquet
in high heaven above.

To God the Father be glory, and to you,
His only Son, with the Spirit Advocate
for all ages ere yet to come. Amen.

COMMON OF SEVERAL OR MANY HOLY WOMEN
EVENING PRAYER I AND II
Christe, Cunctorum Sator et Redemptor / Christ Lord, Creator and Redeemer of All

Christe, cunctorum sator et
redemptor,
siderum, terrae, maris atque rector,
omnium laudes tibi personantum
solve reatum.

Christ Lord,
creator and redeemer of all,
Ruler of the stars,
of the earth, of the sea,
Release from their guilt all who make
their praises of you resound on high.

You conceal precious stones
in fragile vessels,
making chaste women abound
in their hearts with strength untold,
making them bring forth
triumphs brilliant,
triumphs renowned.

Vase qui gemmas fragili recondis,
viribus fluxas animo pudicas
feminas reddens faciensque claros
ferre triumphos.

Quas et in sensu teneras videmus,
praerogativa meriti coronas,
incolas regni facis et perennes
esse superni.

With earthly eyes,
we see these women
as delicate, young, tender:
but you see them and crown them
as first-ranking in merit:
you make them forever citizens
of the heavenly kingdom on high.

To the Father most High
be glory and power;
praise too to you, Holy Son,
and abundant worship.
And to the Holy Spirit be equal praise
and power now
and for ages ere yet to come.
Amen.

Sit Patri summo decus atque virtus,
laus tibi Nato celebrisque cultus,
Flamini Sancto parilis potestas
nunc et in aevum.
Amen.

COMMON OF SEVERAL OR MANY HOLY WOMEN
OFFICE OF READINGS
Hae Feminae Laudabiles / These Holy Women

Hae feminae laudabiles
et honoratae meritis,
ut sanctis pollent moribus,
triumphant sic cum angelis.

These holy women
are most deserving of praise,
most renowned for
what they greatly deserve.
Now, just as they are noted for the
power of their holy ways, so do they
rejoice with the angels above.

Ex corde devotissimo
in flet*u* orantes Dominum,
vigiliis, ieiuniis
haerebant ist*ae* assiduis.

From the depth
of their dedicated hearts
they prayed to God with copious tears
and clung closely to him by vigils well
kept,
by constant fasts observed.

Spernentes mundi gloriam
ac mente semper integra,
perfectam post iustitiam
migrarunt super sidera.

Despising the world's false glories,
and keeping their minds ever pure,
after lives lived in perfect justice,
they took flight to the heavens above.

Quae sanctitatis actibus
sua ditarunt limina,
laetantur nune perpetuis
caelestis aedis praemiis.

By their acts of holiness they enriched
their households on earth; now they
rejoice in the everlasting rewards
of their heavenly home.

Laus un*i* ac trino Domino,
qui nos earum precibus,
peracto vitae termino,
coniungat caeli civibus.
Amen.

Praise be to the Lord of Heaven,
one and three;
may he,
through these women's kindly prayers,
unite us too, when the end of our life
shall have come, with all the denizens
of heaven on high.
Amen.

COMMON OF SEVERAL OR MANY HOLY WOMEN
MORNING PRAYER
Nobiles Christi Famulas Diserta / With Voices Clear and True

Nobiles Christi famulas diserta
voce cantemus, decus aemulatas
feminae fortis, sacra cui profudit
pagina laudes.

With voices clear and true
let us sing of the virtues
of these renowned handmaids
of Christ, the clear-shown equals
of the bravest of women
in the glory that is their due,
and for whom the sacred text
has poured forth its praises.

Non eas mundus laqueis revincit,
iussa quae Patris subeunt volentes,
ut bonum Christi satagant ubique
spargere odorem.

The world does not overcome them
with its snares;
willingly do they embrace
the commands
that are the Father's,
so that they may be occupied in full
in spreading the fragrant scent
of Christ the Lord
throughout this world of ours.

Edomant corpus, precibusque
mentem
nutriunt sanctis; peritura temnunt
lucra, ut inquirant sibi permanentis
praemia vitae.

They overcome the weakness
of their bodies;
with holy prayers they nourish full
their spirits.
Passing treasures they scorn,
so as to seek for themselves
the rewards of life everlasting.

Sit Deo soli decus et potestas,
laus in excelsis honor ac perennis,
qui suis totum moderans gubernat
legibus orbem.
Amen.

To God alone be glory and power,
praise in high heaven,
and honor without end,
to this God of ours who gently rules
the entire world with his merciful laws.
Amen.

COMMON OF ONE HOLY WOMAN
EVENING PRAYER I AND II
Fortem Virili Pectore / That Woman with Courage-Laden Heart

Fortem virili pectore
laudemus omnes feminam,
quae sanctitatis gloria
ubique fulget inclita.

That woman with courage-laden heart:
let us all loudly praise her,
for she shines forth
north, south, east, and west
with the blazing glory of holiness.

By wounds of holy love deep felt,
she trod underfoot
the death-bound things
that belong to this world,
traversed her journey,
harsh though it was,
and came to the bright, the glorious
kingdom of heaven.

Haec sancto amore saucia,
huius caduca saeculi
dum calcat, ad caelestia
iter peregit arduum.

Her flesh she subdued
with penitential fasts;
her spirit she nourished
with the sweet food of prayer.
Now she enjoys the bliss beyond telling
of heaven above.

Carnem domans ieiuniis,
dulcique mentem pabulo
orationis nutriens,
caeli potitur gaudiis.

Christ our King, reason why
brave souls are brave,
You accomplish mighty things
by the power that is yours.
Through the prayer of this holy woman
we ask: graciously hear the pleas
of those who cry to you.

Rex Christe, virtus fortium,
qui magna solus efficis,
huius precatu, quaesumus,
audi benignus supplices.

Jesus, to you be glory,
for you grant that we may hope
for your blessed handmaid's
favor and approval,
and the rewards unending
of heaven above.
Amen.

Iesu, tibi sit gloria,
qui nos beatae servulae
sperare das suffragia
et sempiterna praemia.
Amen.

COMMON OF ONE HOLY WOMAN
OFFICE OF READINGS
Haec Femina Laudabilis / This Holy Woman Is Most Deserving

Haec femina laudabilis
et honorata meritis,
ut sanctis pollet moribus,
triumphat sic cum angelis.

This holy woman
is most deserving of praise,
most renowned
for what she greatly deserves.
Now, just as she is noted
for the power of her holy ways, so
does she rejoice
with the angels above.

Ex corde devotissimo
orans Deum cum lacrimis,
vigiliis, ieiuniis
haerebat haec assiduis.

From the depth of her dedicated heart
she prayed to God with copious tears
and clung close him
by vigils well kept,
by constant fasts observed.

Contemnens mundi gloriam
ac mente semper integra,
perfectam post iustitiam
migravit super sidera.

Spurning the world's false glories,
and keeping her mind ever pure,
after a life lived in perfect justice
she took flight to the heavens above.

By her acts of holiness
she enriched her household on earth;
now she rejoices
in the everlasting rewards
of a heavenly home.

Quae sanctitatis actibus
sua ditavit limina,
laetatur nunc perpetuis
caelestis aedis praemiis.

Praise be to the Lord of Heaven,
one and three;
may he, through this holy woman's
kindly prayers, when the end
of our life shall have come,
unite us too with all the denizens
of heaven on high.
Amen.

Laus uni ac trino Domino,
qui nos eius precatibus,
peracto vitae termino,
coniungat caeli civibus.
Amen.

COMMON OF ONE HOLY WOMAN
MORNING PRAYER
Nobilem Christi Famulam Diserta / With Voices Clear and True

Nobilem Christi famulam diserta
voce cantemus, decus aemulatam
feminae fortis, sacra cui profudit
pagina laudes.

With voices clear and true
let us sing of the virtues
of this renowned handmaid of Christ,
who is the clear-shown equal
of the bravest of women
and for whom the sacred text
has poured forth its praises.

Hers was a faith most lively,
a hope most trusting,
a love for God full burning.
Fecund source were these
of all her good works,
from them, the love for her fellows
came in turn as a matter of course.

Cui fides vivax, pia spes amorque
in Deum fervens, operum bonorum
fertilis radix, amor unde fratrum
nascitur ultro.

Motus illius meritis, remitte
sontibus nobis scelus omne, Iesu,
ut tibi puro resonemus aequas
pectore laudes.

Moved by her merits, O Jesus,
grant to us guilty sinners
the forgiveness of all our crimes,
so that with purified heart
we may once more
sing forth praises
that are truly worthy of you.

To the Father on high
be praise and power;
praise also to you, O holy Son,
and worship most renowned;
and to the sacred Spirit
be equal praise and power
now and for ever more.
Amen.

Sit Patri summo decus atque
virtus,
laus tibi Nato celebrisque cultus,
Flamini Sancto parilis potestas
nunc et in aevum.
Amen.

COMMON OF RELIGIOUS
EVENING PRAYER I AND II and OFFICE OF READINGS
Laeti Colentes Famulum / With Joy We Honor This Servant of Yours

Laeti colentes famulum
qui te perfecte coluit,
tibi gratanter, Domine,
amoris hymnum promimus.

With joy we honor
this servant of yours
who by his (her) life
did so perfectly honor you;
to you, O Lord of all, we happily bring
our song of loving praise.

Christi fidelis assecla,
ultro reliquit gaudia
cuncta quae mundus exhibet
fugaces atque copias.

This faithful follower of Christ the Lord
did, of his (her) own accord
leave behind
whatever joys the world held forth,
did leave as well
the fleeting pleasures of riches,
wealth, and gain.

Tibi se vovit subditum
humilitate oboediens,
Christi, carnis munditie,
sponsi et aemulator virginum.

Tibi placere gestiit
tibique adhaesit unice,
mentem, verba, vel opera
amoris fovens ignibus.

To you he (she) vowed submission,
promising humbly to obey,
promising too,
by cleanliness of the flesh
to imitate Christ,
blissed Spouse of virgins
so holy and so true.

His caritatis vinculis
in terris tibi deditus,
liber ad astra iugiter
triumphaturus prodiit.

He (she) strove to please you alone;
above all others
did he (she) cling to you,
forging his (her) mind, words,
and deeds in the fires of love divine.

Eius exemplis excitos
da gradi nos alacriter,
ut te cum Nato et Spiritu
laudemus hymnis caelicis.
Amen.

[continued]

Laeti Colentes Famulum / With Joy We Honor This Servant of Yours
[concluded]

Bound to you on earth
by these chains of love,
he (she) was,
with no hindrance, no let,
free to hasten to full triumph
in the very heavens above.

By his (her) example are we stirred up,
and we beg:
grant us to come to you eagerly, avidly,
so that we may ever praise you,
may praise too the Son and the Spirit,
with glorious hymns
in high heaven above.
Amen.

COMMON OF RELIGIOUS
MORNING PRAYER
O Redemptoris Pietas Colenda / O Loving Fidelity of the Savior

O Redemptoris pietas colenda,
quae Patri exoptans homines
dicari,
Spiritus miro varioque ducis
pectora nutu!

O loving fidelity of the Savior, truly
to be honored, truly to be praised,
earnestly desiring men and women
to be consecrated to the Father,
you inspire their hearts
with Spirit-movements,
wondrous to know, diverse in kind.

Quos tua lympha facis esse natos
ex Deo vero, nova vis in illis
gratiam crebro dare caritatis
germina, Christe.

Among those you make to be
your children, reborn
of the one true God
at your baptismal font,
ofttimes you desire to grant
within them your graced favor,
a new-budding sprout, whereby

Tu vocas: currunt alacres vocati,
abdicant cunctis, duce te volentes,
calle regali crucis, usque solum
quaerere Patrem.

You send forth your call, and
those who are summoned
run quickly to you in reply.
They cast aside all things, wanting,
with you as their chieftain sublime,
to seek even the Father,
indeed him alone,
along the royal road of the cross.

Caelitus fervens ita sanctus iste
viribus totis tibi amanter haesit,
atque virtutum cupiit tenere
culmina laeta.

This holy, saintly person, so afire
with love from heaven above,
has fondly clung to you with all
his (her) strength, and has striven
to hold fast to the blessed heights
of virtue still to be achieved.

Laus Patri summo, tibi, Christe
princeps,
Flamini Sancto parilis resultet,
parva qui danti, bona corde magno
centupla fertis.
Amen.

[continued]

O Redemptoris Pietas Colenda / O Living Fidelity of the Savior.
[concluded]

O Christ-Prince, let praiseful song
be rendered to the Father on high;
let like hymn be rendered to you and
to the fire-tongued Spirit:
to the triune God
who brings gifts in hundredfold
to the one who gives but a little,
but does so
with great and devoted heart.
Amen.

OFFICE OF THE DEAD
OFFICE OF READINGS
Qui Vivis Ante Saecula / God, O Merciful God, before the Ages Began

Qui vivis ante saecula
vitaeque fons es unicus,
nos, Deus, morti obnoxios
culpaeque reos aspice.

God, O merciful God,
before the ages began,
you are; you are the one source,
the only source of life.
Look upon us, merciful God,
subject as we are to death,
guilty as we are of sin-stained lives.

Peccanti, Pater, homini
poenam sanxisti interitum,
ut, pulvis datus pulveri,
se subderet piaculum.

Vitale sed spiraculum
quod indidisti providus,
aeternitatis permanet
germen immarcescibile.

For the sinner, O Father most high,
you have decreed death
as due punishment;
so that when dust is given over
to dust once more,
that sinner might subject himself
as victim sacrifice.

Haec spes, hoc est solacium:
revirescemus, Domine,
primusque resurgentium
ad te nos Christus rapiet.

[Pro uno vel una]
Hoc vitae regno perfrui
defunctum (-am) praesta
famulum (-am),
quem (quam) Christi fides
imbuit,
quem (quam) almus
unxit Spiritus.

But that life-giving breath-source:
in your loving care, you did instill it;
and it remains in us an unfading font
of the life ere yet to come.

[Pro pluribus]
Hoc vitae regno perfrui
da fratres in te mortuos,
quos Christi fides imbuit,
quos almus unxit Spiritus.

Hoc regnum nobis propera
e terris cum cesserimus,
ut concinamus omnium
te finem, te principem. Amen.

This is our hope,
our rest and comfort blest:
we shall grow strong once more,
Father and Lord,
for Christ, the first-born
of the re-risen, will grasp us
and bring us home to you.
[continued]

Qui Vivis ante Saecula / God, O Merciful God, before the Ages Began
[concluded]

(For one dead person)
Grant that your dead servant
may happily possess this realm of life:
your servant, whom the faith of Christ
has touched, has formed,
whom the kindly Spirit has anointed
with blessed, heavenly oil.

(For several dead persons)
Grant that our brethren,
who have died in you,
may happily possess the realm of life;
the faith of Christ has touched,
has transformed them;
the kindly Spirit has anointed them
with blessed, heavenly oil.

Hasten this life-kingdom for us,
when time comes for us
to depart from earth,
so that we may rightly sing your praises:
you, the final end of each of us all,
you, the leader in our journey of life.
Amen.

OFFICE OF THE DEAD
MORNING PRAYER
Spes, Christe, Nostrae Veniae / We Have Firm Hope

Spes, Christe, nostrae veniae,
tu vita, resurrectio,
ad te sunt corda et oculi
cum mortis dolor ingruit.

Te quoque mortis taedia
passus dirosque stimulos,
Patri, inclinato capite,
mitis dedisti spiritum.

Vere nostros excipiens
languores, pastor miserens,
tecum donasti compati
Patrisque in sinu commori.

Apertis pendens bracchis,
in cor transfixum pertrahis
quos morituros aggravat
morbus vel maeror anxius.

Qui portis fractis inferi
victor pandisti caelicas,
nos nunc dolentes erige,
post obitum vivifica.

[Pro uno(-a) defuncto(-a)]
Sed et qui (quae) frater (soror)
corpore,
nunc dormit pacis requie,
iam te beante vigilet
tibique laudes referat. Amen.

[Pro pluribus defunctis]
Sed et qui fratres corpore
nunc somno pacis dormiunt,
iam te beante vigilent
tibique laudes referant.
Amen.

We have firm hope
that we will be granted
full pardon for our sins:
you, O Christ, are that hope.
You are our life,
our rising from the dead.
Our hearts, our eyes are fixed on you,
e'en when fell fear of dire death
holds us in thrall.

For you, too, suffered
the painful pangs of death,
its fearful torments:
you bowed your head
and, in meekness sublime,
handed over your spirit
to the Father most high.

Most merciful Shepherd, truly
you have taken unto yourself
all our weaknesses.
To share them with you, to endure
death, yes, but to endure it with you
in the very bosom of the Father:
this the favor you have granted
in compassion sublime.

As you hung upon the cross,
arms outstretched, all-embracing,
to your own pierced heart you drew
those for whom
sickness or dreading grief
makes dying e'en yet
more stern and more severe.

[continued]

Spes, Christe, Nostrae Veniae / We Have Firm Hope
[concluded]

Shattered asunder
were hell's grim gates;
flung open wide those of heaven,
by your conquering glory.
Raise us up now in our sorrow:
grant us new life,
after death.

(For one dead person)
But let him (her) who,
as our brother (sister) in the flesh,
now rests in the sleep of peace,
yet keep close watch for when you come
to bring him (her) joy,
to sing your praises without end. Amen.

(For several dead persons)
But let those who,
as our brothers (sisters) in the flesh,
now rest in the sleep of peace,
awaken when you come
to bring them joy,
and sing your praises without end.
Amen.

OFFICE OF THE DEAD
DAYTIME PRAYER
Qui Lacrimatus Lazarum / It Was You, Who, as Human, Wept

Qui lacrimatus Lazarum
gemensque cum sororibus,
ipsum fecisti praepotens
illarum reddi studiis:

It was you,
who, as human, wept over Lazarus,
and shared grief
with his sisters twain;
It was you,
who as the almighty One, saw to it
that he was restored
to their fond and loving care.

Qui petivisti sontibus
benignus, indulgentiam,
ac verba miserantia
dixisti poenae socio:

Qui, moriens, discipulo
matrem donasti Virginem,
tuorum quae fidelium
agon*i* adesset ultimo:

It was you,
who in your kindness great,
sought forgiveness
for those who knew not what they did;
it was you,
who spoke words of mercy
and forgiveness
to the thief who shared
our cross, your pain.

Da nobis, Christe Domine,
tuo redemptis sanguine,
durae mortis tristitiam
in vitae verti gaudium.

It was you,
who, when dying, gave your Mother,
the Virgin blest,
to your disciple, beloved and true,
so that she might be present
to your faithful
whene'er in their final struggle
they bravely contend.

[Pro uno (-a) defuncto (-a)]
Tuum(-am)que voca
famulum(-am)
ex hoc profectum(-am) saeculo,
et ubi mors iam deerit
te vitae canat principem. Amen.

[Pro pluribus]
Tuosque voca famulos,
ex hoc profectos saeculo,
ut ubi mors iam deerit
te vitae canant principem.
Amen.

It is we,
Christ, Lord of all, who are redeemed
by your most precious blood;
grant us, we plead,
that the sadness
of harsh earthly death
may be transformed
into the joy of life eternal.
[continued]

Qui Lacrimatus Lazarum / It Was You, Who, as Human, Wept
[concluded]

(For one dead person)
Summon, then, this servant of yours,
who has now gone forth from this world:
may he (she) be loud in his (her) praises
of you, the Lord of life,
in the land where death
shall be no more. Amen.

(For several or many dead persons)
Summon, then, these servants of yours,
who have now gone forth
from this world;
may they be loud in their praise
of you, the Lord of life,
in the land where death
shall be no more. Amen.

OFFICE OF THE DEAD
EVENING PRAYER
Immensae Rex Potentiae / Christ, King of Limitless Power

Immensae rex potentiae,
Christe, tu Patris gloriam
nostrumque decus moliens,
mortis fregisti iacula.

Infirma nostra subiens
magnumque petens proelium,
mortem qua serpens vicerat,
victor calcasti moriens.

Surgens fortis e tumulo,
paschali nos mysterio
peccato rursus mortuos
ad vitam semper innovas.

Vitam largire gratiae,
ut, sponsus cum redieris,
ornata nos cum lampade
iam promptos caelo invenias.

In lucem nos et requiem
serenus iudex accipe,
quos fides sanctae Triadi
devinxit atque caritas.

[Pro uno(-a) defuncto(-a)]
Tuum[-am]que voca
famulum[-am],
qui [quae] nunc exutus[-a]
corpore
in regna Patris inhiat,
ut te collaudet perpetim. Amen.

[Pro pluribus]
Fratres et omnes advoca
qui nunc exuti corpore
in regna Patris inhiant,
ut te collaudent perpetim.
Amen.

Christ, King of limitless power,
in furthering full the glory
of the Father on high,
and in rebuilding
our own fractured worth,
you have shattered the weapons
that fell death so fiercely bore.

You came to the aid of our weakness,
and sought to endure
that most dread warfare
wherein, as conquerer, yes,
but full-dying conquerer still,
you trampled underfoot the foul death
the serpent had used so long ago
to achieve his dreadful,
deadful triumph drear.

From the rock-hewn tomb
you rise in power sublime;
and forever, by your paschal mystery,
you bring us to a new
and blazing and shining light:
dead though we may all too oft be,
by sin after sin after sin.

Grant us a grace-filled life,
so that when you return
as bridegroom most high,
you will find us full ready
for the heavenly banquet,
with lamps burning steady,
lamps burning bright.

[continued]

Immensae Rex Potentiae / Christ, King of Limitless Power
[concluded]

Blessed and kindly judge,
receive us into light, into rest;
for faith in the holy Trinity
but charity too most high
has bound us together,
bound many into one.

(For one dead person)
Summon this servant of yours:
now bereft of his (her) earthly body,
he (she) gazes eagerly
upon the realm of the Father,
so as to praise you
for time without end. Amen.

(For several or many dead persons)
Summon to you
all your brothers and sisters
who now, bereft of their earthly body,
gaze eagerly upon the realm
of the Father,
so that they might praise you
for time without end. Amen.

INDEXES

INDEX OF LATIN TITLES

INDEX OF ENGLISH TITLES

GENERAL INDEX

INDEX OF LATIN TITLES

INDEX OF ENGLISH TITLES

-O-

-R-

GENERAL INDEX